D0885814

Best Lake Hikes Colorado

HELP US KEEP THIS GUIDE UP TO DATE

Every effort has been made by the authors and editors to make this guide as accurate and useful as possible. However, many things can change after a guide is published—trails are rerouted, regulations change, facilities come under new management, and so forth.

We would love to hear from you concerning your experiences with this guide and how you feel it could be improved and kept up to date. While we may not be able to respond to all comments and suggestions, we'll take them to heart, and we'll also make certain to share them with the authors. Please send your comments and suggestions to the following email address: editorial@falcon.com

Thanks for your input, and happy trails!

Best Lake Hikes Colorado

A Guide to the State's Greatest Lake Hikes

Susan Joy Paul and Stewart M. Green

ESSEX, CONNECTICUT

To everyone who sits on a shoreline and breathes in the life of a lake.

FALCONGUIDES®

An imprint of Globe Pequot, the trade division of The Rowman & Littlefield Publishing Group, Inc.
4501 Forbes Blvd., Ste. 200
Lanham, MD 20706
www.rowman.com

Falcon and FalconGuides are registered trademarks and Make Adventure Your Story is a trademark of The Rowman & Littlefield Publishing Group, Inc.

Distributed by NATIONAL BOOK NETWORK

Copyright © 2022 The Rowman & Littlefield Publishing Group, Inc.

Photos by Susan Joy Paul and Stewart M. Green unless otherwise credited
Maps by The Rowman & Littlefield Publishing Group, Inc.

All rights reserved. No part of this book may be reproduced in any form or by any electronic or mechanical means, including information storage and retrieval systems, without written permission from the publisher, except by a reviewer who may quote passages in a review.

British Library Cataloguing in Publication Information available

Library of Congress Cataloging-in-Publication Data available

ISBN 978-1-4930-4682-9 (paper: alk. paper)
ISBN 978-1-4930-4683-6 (electronic)

∞™ The paper used in this publication meets the minimum requirements of American National Standard for Information Sciences—Permanence of Paper for Printed Library Materials, ANSI/NISO Z39.48-1992.

The authors and The Rowman & Littlefield Publishing Group, Inc. assume no liability for accidents happening to, or injuries sustained by, readers who engage in the activities described in this book.

Contents

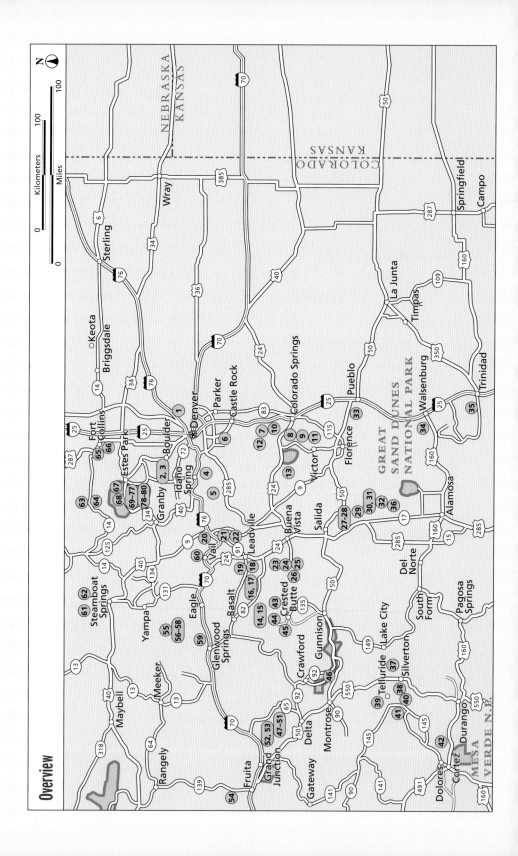

Overview

N

Kilometers
0   100

Miles
0   100

NEBRASKA
KANSAS

COLORADO
KANSAS

Rangely
Maybell
Meeker
Steamboat
Springs
Yampa
Glenwood
Springs
Eagle
Basalt
Fruita
Grand
Junction
Gateway
Delta
Crawford
Gunnison
Montrose
Telluride
Silverton
Lake City
South
Fork
Del
Norte
Pagosa
Springs
Dolores
Cortez
Durango
MESA
VERDE N.P.
Alamosa

Vail
Leadville
Buena
Vista
Salida
Florence
Victor
Colorado Springs
Castle Rock
Parker
Denver
Boulder
Fort
Collins
Estes Park
Idaho
Spring
Granby
Pueblo
Walsenburg
Trinidad
La Junta
Timpas
Springfield
Campo
Sterling
Briggsdale
Keota
Wray

GREAT
SAND DUNES
NATIONAL PARK

61 62
55
56–58
59
60
54
52, 53
47–51
65
66
63
64
68
67
69–77
78–80
2, 3
4
5
1
6
12 7
10
8 9
11
13
14, 15
16, 17
19
18
20
21
22
23
24
26 25
44 43
45
46
92
41
38
40
39
37
42
33
27–28
29
30, 31
32
36
34
35
115
83

Northwestern Colorado
Meeker, Glenwood Springs, Vail, and Steamboat Springs

Northern Colorado
Walden and Fort Collins

Rocky Mountain National Park
Estes Park, Allenspark, and Grand Lake

Acknowledgments

Many thanks to all the people at Rowman & Littlefield Publishing, FalconGuides, the National Book Network, and all of the bookstores and outdoor recreation retailers that create, sell, and support our books and the adventures they provide our readers.

Special thanks to our editor David Legere, production editor Kristen Mellitt, cartographer Melissa Baker, copyeditor Joshua Rosenberg, layout artist Rhonda Baker, and proofreader Steve Arney. We couldn't have done it without you.

—**Susan Joy Paul and Stewart M. Green**

The grassy banks of Hartenstein Lake welcome a picnic lunch with views.

Preface

This book should have been published a long time ago.

When I started writing *Best Lake Hikes Colorado*, I expected to finish the hikes and the manuscript in 1 year—2 tops. Then things happened.

In the spring of 2020, COVID-19 came to Colorado. Shut out of shopping malls and movie theaters, people discovered the outdoors. The state's campgrounds, trails, and parks—already overtaxed by their popularity among locals and out-of-state visitors—were overrun. Land management authorities in places like Brainard Lake, Ice Lake Basin, and Maroon Peak Recreation Areas scrambled to limit access and institute social-distancing measures in Colorado's most popular outdoor places. Public lands that had always been open on a first-come basis now required timed reservations. Time slots, especially those for early in the day, were in high demand, and often impossible to get. Some areas and trailheads were closed down completely.

Then, that summer, Colorado experienced the three worst wildfires in the state's history. The Pine Gulch Fire ravaged land north of Grand Junction. West of Fort Collins, the Cameron Peak Fire crept into Rocky Mountain National Park. Unbelievably, the park would suffer further damage from the East Troublesome Fire. Across Colorado, smoke filled the air, and outdoor activity was deemed unhealthy. There were more fires that year, including the Grizzly Creek Fire that shuttered Glenwood Canyon's iconic Hanging Lake. When it was all over, more than 625,000 acres had burned across the state. By Saturday, August 7, 2020, Denver's air quality index (AQI) had skyrocketed to an eye-watering 167. For a few hours that day, the city achieved the unenviable position of having the worst air quality of any city in the world.

While these wildfires, coupled with a pandemic, created a perfect storm for people wanting to enjoy the outdoors, it made guidebook research nearly impossible. Still, I plugged along on this book, and by the fall of 2020, I was on track to finish it. It would be late, but it would be done, and it would be good.

On October 16, a Friday, I set out to do the Venable-Comanche Loop in the Sangre de Cristo Mountains near Westcliffe. The weather forecast called for 35-mph winds, but I'd hiked in much worse weather. I got an early start to allow plenty of time for the nearly 12-mile loop, along with side trips to Venable Falls, Venable Lakes, and Comanche Lake. Like always, I carried two cameras; a GPS; a map and a compass; extra food, water, and clothing; two headlamps plus extra batteries; and a first aid kit.

The Venable Trailhead sits at about 9,000 feet above sea level and the trail climbs over 4,000 feet, looping around several 13,000-foot mountains on the range crest. The loop hike draws hikers for the exciting Phantom Terrace, a narrow section of trail that contours across the rocky eastern slope of 13,334-foot Venable Peak. The terraced trail was out of the wind that day and mostly dry and snow free. By three o'clock in the afternoon, I had traversed the exposed section, crossed the Custer-Saguache County line, recrossed it back into Custer County, and was heading downhill on the southeast flank of 13,244-foot Spring Mountain. My final destination before returning to the trailhead, Comanche Lake, appeared in the glacial valley far below. I had about 6 miles and 3,000 feet of elevation to descend, but I was making good time and looking forward to getting back to my car before dark.

Suddenly, I was rolling downhill. I twisted hard, forcing myself to stop and sit up. My right side ached, like something was really wrong, and I wondered if I had punctured an organ. My right arm was worse—swollen and ringing with pain. When I was a kid, I held onto a firecracker too long and it went off in my hand. This was the same kind of pain. Throbbing. Electric. Like every nerve was on fire. I lifted my shirt with my left hand to examine my right side, looking for signs of internal damage. No bruising at all, thankfully. But I would have to take care of that arm. I still had my pack on, but my trekking poles were gone.

A few yards below me, the grassy slope dropped away sharply into the Comanche Lake basin. Twisting to the left, I could see the trail about 20 feet above me. My poles were hanging over the edge. With just 3 hours of daylight left, my focus turned from taking care of my injuries to getting back to the trailhead before dark. Clambering upslope to the trail and my poles, I ignored my first aid kit, including the pain medication, and instead organized my gear for the hike out. I stashed one trekking pole in the side pocket of my pack, tucked my useless right arm into my camera strap, and, using my other pole for balance, headed down the trail.

I made good time for the first few miles, but as darkness fell, the trail turned rockier and more rutted. Then I was in a dense forest with no moonlight, and just a circle of light from my headlamp to illuminate my path. I stopped to call my friend Eric, who was my emergency contact that day. He knew that if he didn't hear from me by 10 p.m., he should call 911 and report me missing. I didn't know if I would be out by then and didn't want him to worry, so I told him I might be late and not to wait up. I didn't mention my accident. I didn't want to waste any time at all on the phone explaining what had happened, and there was no sense requesting help since my injuries weren't life-threatening and I could walk out on my own.

Hiking those last couple of miles seemed to take forever. I constantly worried about tripping on a rock or turning my foot in a rut and falling onto my injured arm. Finally, I arrived at the Comanche Trailhead at around 9:30 and, with huge relief, dropped my pack in the backseat and prepared for the 80-mile drive home.

Of course, I had set the emergency brake and couldn't release it, so I walked around from car to car in the parking lot, knocking on windows to see if anyone could help me. They were all empty though, their passengers already up the trail and tucked into tents at Venable Lakes. Eventually, it dawned on me that if I cleared off my front passenger seat I could sit there and release the brake with my left hand. As I arranged my belongings in the front seat, knowing I wouldn't be able to take my one good hand off the steering wheel during the long drive, another friend, Darin, texted me to see how my hike had been. I told him I was just getting out and he wondered why I was so late. Just like my call with Eric, I didn't mention the accident. My first priority was driving home while I was still awake and aware. I didn't want to waste time or energy explaining my accident.

While researching lake hikes for this book, author Susan Joy Paul paused to take a photo of Comanche Lake. Moments later, rockfall knocked her from the trail.

The next day, inspecting the damage to my body, I finally realized what had happened to me on the trail. My left toe was black and there was a dark bruise on the back of my left thigh, like I'd been hit with a baseball. I must have been hit by rockfall. The impact of the rocks, perhaps tumbled down from Spring Mountain, had knocked the poles from my hands and sent me half a dozen yards off the trail. I had fallen hard and fast, put out my hand instinctively, hit the ground, and rolled onto my camera. The arm injury was a classic *FOOSH*: a fall on an outstretched hand.

I headed to the nearest urgent care facility where a doctor confirmed I had broken both the ulna and radius bones in my right arm. Five days later, I got a proper X-ray and a cast, and after another 5 weeks, my arm had healed without surgery.

I couldn't help but consider the "what ifs." What if I had been just 1 foot higher on the trail and the rocks had hit my head? What if I'd been knocked out and unable to stop? Would I have kept tumbling? Would I have survived? I would never know, but none of those things happened so I kept writing this book. My lake hikes, however, were on hold. With just one good hand, everything took longer, including packing and unpacking for hikes, driving to trailheads, and taking photos, tracks, and waypoints. Worse, I had other books in the works too—the second edition of *Hiking Waterfalls Colorado* and the first edition of *Trails to the Top: 50 Colorado Front Range Mountain Hikes*. I felt as if I would never finish any of them.

It was time to bring in the big guns.

I called on my good friend and fellow FalconGuides author Stewart M. Green. How did he feel about coauthoring a few books with me? Sure, he said, when's the deadline? Last year, I said. He chuckled. Then he said yes.

So here we are. A year (2 years? 3?) late but with a book we're both very proud of, after a long, difficult journey to get it done. Thank you, Stewart, for all your work on this book and the others and thanks to our publisher, FalconGuides, for patiently dealing with all the delays.

—Susan Joy Paul

Introduction

Welcome! A Message from Your Lake Guides

Welcome to the delightful world of Colorado's many lakes. We're glad you decided to join us on this glorious journey.

Best Lake Hikes Colorado introduces you to eighty hikes and more than one hundred stunning lakes. The trips include easy strolls on level paths around lakes, moderate hikes you can do in a few hours to glassy lakes amid mountain splendor, and strenuous, all-day treks that lend themselves to backpacking trips with overnight camps beside remote tarns.

We struggled to select the best lakes for this book, not because there aren't enough from which to choose, but because there are so many! While it was tempting to include only the most pristine alpine lakes, the ones that take your breath away, we knew that not everyone could do a 16-mile, 10-mile, or even 5-mile hike to those high-altitude lakes. Those lakes and their trailheads are also locked by snow and ice for at least half of the year, making them inaccessible except by skis or snowshoes. So, we focused on providing a variety of trail distances, elevations, and difficulties, and tried our best to include lakes from each major region of the state.

Colorado's lakes vary in size and appearance, but they're all beautiful. And no matter how easy or difficult they are to reach, sitting beside a shining lake, breathing in the fresh mountain air—perhaps with a sandwich and a thermos full of hot cocoa or cool lemonade—is a delightful way to spend an afternoon.

We hope you enjoy them all as much as we did.

Lake Hike Safety and Protocol

For your own safety, the safety of others, and protection of the environment, a general protocol should be followed when hiking to Colorado's lakes:

- Be prepared with the appropriate clothing, gear, food, water, and supplies you'll need for a safe and enjoyable hike.

- Know where you're going and have adequate directions to get there and the ability to find your way back to the trailhead. Share your plans with someone you trust, along with a "latest time to call" so that—in the event of an accident—someone will know your general whereabouts and can then contact the authorities with that information.

- When driving to your lake trailhead, be aware of changing conditions, especially during inclement weather or natural disasters. Rainfall, snowfall, rockfall, and wildfires can affect your route, so be prepared to turn around if conditions become unsafe.

Keep your distance from animals like this moose on Fern Lake Trail in Rocky Mountain National Park.

- Travel in small groups to lessen impact in the backcountry. In wilderness areas, there is often a limit on the number of people allowed to hike together on a trail. When in doubt, contact the local ranger district for direction.

- Read posted warnings and restrictions at each trailhead, as these vary between public lands and can change based on conditions. It is especially important to be mindful of campfire restrictions and required minimum camping distances from water sources.

- Do not cut switchbacks or hike off-trail where trails exist, which causes erosion and destroys vegetation. Stick to the trail, especially on delicate alpine tundra and desert cryptobiotic soil. If you do have to leave the trail, seek out hard surfaces, such as rocks and stones, to lessen your impact.

- Keep dogs on leash or on voice command, and do not allow them to chase wildlife, which can stress the native animals and cause premature death.

- Do not approach wildlife. Although attacks are rare, they can happen, and are more likely when an animal is provoked or feels threatened. Even small animals carry diseases, so don't try to pet or feed them.

- Beware of mountain beetle–killed trees, and never camp near them or under them. They can fall without warning.

- Take extreme care when crossing streams and do not underestimate the power of a current, especially during Colorado's spring thaw.
- Stay clear of soft or down-sloping edges over creekbeds, as well as wet, icy, or slick rocks and tree limbs on the trail and around the lakes. Stick to dry, solid surfaces if possible, and if the trail is wet or icy, consider using trekking poles for balance and adding traction such as MICROspikes to your boots for a better grip.
- Keep to established trails and avoid traveling off-trail or on social trails. Where the use of side trails is required to view a lake, be sure to adhere to the Leave No Trace principles to lessen your impact and prevent future resource damage. The Leave No Trace (www.LNT.org) principles are easy to follow and ensure a clean and pristine environment for inhabitants and future visitors to the hiking trails.
- Pack out all trash and personal items, including toilet paper. Do not leave behind remnants of your visit, such as painted rocks. Visitors are there to enjoy the natural environment.
- Likewise, leave everything on the trail as you found it. Do not remove rocks, plants, wildflowers, live trees, or historical artifacts from the wilderness, but leave them for others to enjoy.

Hikers climb the trail to Jones Mountain above azure Ptarmigan Lake in the Sawatch Range.

Wildfires and Colorado's Changing Climate

Scientific studies indicate that global warming, caused by greenhouse gas emissions from the burning of fossil fuels, is changing Colorado's climate. These changes include rising temperatures, decreased precipitation, lower snowpack levels, drought, an increase in insects that kill trees, increased aridification, and altered vegetation patterns. Colorado's average temperature has increased 2 degrees, faster than the global rise, since 1990. Stream flows are predicted to decrease as much as 15 percent by 2050.

The increasingly dry and hot conditions and an extended fire season have led to catastrophic wildfires, with the twenty largest fires in Colorado history occurring after 2000, including the three largest in the devastating 2020 season—the Cameron Peak, East Troublesome, and Pine Gulch Fires. Those fires damaged lake hikes in Rocky Mountain National Park.

Hikers need to be aware of wildfire dangers when trekking in Colorado's backcountry. Plan ahead of time and avoid injury by following a few basic safety rules:

- Before hiking, check with land management agencies like the US Forest Service and the Bureau of Land Management for fire restrictions in the area. Campfires may be prohibited due to red-flag fire conditions and high fire danger. Note changing fire restrictions posted on trailhead kiosks.

- Outside of established fire rings in public campgrounds, do not build campfires except in an emergency. Never leave a fire unattended, and ensure your campfire is out completely before abandoning your campsite. Extinguish any smoldering campfires you encounter.

- Avoid hiking when the air is smoke filled and unhealthy.

- Be aware of any active fires adjacent to your hiking location, even if they are many miles away, and monitor their progress in case you need to change plans and return to the trailhead.

- Use extreme caution when hiking in burned forests. Dead and damaged trees create unstable terrain, and a lack of vegetation can make land prone to avalanches, rockslides, landslides, and flooding.

Reservations (May Be) Required

Colorado's population has been steadily increasing by many tens of thousands of people each year. The population growth, coupled with increasing tourism and COVID restrictions, has led to overcrowding and overuse of the state's iconic natural wonders. Increased recreational visits have led to jammed roads, parking lots, and trailheads, trail erosion caused by careless feet cutting switchbacks, and illegal camping and campfires.

In response, some popular Colorado places put limitations on visitation to protect natural resources from damage caused by overuse. Rocky Mountain National Park and Brainard Lake Recreation Area instituted timed-entry reservation systems, and while these systems may be an inconvenience, the benefit to visitors is a better hiking experience. Some other areas require parking and hiking reservations, such as Glenwood Canyon's Hanging Lake. San Juan National Forest is considering a permit system to access Ice Lake Basin, home to a slew of lakes, to alleviate limited trailhead parking and damage to the area's fragile alpine tundra.

Before hiking to a lake, especially the more popular ones, contact the respective land management agency listed in the Land Status detail at the beginning of each hike, or go to the appendix for more contact information including web addresses. Some trailheads may require making camping and hiking reservations weeks or even months in advance. Plan ahead to avoid disappointment.

The distant Wet Mountains rise beyond Lake Pueblo and the Lake Shore Trail.

How to Use This Guide

Each hike includes a short overview followed by details to help you choose the best adventure for you.

Start: The starting point, usually the trailhead, for the hike.

Difficulty: Refer to the level of difficulty as a guide only, as your own level of fitness will ultimately determine your experience.

Trail or Trails: The names and numbers of trails that the hike follows.

Hiking time: The average time it takes to hike the route. The time is based on the total distance, elevation gain, and trail's condition and difficulty. Your fitness level also affects your time.

Distance: The total distance of the recommended route from trailhead to trailhead. This field also specifies the type of hike (out-and-back, loop, or lollipop loop).

Elevation trailhead to lake: The starting elevation at the trailhead and the ending elevation at the lake, along with the difference in elevation between them. This does not include the cumulative elevation gain for a round-trip hike.

Restrictions: General info about fees, parking restrictions, hours, pets, camping, and other restrictions. Note that restrictions change often—contact the land management agency for details.

Amenities: Features at the trailhead and on the trail, including toilets, drinking water, visitor centers, benches, and interpretive signs.

Maps: A list of maps for the trail and trailhead, including the *DeLorme Gazetteer*, 13th edition; Trails Illustrated maps; and USGS topo maps.

County: The name of the county where the trail and lake are found.

Land status: Basic contact information for the trail's land management agency, including phone number. Detailed contact info for each agency, including national parklands, national forests, and state parks, is located in the appendix.

Finding the trailhead: Driving directions and GPS coordinates to the trailhead.

The Hike: A short description of the hike.

Miles and Directions: A step-by-step guide from trailhead to lake including mileage and GPS waypoints at each critical point and trail junction.

How to Use the Maps

Overview map: This map shows the location of each lake hike by hike number.
Trail maps: These maps illustrate the trailheads, roads and trails, points of interest, waterways, landmarks, geographical features, and the lakes.

Packing for Your Lake Hike

You'll want to dress appropriately for your lake hike, but there are other items you should carry for a safe and successful outing.

Start with a comfortable day pack or backpack to fit everything in. You don't have to spend a lot of money to get a pack that will satisfy your needs, and you can upgrade later if you need to. Try it on in the store and make sure it fits your body well, then fill it up and see if it still feels right. If lake hiking becomes a habit, you may be wearing it a lot!

Water is the most important item that goes into your pack, and how much or little you need depends on you and how long your hike is. You can carry it in refillable bottles or use a hydration reservoir that allows you to sip from a tube while you're on the move. For extra-long hikes, carry a water filter, so you can filter water from nearby streams and stay hydrated if your own supply runs out.

Extra clothing is also important, and that starts with a rain jacket. If you get wet on your hike, you will get cold, and that will ruin your day. Also think about carrying extra socks; a warm knit or fleece cap; a ball cap or sun hat with a brim; gloves; a warm top layer, such as a fleece shirt; a neck gaiter, headband, scarf, or "buff"; and water shoes or sandals that you can use for stream crossings, to keep your hiking shoes and boots dry. Staying warm, dry, and thoroughly hydrated is important on any hike, but it's especially critical at higher altitudes and above timberline, when you are even more susceptible to hypothermia, dehydration, and altitude sickness. These conditions can be debilitating and deadly, but can usually be avoided with proper planning, packing, and knowing when to turn around.

A first aid kit is always a good idea. You can buy one or make your own by putting bandages, antibacterial cream, pain reliever, and any other medications that you use in a resealable plastic bag. The bag is also a good place to store a pen and paper with your contact information on it, and that of your emergency contact person. If you have a CORSAR (Colorado Outdoor Recreation Search and Rescue) card, tuck it into the first aid kit. The card may be purchased online or at local businesses, and supports the Search and Rescue Fund, to help reimburse rescue teams that assist hikers who are lost or injured. The CORSAR card is not "rescue insurance," but it is an easy and inexpensive way for responsible Colorado hikers to support backcountry rescue personnel who may one day be called upon to come to their aid.

Invest in a headlamp and extra batteries, or a flashlight. Even the easiest trails are practically impassable in the dark, and there are no streetlights to guide you once the sun goes down. If you are hiking alone, carry two headlamps so you do not have to change batteries in the dark.

Buy a compass and learn how to use it. Should you get off-trail and disoriented, a map and compass—along with route-finding skills—will get you back on the trail and headed in the right direction pronto. You may eventually want to get a GPS too, and a satellite phone, along with extra batteries to go with them. Outdoor recreation schools like NOLS, retailers like REI, and nonprofit organizations like the Colorado Mountain Club offer courses in land navigation and can provide you with the instruction you need to use these tools correctly and confidently.

Food is perhaps the most fun thing to carry on a hike, especially when you get to eat it! A combination of sweet and salty snacks—such as fresh or dried fruit and nuts, or premade, packaged protein bars—will keep you alive and alert. For longer hikes, bring a lunch. Sandwiches travel well and taste great, and you can pack them in foil and plastic bags, along with a cold pack to keep them fresh and cool. Add a bottle of your favorite beverage like juice or an electrolyte drink in summer, or a thermos full of hot chocolate or tea in colder months.

Sun protection is important, even on cloudy days. Along with your hat, pack sunglasses, sunscreen, and lip balm, and reapply during your hike.

Insect repellent isn't always necessary in Colorado's backcountry, but if you end up near standing, swampy water in the summertime, you will be glad to have packed it.

Be sure to use the toilet before your hike, but if you should require a bathroom break along the trail, be prepared with a kit that includes toilet paper or wet wipes, plus—for women—feminine products, and—for men—anti-chafing powder, cream, or stick. Double bag it all in resealable plastic bags to keep the items fresh and dry, step off the trail to use them, bury all solid waste, and pack out all used items including toilet paper in an extra plastic bag. Certain locations require that you pack out your solid waste as well, so if that is the case, be prepared with a suitable, disposable container or use a Wag Bag, a human waste disposal system that can be carried out and disposed of properly.

Winter conditions demand even more gear than summer hikes, including additional clothing layers like a face mask, windproof pants and gloves, and ski goggles for extreme cold and wind, a puffy jacket to keep you warm during breaks, plus MICROspikes or other portable traction devices to slip over your boots for safe passage on icy trails and frozen stream crossings, and even gaiters and snowshoes to keep you high and dry in deep powder.

Extra items might include trekking poles—especially if your hike includes a lot of elevation gain or stream crossings—a camera or your cellphone with camera, and, of course, a copy of *Best Lake Hikes Colorado*. Copy or take a picture of the pages you need or pack the whole book in a resealable plastic bag to keep it safe and dry for your next hike.

Final Preparations

Once you've selected your lake hike and you're packed up and ready to go, there are just a few more things you should know.

Check the CDOT (Colorado Department of Transportation) site at www.cotrip .org for road conditions and closures along your driving route to the trailhead.

Check the NOAA (National Oceanic and Atmospheric Administration) site at www.noaa.gov for weather conditions and be sure that you won't be hiking through open areas or above treeline in inclement weather, especially if there's a danger of lightning. If stormy conditions do arise, be prepared to descend to the trailhead immediately.

If you plan on camping at a campground, check www.recreation.gov for availability and reservations.

If you're traveling on snow, check the Colorado Avalanche Information Center site at https://avalanche.state.co.us/index.php and avoid areas subject to avalanche danger. A thorough discussion of avalanche safety is beyond the scope of this book, but if avalanche danger exists on your planned hike, seek out the advice of an expert to determine an alternate route, choose another hike, or hike on another day.

Check the websites or call the phone numbers listed in the Land status detail for each hike for notifications or changes in restrictions. In the winter or springtime, ask about the effects of snow on the road to the trailhead, as some may be closed and gated, adding extra miles to your hike. Also find out about avalanche danger on the trail, and if there's a "winter route" that avoids that danger. Call the ranger station to get all your questions answered before you go.

If you're visiting a fee area, call ahead to find out how much it costs. Many of the parks offer annual passes, and if you plan to visit them often it may make sense to invest in an annual national park pass and a Colorado state park pass. These may be purchased at the parks, online, and at local businesses around the state. Also, bring cash or checks in case the entrance gate is unattended and you have to pay at a self-serve kiosk. Some kiosks also accept credit and debit cards. Contact information for purchasing park passes can be found in the appendix of this book.

For extra-long drives, bring a cooler with drinks and snacks, and two bags for your trash: one for recycling and one for composting. Carry some loose change or small bills too, so you can stop at small grocers or gas stations and buy items like drinks or postcards, and then use the restrooms.

Plan on the drive and the hike taking longer than you expect, especially if you're traveling with others. Stops for gas, snacks, and restroom breaks take time, and you should work these into your schedule. Expect them and you won't be stressed out when they happen.

Lake hikes may become a habit, and your favorite part of the whole week. Keep them fun, safe, and healthy, and you'll keep yourself happy doing them.

Map Legend

Transportation

- =🛡70🛡= Interstate Highway
- =〈24〉= US Highway
- =〈13〉= State Road
- =〔09〕= Local/County Road
- = = = : Unpaved Road
- ├──┼──┤ Railroad
- •─•─•─• Power Line
- ─ ·· ─ ·· ─ State Boundary

Trails

- ------- Featured Trail
- - - - - - Trail or Fire Road

Water Features

- Body of Water
- Glacier
- River/Creek
- Intermittent Stream
- ⌇ Waterfall

Symbols

- ≍ Bridge
- ■ Building/Point of Interest
- ▥ Boardwalk
- ▲ Campground
- ▲ Campsite (backcountry)
- •─• Gate
- ▭ Inn/Lodging
- 🅿 Parking
- 🛆 Picnic Area
- 🛈 Ranger Station/Park Office
- 🛆 Scenic View
- ○ Town
- ㉑ Trailhead
- ❓ Visitor/Information Center

Land Management

- National Park/Forest
- National Monument/ Wilderness Area
- State/County Park
- Natural Area

Denver and Boulder Area

Brighton, Ward, Idaho Springs, Georgetown, and Littleton

Mount Blue Sky, the thirteenth-highest mountain in Colorado, towers above a wetland on the southern shoreline of Summit Lake.

1 Barr Lake

Barr Lake, a high-plains reservoir that stores water for irrigation, is a bird-watcher's paradise with its crucial wetland habitats. Explore the wildlife refuge at the lake's southern half on several trails to scenic overlooks, bird blinds, and a gazebo in the lake.

Start: Trailhead at Nature Center
Difficulty: Easy
Trails: Barr Lake Perimeter Trail, Niedrach Nature Trail, Fox Meadow Trail, Gazebo Boardwalk Trail
Hiking time: About 2 hours
Distance: 3.4 miles out-and-back
Elevation trailhead to lake: 5,103 to 5,098 feet at gazebo on lake
Restrictions: Fee area; day-use only; open 5 a.m. to 10 p.m.; no dogs allowed at wildlife refuge; stay on designated trails and boardwalks; no fires; boating, fishing, swimming, and wading prohibited in wildlife refuge; no collecting plants, animals, or natural objects; watch wildlife from a distance
Amenities: Restrooms at trailhead area; visitor center; picnic area; interpretive and nature programs; services in Brighton
Maps: *DeLorme*: Page 40, A5; Trails Illustrated none; USGS Brighton, Mile High Lakes; Barr Lake State Park map
County: Adams
Land status: Barr Lake State Park, (303) 655-1495

Finding the trailhead: From north Denver, head northeast on I-76 and take exit 22 onto Bromley Lane/E. 152nd Avenue. Drive east for 0.9 mile to Picadilly Road and turn right. Drive south for 1.9 miles to the park entrance on the right. From E-470, a toll beltway around east Denver, take exit 34 onto 120th Avenue. Drive east on E. 120th Avenue for 0.6 mile to Tower Road and turn left on Tower Road. Drive north for 3 miles, making a right bend onto E. 128th Avenue and drive to Picadilly Road. Go left on Piccadilly and drive 1.1 miles to the park entrance on the left. Follow the park road through the entrance station for 1.3 miles to a parking area at the Nature Center. The trailhead is on the west side of the lot (GPS: 39 56.2946, –104 45.1144).

The Hike

Barr Lake, the centerpiece of Barr Lake State Park northeast of Denver, is a 1,307-acre reservoir that sprawls alongside I-76 and the nearby South Platte River. The prairie lake, originally a buffalo wallow, is a warm-water oasis that is a bird-watching wonderland. Considered one of Colorado's premier birding areas, naturalists have spotted over 360 of the state's 440 bird species at the lake, including shorebirds, waterfowl, songbirds, and raptors. It also is a critical refuge for reptiles, amphibians, and mammals with diverse habitats, including marshes, cottonwoods, grasslands, and the large lake. The lake's southern half is a designated wildlife refuge, while the northern part is open to low-powered boats and recreation. It is best to visit Barr Lake in early summer when South Platte water fills it. Later in the season, water drains out for irrigating farmland.

Looping around the lake for 8.8 miles, the level Barr Lake Perimeter Trail makes a perfect hike for walkers, but the trail's best section threads along the southeastern shore of the wildlife area. This 3.4-mile round-trip segment, closed to dogs, offers wildlife blinds, boardwalks onto the lake, and observation points to spot birds. The described hike follows the best part of the trail, stopping at blinds to glimpse shy birds, edging past ponds alive with chorus frogs, and a long boardwalk that ends at a gazebo surrounded by water.

After checking out the Nature Center, cross the Denver and Hudson Canal on a bridge, and turn south on the Perimeter Trail. The next section follows the Niedrach Nature Trail on a boardwalk along the lake's edge before rejoining the main trail. Continue southwest on the trail between the lake and canal, passing bird blinds and viewpoints, to Fox Meadow Trail, a shoreline open loop. Continue on the Perimeter Trail to the Gazebo Boardwalk Trail. This elevated walkway, loved by kids, hovers above the water as it jogs almost a quarter mile into the lake. The shady gazebo is a perfect place for a picnic and to watch pelicans, herons, ducks, and grebes. Afterwards, head back north to the Nature Center with one final boardwalk on the return leg of Niedrach Nature Trail. For a longer hike, continue southwest on the Perimeter Trail for another mile to a spur path that leads to a viewpoint of the park's heron rookery at the lake's south end.

Silvered cottonwood tree trunks line the eastern shoreline of Barr Lake, one of Colorado's best birding areas.

Barr Lake

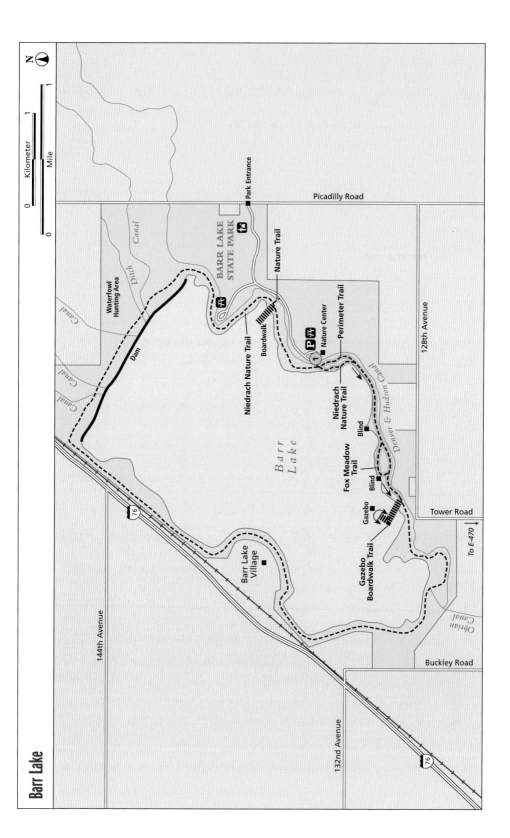

Miles and Directions

0.0 Start at the trailhead on the west side of the parking lot at the Nature Center. Walk west and cross a bridge over a canal.

0.04 Reach a junction with the Perimeter Trail. Go left.

0.06 Reach a junction on the right with Niedrach Nature Trail. Go right on the nature trail.

0.1 Arrive at the junction at the start of the Niedrach loop. Keep right and follow the trail to a boardwalk on the lake's edge.

0.3 Reach the end of Niedrach loop (GPS: 39 56.0558, –104 45.1541). Keep right and hike 0.05 mile to the Perimeter Trail. Go right and hike along the trail between the lakeshore and canal.

0.8 Junction with a short trail that goes right to a wildlife blind. Return to the Perimeter Trail and continue southwest.

1.0 Arrive at a junction with Fox Meadow Trail on the right (GPS: 39 55.8942, –104 45.731). Go right on it and follow the loop along the lake edge.

1.2 Pass a wildlife blind building on the right. Continue straight.

1.3 Return to the Perimeter Trail and go right. Hike along the lake edge.

1.55 Reach a junction on the right with the Gazebo Boardwalk Trail (GPS: 39 55.8579, –104 46.1264). Pass a toilet and interpretive signs and follow the boardwalk onto Barr Lake.

1.8 Arrive at the gazebo and turnaround point (GPS: 39 55.9769, –104 46.179). Look for birds and rest on shady benches. Then return on the boardwalk to shore.

2.0 Reach the Perimeter Trail. Go left toward the Nature Center past Fox Meadow Trail to Niedrach Nature Trail.

3.0 Reach a Y-junction with the Niedrach Nature Trail. Go left to complete its loop. Keep right at the next junction and follow a boardwalk through cottonwoods.

3.3 Arrive at the junction with the Perimeter Trail. Go left, cross the canal bridge, and hike toward the parking lot.

3.4 Arrive back at the trailhead (GPS: 39 56.2946, –104 45.1144).

A Canada geese family floats across Barr Lake, the gleaming water covered with cottonwood "cotton."

2 Lake Isabelle

Turquoise gems sprawled in a glacier-sculpted cirque, Lake Isabelle and Long Lake sit at the foot of rugged peaks in the Indian Peaks Wilderness Area.

Start: Long Lake Trailhead
Difficulty: Easy
Trails: Jean Lunning Trail #907.1, Pawnee Pass Trail #907, Isabelle Glacier Trail #908, Niwot Cutoff Trail #907.2 (alternative start at Niwot Cutoff Trailhead)
Hiking time: About 3 hours
Distance: 4.6 miles loop
Elevation trailhead to lakes: 10,510 to 10,890 feet at lake overlook
Restrictions: Timed entry reservations are required to enter Brainard Lake Recreation Area and to access the trailhead; visit recreation.gov for the permit and fee info; trailhead parking usually is closed until late June; park only in designated lots; no roadside parking; observe wilderness regulations; no motorized vehicles or equipment; dogs must be leashed; in winter, park at the free Brainard Gateway Lot before the entrance station and snowshoe or ski on road for 3.1 miles to the trailhead.
Amenities: Restrooms, picnic table, info signs at trailhead; services in Nederland
Maps: DeLorme: Page 29, E6; Trails Illustrated 102: Indian Peaks, Gold Hill; USGS Ward
County: Boulder
Land status: Brainard Lake Recreation Area; Indian Peaks Wilderness Area; Roosevelt National Forest, (970) 295-6600; Boulder Ranger District, (303) 541-2500

Finding the trailhead: From the junction of CO 119 and CO 72 in Nederland, turn on West 2nd Street/CO 72 (Peak to Peak Highway) and drive north for 11.8 miles to a left turn on signed Brainard Lake Road. From the junction of CO 72 and CO 7 between Allenspark and Lyons, turn south on CO 7 and drive 9.9 miles to a right turn on Brainard Lake Road. Drive west on Brainard Lake Road/CR 112 for 5.3 miles, passing the entrance station, Pawnee Campground, and Brainard Lake, to a junction with Mitchell Lake Road. Go left on it and drive 0.1 mile to a left turn on Long Lake Road. Go left on it and drive 0.4 mile to a parking lot and the Long Lake Trailhead (GPS: 40 4.6705, -105 35.0768).

The Hike

Lake Isabelle, a glistening reservoir tucked below soaring mountain peaks, is a deservedly popular hike in the 76,711-acre Indian Peaks Wilderness Area, the most visited wilderness area in the United States. The lake hike, beginning at Brainard Lake Recreation Area, passes Long Lake and then climbs easy grades to Lake Isabelle and stunning scenic views. A row of sawtoothed mountains looms above the lake, including 13,409-foot Navajo Peak, 13,441-foot Apache Peak, and 12,967-foot Shoshoni Peak, while Isabelle Glacier, the headwaters of the lake and South St. Vrain Creek, is plastered against the Continental Divide. This shrinking glacier is the last remnant of a huge glacier that once filled the valley. The original lake was enlarged as a reservoir to store water for agriculture, so it is often drawn down by late summer. Besides stellar views, this loop hike offers wildflowers in summer and moose munching willows in wetlands along the creek.

The Brainard Lake Recreation Area, an hour's drive from Denver, is busy during its snow-free months from late June until mid-October. To protect the area from being loved to death, the US Forest Service instituted a paid, timed-entry reservation system for all visitors to park at any of the lots in the area. Make a reservation at recreation.gov. The only free lot is at Brainard Gateway Trailhead before the entrance station. The seasonal entrance gate is open from mid-June to mid-October. The Long Lake Trailhead for the Lake Isabelle hike is closed until late June to protect muddy trails from damage.

The hike to Lake Isabelle is mostly easy with minimal elevation gain except for the last section, easy to follow, and marked with directional signs. Starting at the Long Lake Trailhead, the hike heads west to Long Lake on Pawnee Pass Trail, which leads to a junction with Isabelle Glacier Trail above Isabelle Lake. The return loop heads east and then follows Jean Lunning Trail around the south side of Long Lake before returning to Pawnee Pass Trail near the trailhead. If you're unable to obtain a parking reservation for Long Lake Trailhead, reserve at Niwot Picnic Area and hike the Niwot Cutoff Trail to the Jean Lunning Trail.

Clouds wreath Navajo and Apache Peaks above Lake Isabelle in the Indian Peaks Wilderness Area.

Lake Isabelle; Mitchell Lake and Blue Lake

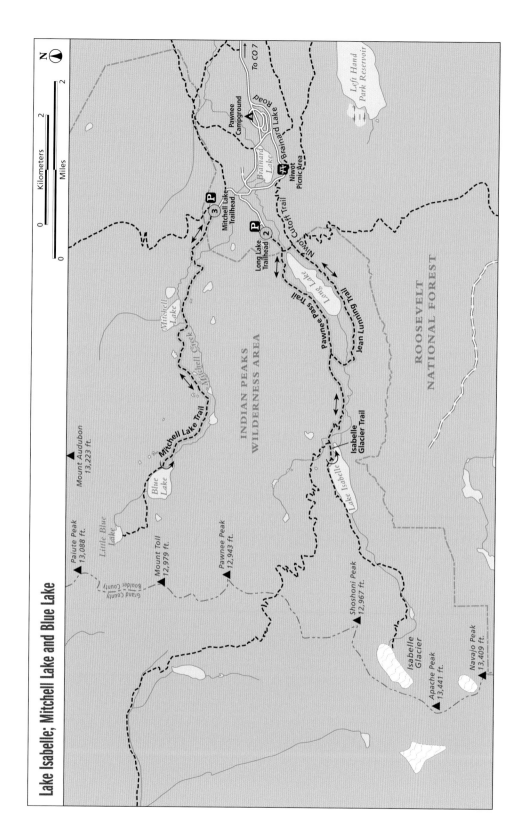

Miles and Directions

0.0 Start at the Long Lake Trailhead and hike west on wide Pawnee Pass Trail through forest.

0.2 Reach a junction on the left with Jean Lunning Trail (GPS: 40 4.5502, –105 35.2221), which is the hike's return loop. Continue straight on wide Pawnee Pass Trail through forest along the northern edge of Long Lake with views south of the lake and Niwot Ridge.

1.2 West of Long Lake, reach a second junction with Jean Lunning Trail on the left (GPS: 40 4.2271, –105 36.0827), which is the start of the return loop. Continue straight on Pawnee Pass Trail.

2.0 Reach a junction with Isabelle Glacier Trail going straight and Pawnee Pass Trail to the right (GPS: 40 4.2228, –105 36.8754). Keep straight on Isabelle Glacier Trail.

2.1 Go left on a side trail that goes left to Lake Isabelle.

2.15 Arrive at viewpoint on rock outcrop above Lake Isabelle's north shore (GPS: 40 4.201, –105 36.9801). Return to main trail and go right to junction with the Pawnee Pass Trail. Continue straight and hike east on Pawnee Pass Trail.

3.1 Reach a junction with Jean Lunning Trail on the right. Go right and hike south on Jean Lunning Trail, crossing a footbridge over South St. Vrain Creek, and continue east and then northeast on the trail south of Long Lake.

4.3 Reach a junction with Niwot Cutoff Trail (GPS: 40 4.4807, –105 35.1845), which goes straight. Go left on Jean Lunning Trail and cross a bridge over Long Lake's outlet stream.

4.4 Reach a junction with Pawnee Pass Trail and go right. Hike east on the wide trail.

4.6 Arrive back at the trailhead (GPS: 40 4.6705, –105 35.0768).

Alternative start: If you're unable to get a parking reservation for Long Lake Trailhead, get one for Niwot Picnic Area in the Brainard Lake Recreation Area.

- Start across the road from the parking area at Niwot Cutoff Trailhead.
- Follow Niwot Cutoff Trail for 0.6 mile to its junction with Jean Lunning Trail.
- Go left and hike west on Jean Lunning Trail to Pawnee Pass Trail.
- Go left on it and hike 1.05 miles to Lake Isabelle.
- To return, hike east on Pawnee Pass Trail to its second junction with Jean Lunning Trail. Go right on it to Niwot Cutoff Trail and return 0.6 mile to the trailhead.

Winter start: The trailheads and Brainard Lake area are inaccessible much of the year due to heavy snowfall. They usually open in late June. For a winter hike, park at the Brainard Gateway Trailhead before the entrance station on Brainard Lake Road. The gate is closed, and no fee is charged to enter the area. Follow Brainard Lake Road for 3.1 miles to the Long Lake Trailhead and follow above directions.

3 Mitchell Lake and Blue Lake

Lying amid mountain splendor, Mitchell, Blue, and "Little Blue" Lakes glisten in a deep, glaciated valley beneath towering peaks in the Indian Peaks Wilderness Area northwest of Boulder and Denver.

See map on page 8.
Start: Mitchell Lake Trailhead
Difficulty: Moderate
Trail: Mitchell Lake Trail #912
Hiking time: About 2 hours
Distance: 4.8 miles out-and-back
Elevation trailhead to lake: 10,500 to 10,700 feet at Mitchell Lake (+200 feet); 11,310 feet at Blue Lake (+810 feet)
Restrictions: Timed entry reservations are required to enter Brainard Lake Recreation Area and to access the trailhead; visit recreation.gov for permit and fee info; trailhead parking usually is closed until late June; park only in designated lots; no roadside parking; observe wilderness regulations; no motorized vehicles or equipment; leashed dogs only; in winter, park at the free Brainard Gateway Lot before the entrance station and snowshoe or ski on the road for 2.9 miles to the trailhead.
Amenities: Restrooms, picnic tables, info signs at trailhead; services in Nederland
Maps: DeLorme: Page 29, E6; Trails Illustrated 102: Indian Peaks, Gold Hill; USGS Ward, Monarch Lake
County: Boulder
Land status: Brainard Lake Recreation Area; Indian Peaks Wilderness Area; Roosevelt National Forest, (970) 295-6600; Boulder Ranger District, (303) 541-2500

Finding the trailhead: From the junction of CO 119 and CO 72 in Nederland, turn on West 2nd Street/CO 72 (Peak to Peak Highway) and drive north for 11.8 miles to a left turn on signed Brainard Lake Road. From the junction of CO 72 and CO 7 between Allenspark and Lyons, turn south on CO 7 and drive 9.9 miles to a right turn on Brainard Lake Road. Drive west on Brainard Lake Road/CR 112 for 5.3 miles, passing the entrance station, Pawnee Campground, and Brainard Lake, to a junction with Mitchell Lake Road. Go left on it and drive 0.1 mile to a junction with Long Lake Road (goes to Long Lake Trailhead). Continue straight on Mitchell Lake Road for 0.3 mile to a parking lot and the Mitchell Lake Trailhead (GPS: 40 4.9993, –105 34.9091).

The Hike

A gleaming string of three lakes—Mitchell, Blue, and "Little Blue" Lakes—scatter along the floor of a wide glaciated valley in the Indian Peaks Wilderness Area. Popular Mitchell Lake, reached by a short hike, nestles against the southern flank of 13,223-foot Mount Audubon. Mitchell Lake, surrounded by forest, meadows, and a talus field below Audubon, is a perfect family-friendly hike with easy hiking and minimal elevation gain. The trail to Blue Lake is tougher, threading around hummocky hills on the valley floor and then steeply climbing rocky, tundra-clad slopes above timberline to the gorgeous lake. A parade of high peaks encase Blue Lake, including Mount Audubon to the north and 13,088-foot Paiute Peak, 12,979-foot

Mount Toll, and 12,943-foot Pawnee Peak on the Continental Divide above the lake. For extra credit, a rough trail scrambles to rockbound "Little Blue Lake" at 11,833 feet. Like the Lake Isabelle hike in the next valley south, the lakes and trail offer stunning scenery, riotous wildflowers in summer, and moose wading through wetlands and willows along Mitchell Creek.

The trail starts at the Brainard Lake Recreation Area on the eastern edge of the Indian Peaks Wilderness Area. The area is busy during its snow-free months from late June until mid-October. To protect the area from being overrun with hikers and tourists, the US Forest Service has a paid, timed-entry reservation system for all visitors to park at any of the designated parking lots. Make daily reservations at recreation.gov. If you're unable to obtain a parking reservation for Mitchell Lake Trailhead, reserve at Niwot Picnic Area and hike up the road to the trailhead or at Brainard Lake and follow trails around the lake's north side and then to the trailhead. The only free lot is at Brainard Gateway Trailhead before the entrance station. The seasonal entrance gate is open from mid-June to mid-October, and then closed in winter. To reach the lakes and trail in the snowy months, hikers must park before the gate and hike, snowshoe, or ski up the road or trails to the trailhead, adding 5 to 6 extra miles to the overall distance.

The Mitchell Lake Trail, one of Colorado's classic lake hikes, is easy to follow and marked with directional signs. The first trail section winds through forest to the south side of Mitchell Lake. This is the turnaround point for casual hikers. The second section gently ascends the valley past wetlands and ponds, to a final steep pull to Blue Lake. Snow often covers this final section in June, making it hard to follow the trail. Bring poles and MICROspikes for traction on snowdrifts.

Forest-fringed Mitchell Lake lies against the long east ridge of Mount Audubon.

Miles and Directions

0.0 Start at the Mitchell Lake Trailhead on the west side of the parking lot. Hike west on the Mitchell Lake Trail.

0.4 Cross a footbridge over Mitchell Creek and enter the Indian Peaks Wilderness Area after 100 feet. Continue southwest and then northwest on the well-trod trail.

0.9 Reach a trail junction (GPS: 40 5.2184, –105 35.741). Go right for 125 feet to the south shore of Mitchell Lake. Return to the junction and go right (west) toward Blue Lake.

1.0 Cross Mitchell Creek south of Mitchell Lake (GPS: 40 5.1678, –105 35.8584). Continue west and then southwest on the trail, skirting low glaciated hills and then traversing across a hillside above a wide valley and Mitchell Creek. Look down at the extensive wetland and five ponds along Mitchell Creek to spot grazing moose. The trail continues traversing the hillside above the valley, passing a large pond flanked by talus slopes, and then climbs past a cascading waterfall. The trail's angle lessens as it rolls across tundra-clad slopes to a final steep ascent up a rocky slope.

2.4 Reach a spectacular viewpoint on the east side of Blue Lake (GPS: 40 5.3148, –105 37.0425). After a snack, head back down the trail.

4.8 Arrive back at the trailhead (GPS: 40 4.9993, –105 34.9091).

EXTRA CREDIT: "LITTLE BLUE LAKE"

Reach "Little Blue Lake," a pretty tarn on a shelf below Piute Peak, by an unmaintained 0.8-mile trail that follows the north shore of Blue Lake and then skirts cliffs before climbing steeply up tundra and talus slopes to the lake. The trail, gaining over 400 feet of elevation, is hard to follow in places and hiking over the talus is laborious. Snowfields cover the trail for most of the year, so bring trekking poles, MICROspikes, and an ice axe, depending on snow and weather conditions.

4 Summit Lake

Two trails explore Summit Lake, one of Colorado's highest lakes, on the floor of an alpine cirque below cliffs and couloirs on Mount Blue Sky, formerly called Mount Evans.

Start: Summit Lake Trailhead
Difficulty: Easy
Trails: Chicago Lakes Overlook Trail; Summit Lake Loop Trail
Hiking time: About 30 minutes
Distance: Chicago Lakes Overlook Trail: 0.5 mile out-and-back; Summit Lake Loop Trail: 0.18 mile lollipop loop
Elevation trailhead to lake: 12,856 to 12,840 feet at lake (-16 feet)
Restrictions: Highway fee; timed-entry passes required to drive Mount Evans Highway to Summit Lake; buy passes at recreation.gov reservation system; stay on trails to avoid fragile plants; usually accessible Memorial Day to Labor Day; vault toilets at trailhead; services in Idaho Springs
Amenities: Vault toilets at trailhead; services in Idaho Springs
Maps: *DeLorme*: Page 39, E5 and E6; Trails Illustrated 104: Idaho Springs, Loveland Pass; USGS Mount Evans
County: Clear Creek
Land status: Denver Mountain Parks, (720) 865-0900; park rangers, (720) 913-1311

Finding the trailhead: Summit Lake Mountain Park is 60 miles west of Denver. Drive on I-70 to Idaho Springs and take exit 240. Follow CO 103 for 15 miles to Echo Lake. Go right on Mount Evans Highway/CO 5 and drive 15 miles to the signed Summit Lake turnoff on the right. The trailhead is on the north side of the parking lot (GPS: 39 35.926, -105 38.4271).

The Hike

Summit Lake, the thirteenth-highest lake in the United States at 12,830 feet above sea level, tucks into a cliff-rimmed alpine cirque below 14,271-foot Mount Blue Sky and 13,842-foot Mount Spalding. The glacier-created lake is the shining gem of 150-acre Summit Lake Park, part of Denver's mountain park system and the highest city park in the nation. Designated as Colorado's first National Natural Landmark in 1965, the park's high meadows surrounding the lake are a superb example of alpine tundra, an ecosystem of plants and grasses that grow above treeline. Summit Lake Flats east of the lake is one of the few permafrost areas outside of Alaska. Besides the lake, the park includes a parking lot, stone shelter built in the 1930s, restrooms, and two trails. Mount Blue Sky is often climbed on a trail that begins at Summit Lake and climbs Mount Spalding and then the skyline ridge to Blue Sky's summit.

The Chicago Lakes Overlook Trail and Summit Lake Loop Trail explore the lake's eastern shore. The overlook trail contours above the lake to a dramatic viewpoint above a glaciated gorge and the Chicago Lakes. Besides great views, the fenced overlook features interpretive signs. The loop trail gently descends to the lake's southeastern shoreline by Bear Creek, the outlet stream, and offers spectacular views of looming Mount Blue Sky. Stay on both trails to avoid damaging tundra plants.

Summit Lake sprawls across an alpine cirque below Mount Spalding.

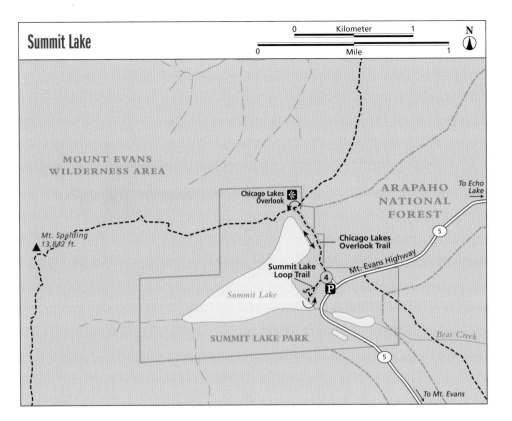

0   Kilometer   1

0   Mile   1

N

MOUNT EVANS
WILDERNESS AREA

Chicago Lakes
Overlook

ARAPAHO
NATIONAL
FOREST

To Echo
Lake

Mt. Spalding
13,842 ft.

Chicago Lakes
Overlook Trail

5

Summit Lake
Loop Trail

Mt. Evans Highway

4

P

Summit Lake

SUMMIT LAKE PARK

Bear Creek

5

To Mt. Evans

Miles and Directions

Chicago Lakes Overlook Trail

0.0 Start at trailhead on north side of parking lot and left of restrooms. Hike north on the trail.

0.25 Reach Chicago Lakes Overlook and start of Mt. Blue Sky Trail (GPS: 39 36.1066, –105 38.539).

0.5 Arrive back at the trailhead (GPS: 39 35.926, –105 38.4271).

Summit Lake Loop Trail

0.0 Begin at trailhead on west side of parking lot (GPS: 39 35.913, –105 38.4503). Hike west toward lake.

0.03 Reach a junction and start of loop trail after 160 feet. Keep right.

0.06 Arrive at Summit Lake shoreline. Go left.

0.08 Reach a three-way junction. Go right to overlook.

0.1 Admire the lake and Mt. Blue Sky from shoreline, then return back to junction and hike east on the trail to the first junction.

0.15 Reach a junction. Continue straight to the parking lot.

0.18 Arrive back at the trailhead (GPS: 39 35.926, –105 38.4271).

5 Square Top Lakes

The twin Square Top Lakes hide in an alpine cirque on the east flank of Square Top Mountain, offering gorgeous reflections of peak and sky, and spectacular views of Mount Bierstadt and Mount Blue Sky, formerly called Mount Evans.

Start: South Park Trailhead
Difficulty: Moderate
Trail: South Park Trail #600
Hiking time: About 3 hours
Distance: 4.5 miles out-and-back
Elevation trailhead to lake viewpoints:
11,720 to 12,046 feet at lower lake (+326 feet); 12,263 feet at upper lake (+543 feet)
Restrictions: No motorized vehicles or mountain bikes; dogs must be under control

Amenities: Vault toilets at trailhead; services in Georgetown
Maps: *DeLorme*: Page 39, E5; Trails Illustrated 104: Idaho Springs, Loveland Pass; USGS Mount Evans
County: Clear Creek
Land status: Pike National Forest, (719) 553-1400; South Park Ranger District, (719) 836-2031; Guanella Pass travel info: (303) 679-2312 or (303) 679-2422 x2

Finding the trailhead: From I-70 west of Denver, take exit 228 toward Georgetown and follow sign to CR 381/Guanella Pass Road. From the junction of Second and Rose Streets on the south side of Georgetown, go left on Guanella Pass Road and drive 10.6 miles, passing the top of the pass to a right turn. Drive a side road for 0.2 mile to a parking lot and the South Park Trailhead for Square Top Lakes (GPS: 39 35.8306, -105 42.7816). From Fairplay, drive north on US 285 for 27.8 miles and turn left on CR 62/Guanella Pass Road. Drive 13.0 miles north to a left turn to the trailhead and parking.

The Hike

Lower and Upper Square Top Lakes nestle in a glacier-carved basin below the east face of 13,794-foot Square Top Mountain, Colorado's 111th-highest peak. Tundra meadows, blotched with wildflowers in midsummer, and low clumps of willows surround both alpine lakes. Beginning at a parking lot above Guanella Pass, the South Park Trail twists west below Square Top's long east ridge, slowly climbing to the high lakes. The popular trail is easy to follow, runs entirely above treeline, has a footbed of rocks and dirt, and has only three steep sections. The trail offers spectacular views east of 14,065-foot Mount Bierstadt, the dramatic Sawtooth ridge, and 14,265-foot Mount Blue Sky. The parking lot, used for overflow parking for Bierstadt hikers, fills on weekends so plan on an early arrival. Guanella Pass Road's upper section closes during the winter from late November until late May.

Upper Square Top Lake lies below a glacier-carved cirque on Square Top Mountain.

Square Top Lakes

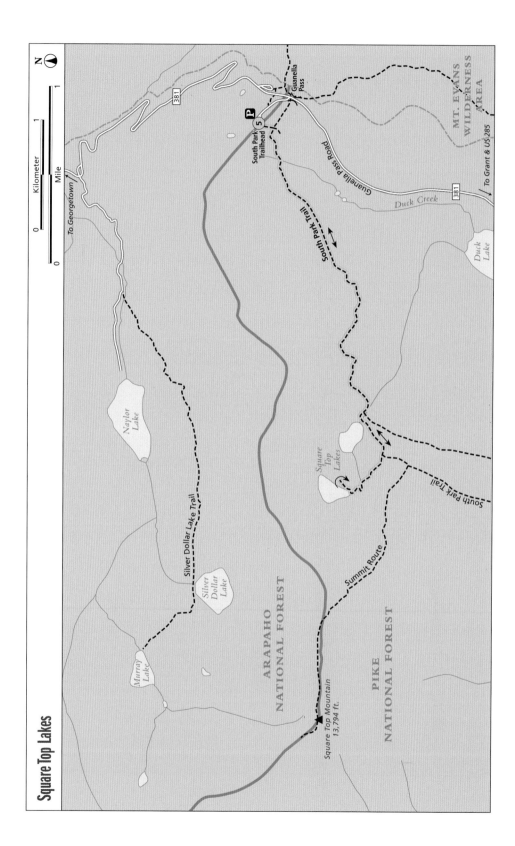

Miles and Directions

0.0 Start at South Park Trailhead at southwest corner of parking lot by the toilets. Hike southwest on signed trail to a fork.

0.1 At junction, go right and descend west on the trail. The other trail goes straight to an overlook.

1.7 Cross rocks across a creek. Continue straight.

1.75 Cross a creek, follow trail for 100 feet through willows, and turn right on side trail. Hike 75 feet to east shore of Lower Square Top Lake (GPS: 39 35.4178, -105 44.3377). Return to main trail and continue southwest up steep trail.

1.95 Reach a signed junction for Square Top Lakes; continue straight on the trail and hike northwest up slopes. *Option:* A left turn on South Park Trail climbs steep slopes for 1.4 miles to summit of Square Top Mountain.

2.15 Reach a wetland. Keep left and hike clockwise on the trail along left edge of wetland for dry feet and to avoid damage to marsh.

2.25 Arrive at south shore of Upper Square Top Lake (GPS: 39 35.4637, -105 44.6881). The trail continues right onto a bluff above the lake and offers views east of lower lake. Return the way you came.

4.5 Arrive back at the trailhead (GPS: 39 35.8306, -105 42.7816).

Square Top Mountain, the 111th-highest peak in Colorado, rises above Lower Square Top Lake near Guanella Pass.

6 Chatfield Reservoir and Audubon Nature Center Ponds

Several trails explore the edges of ponds and the South Platte River in the Audubon Nature Center wildlife area in the southern part of Chatfield State Park southwest of Denver. An extra credit hike follows an easy, paved trail around Chatfield Reservoir.

Start: Trailhead at Audubon Nature Center
Difficulty: Easy
Trails: Southeast Short Loop Trail, Audubon Discovery Loop, Muskrat Trail, Blackbird Pond Trail, Cottonwood Loop Trail, Old River Trail, Wetlands Connector Trail
Hiking time: About 2 hours
Distance: 3.1 miles loop
Elevation trailhead to lake: 5,510 to 5,470 feet at Muskrat Pond

Restrictions: Open year-round; daylight hours only; leashed dogs only
Amenities: Toilets near trailhead; interpretive information; nature center; ADA accessible facilities; picnic area
Maps: *DeLorme*: Page 40, E2 and page 50, A2; Trails Illustrated none; USGS Kassler
County: Jefferson
Land status: Chatfield State Park, (303) 791-7275; Audubon Nature Center, (303) 973-9530

Finding the trailhead: From the junction of I-25 and C-470 in south Denver, drive west on C-470 for 12 miles and take the exit for Wadsworth Boulevard/CO 121. Drive south on Wadsworth, passing the entrance to Chatfield State Park. Continue south to 11280 Waterton Road, Littleton. Turn left on Waterton Road and drive east to a left turn into the parking lot and trailhead at the Audubon Nature Center (GPS: 39 29.6056, –105 5.5409).

The Hike

Chatfield State Park is a recreational playground surrounding 1,423-surface-acre Chatfield Reservoir about 15 miles southwest of Denver. The southern part of the park operates as the Denver Audubon Nature Center, a natural preserve for wildlife, including 345 bird species, and a variety of habitats from grasslands and wetlands to the South Platte River corridor. A network of easy trails explore the nature center, passing four ponds—Muskrat, Blackbird, Cigar, and Gravel.

The described hike, a family-friendly adventure, follows a series of trails past the ponds, across open meadows, along a cottonwood-shaded path beside the river, and through wetlands teeming with birds to add to your life list. Not all of the trails and junctions are marked, but route-finding is easy. If the nature center is open (call ahead for hours), begin your adventure there with programs and hands-on exhibits to learn about area wildlife, ecology, and life zones.

Chatfield Reservoir, watery centerpiece of the state park, was built for flood control after several devastating floods, including one in 1965, led to the construction

Cattails line the edge of Muskrat Pond along Muskrat Trail at the Audubon Nature Center, part of Chatfield State Park.

of the huge dam and lake. One of Colorado's most popular lakes, Chatfield offers boating, waterskiing, a swim beach, picnic areas, campgrounds, and hiking on over 26 miles of trails. A good extra credit hike follows the paved, 10-mile Chatfield Perimeter Trail and the 2.4-mile Chatfield Dam Trail around the lake for a 12.4-mile loop hike. For a shorter lake hike, park near the headquarters building on the southeast lakeshore and hike south on the easy Chatfield Perimeter Trail for a couple of miles, passing a heron rookery and wildlife-viewing areas, then turn around and return back to the trailhead.

A boater floats on Gravel Pond, a former gravel pit that is the largest pond at Chatfield State Park.

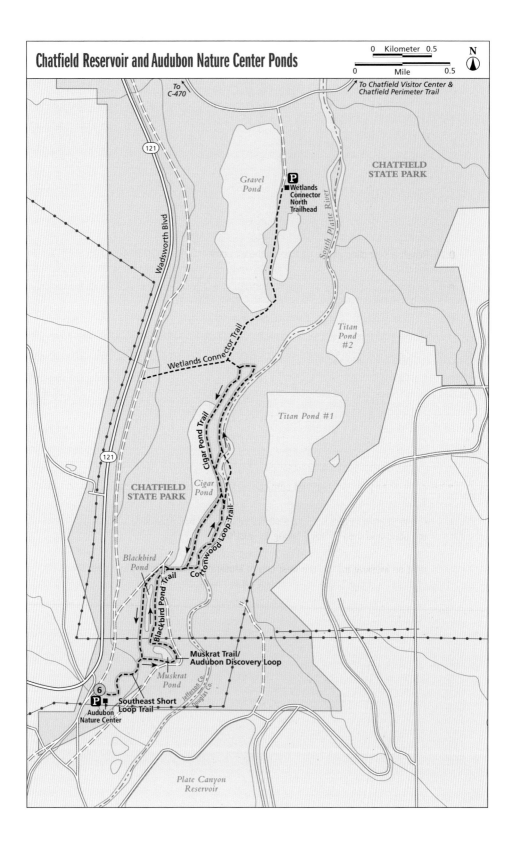

Chatfield Reservoir and Audubon Nature Center Ponds

0   Kilometer   0.5

0   Mile   0.5

N

To C-470

To Chatfield Visitor Center & Chatfield Perimeter Trail

121

CHATFIELD STATE PARK

Gravel Pond

P Wetlands Connector North Trailhead

South Platte River

Wadsworth Blvd

Wetlands Connector Trail

Titan Pond #2

Cigar Pond Trail

Titan Pond #1

121

CHATFIELD STATE PARK

Cigar Pond

Cottonwood Loop Trail

Blackbird Pond

Blackbird Pond Trail

Muskrat Trail/ Audubon Discovery Loop

Muskrat Pond

Jefferson Co. Douglas Co.

6 P Audubon Nature Center

Southeast Short Loop Trail

Plate Canyon Reservoir

Miles and Directions

0.0 Start at the trailhead on the south side of the nature center building. Hike east past the building and go left past Discovery Plaza, an area enclosed by a wall, on Southeast Short Loop Trail. Hike north to a junction by restrooms. Go right to another junction above Muskrat Pond.

0.2 Turn right on unmarked Muskrat Trail and hike around Muskrat Pond to a junction on its northwest side.

0.45 Reach a three-way junction. Go right on unmarked Blackbird Pond Trail. Hike north on the east side of the long, narrow pond.

0.7 Past the pond, reach a junction. Go right on unmarked Cottonwood Loop Trail and hike east by a fence along the southern edge of Cigar Pond.

0.75 Reach a Y-junction at the pond's southeast corner (GPS: 39 29.9446, –105 5.2512). Go right.

0.8 Reach the west bank of the South Platte River and turn left on unmarked Cottonwood Loop Trail. Hike north alongside the river.

1.1 Reach a junction with Cigar Pond Trail (GPS: 39 30.1215, –105 5.1121). Go straight (north) on it between Cigar Pond on the left and the South Platte River on the right.

1.2 Reach a Y-junction with Cottonwood Loop Trail on the right (GPS: 39 30.2208, –105 5.1398). Go right on it and hike along the river's west bank.

1.5 Arrive at a junction and go left (GPS: 39 30.4954, –105 4.9941). Hike 250 feet west and turn left on a wide trail. Hike south through trees to the east side of Cigar Pond and continue south on the trail. The right trail continues along the riverbank.

1.9 Reach a junction and continue south between Cigar Pond on the right and the South Platte River on the left on Cottonwood Loop Trail.

2.4 Meet a Y-junction and keep right along Cigar Pond.

2.45 Arrive at another junction and continue west on the south edge of Cigar Pond on Cottonwood Loop Trail.

2.5 Reach a junction and keep right on Blackbird Pond Trail. Hike west to the north end of the pond and then go south along its west bank.

2.8 Reach a junction with a boardwalk between Blackbird Pond and Muskrat Pond. Keep right on Muskrat Trail on the west end of Muskrat Pond and hike south past a viewing platform to a junction. Keep right and climb timber steps up a hill.

2.9 Reach junction at the start of Audubon Discovery Loop. Keep right and return to the nature center and trailhead.

3.1 Arrive back at the trailhead (GPS: 39 29.6056, –105 5.5409).

Colorado Springs Area

Palmer Lake, Cascade, Colorado Springs, Woodland Park, and Lake George

Fleecy clouds reflect in Manitou Lake's calm waters north of Woodland Park.

7 Palmer Lake Reservoirs

Lower and Upper Palmer Reservoirs, part of the Palmer Lake water supply, hide in a wooded canyon carved by North Monument Creek on the eastern flank of the Rampart Range north of Colorado Springs.

Start: Reservoir Trailhead
Difficulty: Moderate
Trail: Palmer Reservoir Trail
Hiking time: About 2 hours
Distance: 3.2 miles out-and-back
Elevation trailhead to lakes: 7,225 to 7,750 feet at upper lake (+525 feet)
Restrictions: Lower canyon is in the Palmer Lake watershed; pedestrian use only; open day and night year-round; no dogs allowed on trails or in lakes (strictly enforced and punishable with fines); no firearms, horses, motor vehicles, camping, fishing, or swimming
Amenities: Services in Palmer Lake and Monument
Maps: *DeLorme*: Page 50, D3 and D4; Trails Illustrated 137: Pikes Peak, Cañon City; USGS Palmer Lake
County: El Paso
Land status: Pike National Forest; Pikes Peak Ranger District, (719) 636-1602; Town of Palmer Lake, (719) 481-2953

Finding the trailhead: From Colorado Springs, drive north on I-25 to Monument and take exit 161. Drive west on CO 105 for 3.5 miles to Palmer Lake. Turn left (west) on South Valley Road in Palmer Lake and continue west for 0.35 mile. Turn left (south) on Old Carriage Road and drive 0.2 mile to a large roadside parking area and the trailhead in the valley below (GPS: 39 7.1212, –104 55.2673).

The Hike

The twin Palmer Reservoirs, formed by dams blocking North Monument Creek, are reached by a popular hike up a closed utility road from the southwestern edge of the town of Palmer Lake. Named for General William Jackson Palmer, the founder of Colorado Springs, the shiny lakes hide in a steep-walled canyon lined with ponderosa pines, Douglas fir, and Engelmann spruce. The trail steadily climbs uphill from the trailhead and then evens out at the lakes. A hike to the lakes is also the jumping-off point for more hiking adventures up Ice Cave Creek Trail, Winding Stairs Trail, and Balanced Rock Trail. Peakbaggers scramble up Chautauqua and Sundance Mountains for views east to the high prairie or climb to the rocky top of Cap Rock. When you reach the lakes, remember that people cannot swim or wade in the reservoirs, which is stored drinking water for the Town of Palmer Lake.

Palmer Lake Reservoirs

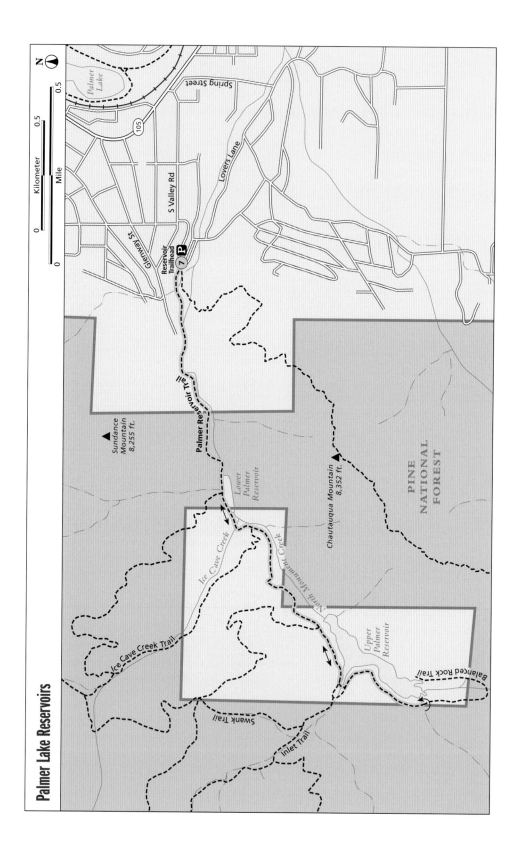

Palmer Lake

105

Glenway St

S Valley Rd

Reservoir Trailhead

7 P

Spring Street

Lovers Lane

Sundance Mountain 8,255 ft.

Palmer Reservoir Trail

Lower Palmer Reservoir

Ice Cave Creek

Ice Cave Creek Trail

North Monument Creek

Chautauqua Mountain 8,352 ft.

Upper Palmer Reservoir

Balanced Rock Trail

Swank Trail

Inlet Trail

PINE NATIONAL FOREST

N

Kilometer   0   0.5   0.5

Mile   0   0.5

Miles and Directions

0.0 Start from Reservoir Trailhead on Old Carriage Road in Palmer Lake. Hike west on Palmer Reservoir Trail, a closed road, up North Monument Creek's canyon.

0.3 Climb a short singletrack trail and reach a utility road (GPS: 39 7.1212, -104 55.532). Hike up the road (Palmer Reservoir Trail), pass through a gate, and continue up the steep road.

0.6 Reach the dam at Lower Palmer Reservoir (GPS: 39 7.0282, -104 55.8802). Hike west on the road along the north side of the lake.

0.8 Past the west end of the lower lake, reach Ice Cave Creek Trail on the right (GPS: 39 6.9559, -104 56.0276).

1.1 Reach the east end of the upper reservoir. Continue southwest along the north side of the lake.

1.3 Reach a junction on the right with the Inlet Trail (GPS: 39 6.8358, -104 56.5932). Continue on the wide trail, which bends south along the lakeshore.

1.6 Reach the lake's south side and the end of the trail (GPS: 39 6.5601, -104 56.5311). The trail continues south from here along North Monument Creek as Balanced Rock Trail. Turn around and retrace the trail back past the lakes.

3.2 Arrive back at the trailhead (GPS: 39 7.1212, -104 55.2673).

Sundance Mountain rises beyond Upper Palmer Reservoir in the Rampart Range above Palmer Lake.

8 Crystal Creek Reservoir

This scenic hike, edging along the north shore of Crystal Creek Reservoir, offers postcard-worthy views of the towering North Face of Pikes Peak.

Start: Crystal Trailhead at Crystal Reservoir Visitor Center
Difficulty: Easy
Trail: Crystal Trail
Hiking time: About 2 hours
Distance: 3.4 miles out-and-back
Elevation trailhead to lake: 9,234 to 9,226 feet at trail's end
Restrictions: Open May 1 through the third Sun in Oct with hours between 7:30 a.m. and 7 p.m. depending on the time of year, and with last gate entry 1 hour before closing; closed for the Hill Climb; day-use fee; ask at toll gate for pass only to North Slope Recreation Area, not the summit; toilets at trailhead; dogs allowed on leash but not in water; no hunting or firearms; no alcohol or smoking except in designated areas; no open fires; no swimming, wading, boating, or horseback riding
Amenities: Restrooms at trailhead; gift shop and snack bar at trailhead; services in Cascade and Green Mountain Falls
Maps: *DeLorme*: Page 62, A3; Trails Illustrated 137: Pikes Peak, Cañon City; USGS Woodland Park
County: El Paso
Land status: North Slope Recreation Area; Colorado Springs Parks, Recreation and Cultural Services, (719) 385-5940; Pikes Peak Highway, (719) 385-7325

Finding the trailhead: From Colorado Springs and I-25, drive west on US 24 for about 11 miles to Cascade. Turn left on Fountain Avenue and drive to a left turn on Pikes Peak Highway. Continue to the highway toll gate and pay the entrance fee. Ask for a discounted price to the North Slope Recreation Area, not the summit toll. From the gate, drive 5.2 miles to a marked left turn to the Crystal Reservoir Visitor Center and a parking lot. The Crystal Trailhead is on the right side of the building (GPS: 38 55.2686, -105 1.5545).

The Hike

Crystal Creek Reservoir, a 136-acre lake at the North Slope Recreation Area, stretches southwest from the Pikes Peak Highway in a drowned valley. Starting at the Crystal Reservoir Visitor Center on the west side of the dam, Crystal Trail follows the twisting western shoreline of the lake. The trail offers stunning views of the North Face of 14,115-foot Pikes Peak to the south. The best season to hike is May and June when snow blankets the peak and late September when golden aspens shimmer on hillsides. The visitor center, selling snacks and souvenirs, offers ample spaces for hikers and picnickers. After enjoying the hike, drive the rest of the Pikes Peak Highway to the summit for spacious views across Colorado. Timed reservations are required to drive to the summit during the summer months.

U R Stickers.

PREMIUM QUALITY STICKERS
REMOVABLE & RESTICKABLE

Stick on Auto, Home, Computers, Books, Doors, Walls and Anywhere
RE-STICK Again!

INDOOR & OUTDOOR USE

Made in the USA

Summit Canyon
Mountaineering

GLENWOOD CANYON COLORADO

To Remove
Sticker
Peel From
Inner Cut Line

www.urstickers.com

U R Stickers®

To Remove Sticker Peel From Inner Cut Line

PREMIUM QUALITY STICKERS
REMOVABLE & RESTICKABLE

Stick on Auto, Home, Computers, Books, Doors, Walls and RE-STICK Anywhere Again!

INDOOR & OUTDOOR USE

Made in the USA

Summit Canyon
Mountaineering

GLENWOOD CANYON COLORADO

www.urstickers.com

U R Stickers.

PREMIUM QUALITY STICKERS
REMOVABLE & RESTICKABLE

Stick on Auto, Home,
Computers, Books,
Doors, Walls and
RE-STICK
Anywhere
Again!

INDOOR & OUTDOOR USE

Made in the USA

Summit Canyon
Mountaineering

GLENWOOD CANYON COLORADO

To Remove
Sticker
Peel From
Inner Cut Line

www.urstickers.com

The North Face of Pikes Peak towers above Crystal Creek Reservoir at the North Slope Recreation Area near Colorado Springs.

Crystal Trail skirts gleaming Crystal Creek Reservoir on the north slope of Pikes Peak.

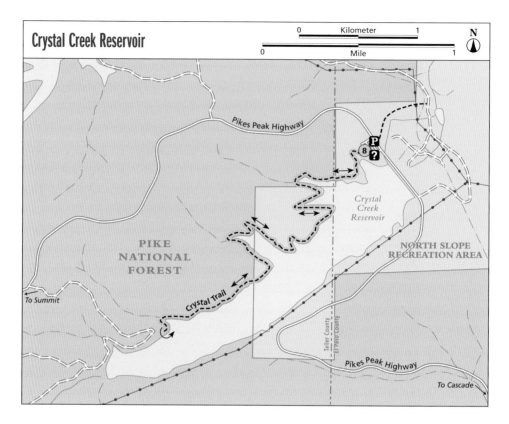

Crystal
Creek
Reservoir

PIKE
NATIONAL
FOREST

NORTH SLOPE
RECREATION AREA

To Summit

Crystal Trail

Teller County
El Paso County

Pikes Peak Highway

Pikes Peak Highway

To Cascade

0   Kilometer   1
0   Mile   1

N

Miles and Directions

0.0 Start at the Crystal Trailhead on the right side of the visitor center. Follow a paved trail downhill for 200 feet to restrooms. Bend left on the trail, which becomes dirt, and hike southeast past floating docks (if lake is full).

0.1 Reach a junction. Go right and follow a wide trail.

0.15 Reach another junction (GPS: 38 55.214, –105 1.578). Go right or west on a singletrack trail across a hillside. The wide trail goes straight to a dock and then follows the shore to rejoin the hike.

0.2 Trail reaches the shoreline when the lake is full. Continue west along the north shore.

0.3 Reach a junction on the north side of an inlet. Go left across the top of the inlet and follow the trail along the edge of the lake. The other trail goes west up a valley and meets the Pikes Peak Highway.

1.0 Reach the western edge of an inlet (GPS: 38 55.085, –105 1.9531). Continue southwest along the lakeshore.

1.7 Reach the trail's end at a utility road which follows the lake's edge to the southwest (GPS: 38 54.8084, –105 2.2199). Turn around at the road and return to the trailhead.

3.4 Arrive back at the trailhead (GPS: 38 55.2686, –105 1.5545).

9 North and South Catamount Reservoirs

North and South Catamount Reservoirs, part of the Colorado Springs water supply, tuck into high valleys in the North Slope Recreation Area off the Pikes Peak Highway north of 14,115-foot Pikes Peak.

Start: North Catamount Reservoir Trailhead, North and South Catamount Reservoir parking lot
Difficulty: Easy
Trails: Ridge Trail, South Catamount Creek Trail, Kinnikinnik Trail
Hiking time: About 2 hours
Distance: 2.9 miles loop
Elevation trailhead to lakes: 9,352 to 9,225 feet at South Catamount Reservoir
Restrictions: Open May 1 through the third Sun in October with hours between 7:30 a.m. and 7 p.m. depending on the time of year, and with last gate entry 1 hour before closing; closed for the Hill Climb; day-use fee; ask at toll gate for pass only to North Slope Recreation Area, not the summit; parking limited to 120 vehicles; dogs allowed on leash but not in water; no hunting or firearms; no alcohol or smoking except in designated areas; no open fires; no swimming, wading, boating, horseback riding
Amenities: Vault toilets at trailhead; picnic tables; services in Cascade and Green Mountain Falls
Maps: *DeLorme:* Page 62, A2; Trails Illustrated 137: Pikes Peak, Cañon City; USGS Woodland Park
Counties: El Paso, Teller
Land status: North Slope Recreation Area; Colorado Springs Parks, Recreation and Cultural Services, (719) 385-5940; Pikes Peak Highway, (719) 385-7325

Finding the trailhead: From Colorado Springs, drive west on US 24 for about 11 miles to Cascade. Turn left on Fountain Avenue and drive to a left turn on Pikes Peak Highway. Continue to the highway toll gate and pay the entrance fee. Ask for a discounted price to the North Slope Recreation Area, not the summit toll. From the gate, drive 10.7 miles to a marked right turn to Catamount Reservoirs. Drive north on narrow, dirt Catamount Loop Road, keeping left at a Y-junction at 0.1 mile, for 1.3 miles to the North Catamount Reservoir parking lot and the trailhead (GPS: 38 55.7024, -105 3.2011).

The Hike

This hike on Pikes Peak passes two reservoirs—210-acre North Catamount and 120-acre South Catamount—on the Ridge and South Catamount Creek Trails, which are connected by 0.18-mile Kinnikinnik Trail. Start at a trailhead by North Catamount Reservoir's dam and hike west for 1.1 miles on Ridge Trail, a closed utility road that rolls along a wooded ridge between the lakes. The hike's 1.6-mile second leg, following South Catamount Creek Trail, descends a closed road to the lake and then twists along a singletrack trail on South Catamount's northern shoreline. Finish up on Kinnikinnik Trail to the parking lot. The well-marked trails are easy to follow and rarely crowded.

Raspberry Mountain lifts wooded slopes on the western end of North Catamount Reservoir on Pikes Peak's north slope.

The North Slope Recreation Area offers plenty of other good trails, mostly in the hills north of North Catamount Reservoir. From a trailhead on the north side of the dam, follow the fabulous 2.3-mile Mackinaw Trail along the shoreline. When it ends, reverse the trail, or create a longer loop by hiking Blue River, Mule Deer, Limber Pine, or Catamount Trails. Visit the recreation area's third reservoir by hiking Crystal Trail on the north side of Crystal Creek Reservoir (Hike 8).

A hiker follows South Catamount Creek Trail alongside South Catamount Reservoir.

Pikes Peak towers above windswept South Catamount Reservoir at the North Slope Recreation Area.

North and South Catamount Reservoirs

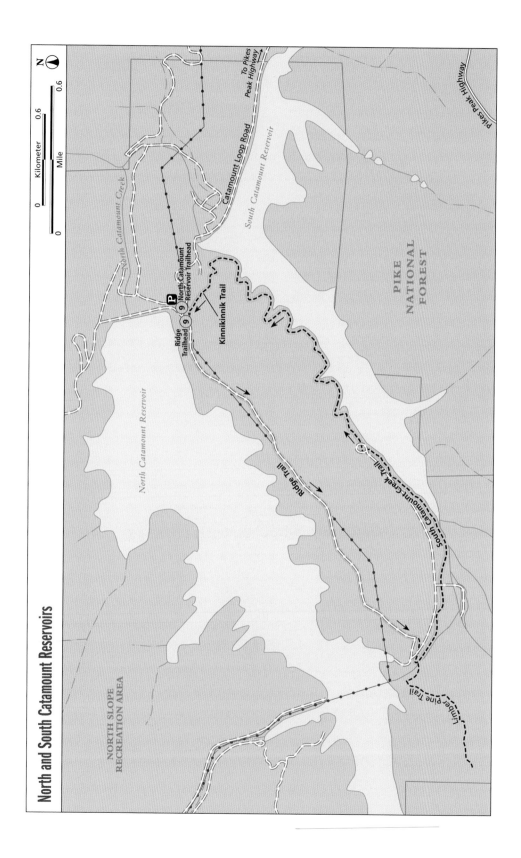

N

0   0.6   Kilometer
0   0.6   Mile

NORTH SLOPE
RECREATION AREA

North Catamount Reservoir

Ridge Trail

Kinnikinnik Trail

Ridge Trailhead

9   North Catamount
     Reservoir Trailhead

P

North Catamount Creek

Catamount Loop Road

South Catamount Reservoir

To Pikes
Peak Highway

South Catamount Creek Trail

Limber Pine Trail

PIKE
NATIONAL
FOREST

Pikes Peak Highway

Miles and Directions

0.0 Start at Ridge Trailhead and hike southwest on Ridge Trail, a closed utility road, along a ridge-top between North and South Catamount Reservoirs (GPS: 38 55.7024, -105 3.2011).

0.4 Reach the head of a bay with scenic views across North Catamount. A short trail descends north to the bay.

1.1 At the two-way road/trail junction with Limber Pine Trail, take a sharp left onto South Catamount Creek Trail and head southeast down a steep road (GPS: 38 55.1972, -105 4.1297).

1.4 The trail reaches the western end of South Catamount Reservoir at the inlet stream (GPS: 38 55.1423, -105 3.7778). Hike east on a utility road along the lake's northern edge.

1.55 Reach a junction with a singletrack trail at the end of the road (GPS: 38 55.2032, -105 3.6716). Go straight on the lakeside trail.

2.6 The trail leaves the lakeshore and climbs northeast up a hill (GPS: 38 55.6383, -105 3.0221). A right turn here goes east to a picnic area.

2.7 At the junction, go left onto Kinnikinnik Trail and hike uphill to return to the trailhead (GPS: 38 55.6562, -105 3.0354). Alternatively, continue straight and hike up the shoulder of the road.

2.9 End the hike after leaving the forest opposite the entrance to the parking lot. Arrive back at the trailhead (GPS: 38 55.7112, -105 3.1595).

A hiker strides along South Catamount Creek Trail above South Catamount Reservoir.

10 Rampart Reservoir

Rampart Reservoir, a 500-acre lake in Rampart Reservoir Recreation Area northwest of Colorado Springs, offers several popular trails including Rainbow Gulch and Rampart Reservoir Trails. The lake, part of the Homestake Water System, is part of Colorado Springs's water supply.

Start: Rainbow Gulch Trailhead
Difficulty: Easy for Rainbow Gulch Trail; moderate for Rampart Reservoir Trail
Trails: Rainbow Gulch Trail #714, Rampart Reservoir Trail #700
Hiking time: 1 to 2 hours for Rainbow Gulch Trail; 5 to 8 hours for Rampart Reservoir Trail
Distance: 3.4 miles out-and-back on Rainbow Gulch Trail; 13.9 miles lollipop loop on Rainbow Gulch Trail and Rampart Reservoir Trail
Elevation trailhead to lake: 9,275 to 9,000 feet at Rampart Reservoir (-275 feet)
Restrictions: No fee at trailhead; reservoir open seasonally Thurs through Sun from the Thurs before Memorial Day through the last

Sun in Sept from 7:30 a.m. to 2:30 p.m., weather permitting; preregistration required to access reservoir area; day-use fee to park at Rampart Reservoir; road across dam open 7 a.m. to 5 p.m.; leashed dogs allowed; no swimming, wading, or waterskiing
Amenities: Potable water, toilets, picnic areas, seasonal campgrounds at recreation area; services in Woodland Park
Maps: *DeLorme*: Page 62, A3; Trails Illustrated 137: Pikes Peak, Cañon City; USGS Pikes Peak
County: El Paso
Land status: Rampart Reservoir Recreation Area; Pike National Forest, (719) 553-1400; Pikes Peak Ranger District, (719) 636-1602

Finding the trailhead: From Colorado Springs, take US 24 West for about 15 miles to Woodland Park. Turn right on South Baldwin Street, which becomes CR 22, and drive 2.9 miles to a Y-fork in the road. Bear right on Loy Creek Road and drive 1.5 miles to a four-way junction. Turn right on unpaved Rampart Range Road/FR 300. Continue 2.7 miles south to an unsigned dirt parking area on the left for Rainbow Gulch Trailhead (GPS: 38 58.6689, -105 0.5418).

The Hike

Rampart Reservoir, a large lake with nine distinct inlets, offers plenty of recreation, including three campgrounds and a trail network. Rainbow Gulch and Rampart Reservoir Trails are the best hikes to explore the lake and enjoy brilliant views of Pikes Peak. Both trails are shared with mountain bikers.

Rainbow Gulch Trail is an easy, family-friendly hike that provides free access to the lake. Follow the wide path down pastoral Rainbow Gulch, a valley bordered by aspens, pine, and fir trees and littered with chunks of granite, to its junction with Rampart Reservoir Trail. Turn around here and return to the trailhead or take a longer stroll on Rampart Reservoir Trail until you want to turn around. The north or left side of the lake offers better views of Blodgett Peak and Ormes Peak and more

A long hiking trail encircles glassy Rampart Reservoir on the Rampart Range northwest of Colorado Springs.

An arm of Rampart Reservoir reflects clouds and sky at the end of the Rainbow Gulch Trail.

sunshine than the south side. Hike to the first inlet for great views and floating flocks of ducks and geese and then turn around.

For a longer lake hike, take the Rampart Reservoir Trail. At the end of Rainbow Gulch Trail, go left on the twisting trail past inlets on the lake's north shore to a dam. Cross the dam to its south side and pick up the trail again on the right. The trail dips and weaves along the south shoreline, passing through a shady forest and an area burned in the 2012 Waldo Canyon Fire.

Granite boulders scatter along the edge of Rampart Reservoir below the Rampart Reservoir Trail.

Rampart Reservoir

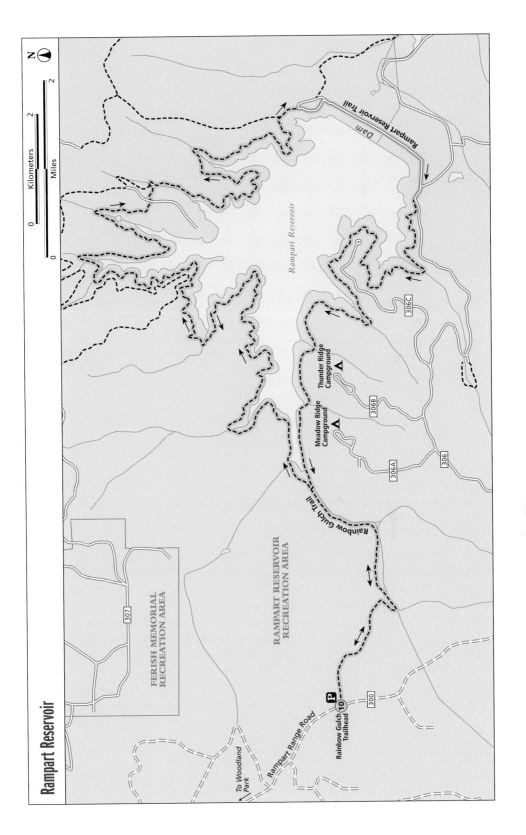

FERISH MEMORIAL RECREATION AREA

307

RAMPART RESERVOIR RECREATION AREA

Rampart Reservoir

Meadow Ridge Campground

Thunder Ridge Campground

306A

306B

306C

306

Rainbow Gulch Trail

Rampart Reservoir Trail

Dam

Rampart Range Road

To Woodland Park

Rainbow Gulch Trailhead 10

P

300

Kilometers

Miles

N

Hikers walk through an aspen grove on the south shore of Rampart Reservoir.

Miles and Directions

Rainbow Gulch Trail

0.0   Start at the Rainbow Gulch Trailhead. Hike east down a valley on the trail from a gate between two posts.

1.4   Reach a footbridge on the right and a junction with the Rampart Reservoir Trail (GPS: 38 58.7843, –104 59.4695). Go straight on the trail to the lake's western inlet.

1.7   Arrive at the far west end of Rampart Reservoir. Walk along either the north or south shore on Rampart Reservoir Trail for good lake views and turn around at your convenience. Return back on the trail.

3.4   Arrive back at the trailhead (GPS: 38 58.6689, –105 0.5418).

Rampart Reservoir Trail

0.0   Start at the Rainbow Gulch Trailhead. Hike east down a valley on Rainbow Gulch Trail.

1.4   Reach a footbridge on the right and a junction with Rampart Reservoir Trail (GPS: 38 58.7843, –104 59.4695). Go straight on the trail to the lake's western inlet and hike left along the lake's north shoreline.

8.6   Arrive at a large parking lot and boat ramp at the north end of the reservoir's dam (GPS: 38 58.8395, –104 57.5455). Walk southwest on FR 306 along the top of the dam.

8.8   Reach the south end of the dam. Cross the road to the first parking pullout on the right (GPS: 38 58.3569, –104 58.0112) and pick up the Rampart Reservoir Trail and hike west.

12.5 Continue on the winding trail to the footbridge over a creek and the junction with Rainbow Gulch Trail (GPS: 38 58.7843, –104 59.4695). Go left and hike up the valley to the trailhead.

13.9 Arrive back at the trailhead (GPS: 38 58.6689, –105 0.5418).

11 Mason and Boehmer Reservoirs

The Mason Trail climbs through conifer forests and wetlands to two scenic reservoirs, part of the Colorado Springs water supply, in the remote and seldom visited South Slope Recreation Area on Pikes Peak.

Start: South Slope Recreation Area Trailhead
Difficulty: Moderate
Trail: Mason Trail
Hiking time: 6 to 7 hours
Distance: 9.4 miles out-and-back to Boehmer Reservoir, 2.4 miles out-and-back to Mason Reservoir
Elevation trailhead to lake: 10,950 to 11,305 feet at Boehmer Reservoir (+355 feet)
Restrictions: Area is open from the third Thurs in May until the last Sun in Sept, weather permitting; open Thurs through Sun from 7:30 a.m. to 3 p.m.; ranger is at the gate from 7:30 a.m. to 8 a.m., then gate is locked; hikers must be at the gate by 3 p.m. to leave; gate is locked at 3 p.m.; open by online reservation only; no on-site permits sold; limited number of vehicles and people are allowed daily; fee is charged for up to 8 people per vehicle; permits are available on a first-come, first-served basis; no body contact with water; fishing restrictions; no fires, smoking, fireworks, alcoholic beverages, or dogs allowed.
Amenities: Vault toilets at trailhead; services in Cripple Creek
Maps: *DeLorme*: Page 62, B3 and C3; Trails Illustrated 137: Pikes Peak, Cañon City; USGS Pikes Peak
Counties: El Paso, Teller
Land status: South Slope Recreation Area; Colorado Springs Parks, Recreation and Cultural Services, (719) 385-5940; reservations and permits: coloradosprings.gov/southslope; call (719) 385-7707 for assistance

Finding the trailhead: From Colorado Springs and I-25, drive west on US 24 for 27 miles to Divide. Turn left or south on CO 67 and drive south for 13.5 miles to Teller CR 81 at Gillette. Turn left on CR 81 and drive 3 miles to CR 8/Gold Camp Road. Turn left on Gold Camp Road and drive 7.5 miles on the dirt road to FR 376. Turn left on FR 376 and drive the steep road for 3.2 miles to the entrance gate at South Slope Recreation Area. After the ranger checks your permit, follow road to a parking lot and trailhead right of the toilets (GPS: 38 46.5337, -105 0.5599).

The Hike

The 4.7-mile Mason Trail, one of the best lake hikes in the Pikes Peak region, passes 10,910-foot Mason Reservoir, climbs through old-growth spruce forests, crosses wetlands and meadows, and ends at the rocky rim of Boehmer Reservoir tucked against the hidden south face of Pikes Peak. The trail, gaining over 1,000 feet of elevation round-trip, threads through the South Slope Recreation Area, which includes three reservoirs managed for Colorado Springs's drinking water. The area, closed to the public until 2014, is open for limited recreation by hikers.

Driftwood scatters along the shoreline of Boehmer Reservoir below the south face of Pikes Peak.

Mason Reservoir reflects wooded slopes and Pikes Peak in its still waters.

Start at the Mason Trailhead and hike across Middle Beaver Creek to sparkling 110-acre Mason Reservoir, a long lake that reflects Pikes Peak. Stop at an excellent viewpoint on the south shore before heading west across wooded slopes and open meadows to the trail's 11,490-foot highpoint. The last trail section climbs through spruce and limber pine to the southeast shore of Boehmer Reservoir, one of the Peak's unseen beauty spots with granite cliffs rising above wooded hollows. After a lakeside lunch, head back down the trail. Plan on leaving the lake by 12:30 p.m. at the latest to reach the exit gate by 3 p.m.

Although you can do most of the hike when the South Slope Recreation Area opens in late May, the last 0.4 mile is off-limits behind a locked gate during bighorn sheep lambing season, so wait until that section is opened to complete the hike to Boehmer Reservoir. Black bear, elk, and moose also inhabit the area. Watch for scat and tracks on the trail.

For a shorter, family-friendly hike, follow the Mason Trail for 1.2 miles to the lakeside cutoff trail and then return for a 2.4-mile, round-trip hike.

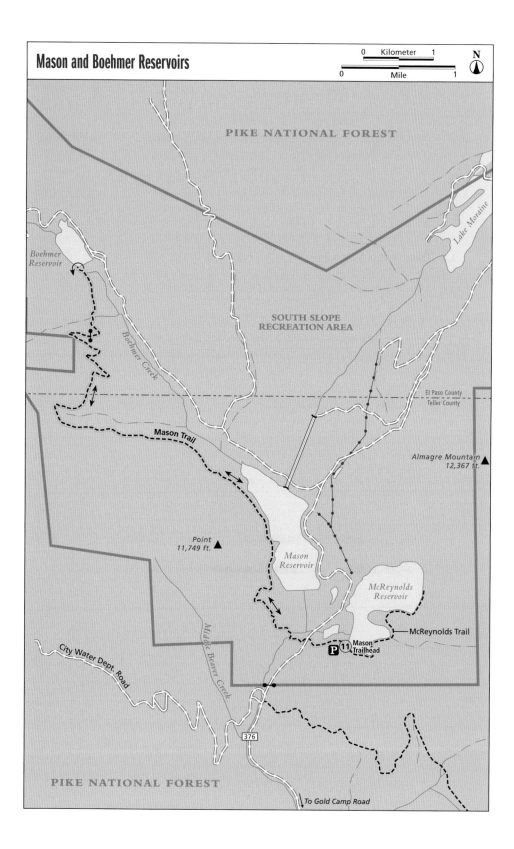

Mason and Boehmer Reservoirs

0 Kilometer 1

0 Mile 1

N

PIKE NATIONAL FOREST

Boehmer Reservoir

Lake Moraine

SOUTH SLOPE
RECREATION AREA

Boehmer Creek

El Paso County
Teller County

Mason Trail

Almagre Mountain ▲
12,367 ft.

Point ▲
11,749 ft.

Mason Reservoir

McReynolds Reservoir

McReynolds Trail

City Water Dept. Road

Middle Beaver Creek

P 11 Mason
Trailhead

376

PIKE NATIONAL FOREST

To Gold Camp Road

Miles and Directions

0.0 Start at the South Slope Recreation Area Trailhead right of the restrooms on the northeast side of the parking lot. Follow the Mason Trail behind the restrooms and walk west through forest. Pikes Peak is visible ahead.

0.2 Cross Service Road 376 and continue west on the other side (GPS: 38 46.5505, −105 0.8065).

0.4 Cross two footbridges over wetlands and Boehmer Creek.

1.1 Reach the western shoreline of Mason Reservoir.

1.2 Step right on a signed cutoff trail to a peninsula on Mason's south shoreline and views of Pikes Peak (GPS: 38 47.0543, −105 1.0408). Admire a scenic view of Pikes Peak and the north side of the lake. Return to Mason Trail and continue west.

1.5 Open views of Mason Reservoir, Windy Point, and the Cog Railway, framed by 12,590-foot Sachett Mountain.

3.0 Cross a wetland in a broad valley and hike northeast across dry slopes (GPS: 38 47.7502, −105 2.5281).

3.7 Reach the trail's highpoint at 11,490 feet before dropping west to Boehmer Reservoir. You regain 185 feet of elevation on the way back, the toughest part of the hike.

4.3 Go through a gate and cross a bridge over an unnamed creek (GPS: 38 48.1894, −105 2.2734). The area beyond gate is closed for bighorn sheep lambing until July 15.

4.6 Cross a footbridge and reach the southeast edge of Boehmer Reservoir on the south end of a dam (GPS: 38 48.4578, −105 2.3713). Return to the trailhead on the Mason Trail.

9.4 Arrive back at the trailhead (GPS: 38 46.5337, −105 0.5599).

Boehmer Reservoir tucks into a glaciated valley below the south face of Pikes Peak.

12 Manitou Lake

An easy trail encircles glassy, 7,735-foot Manitou Lake, a 5-acre reservoir north of Woodland Park and Pikes Peak. It's an ideal hike for children with easy grades, nature study, and scenic views.

Start: Trailhead opposite restrooms at northwest edge of lake
Difficulty: Easy
Trail: Manitou Lake Trail (#670)
Hiking time: About 1 hour
Distance: 0.8 mile loop
Elevation trailhead to lake: 7,748 to 7,740 feet at lake boardwalk (-8 feet)
Restrictions: Open year-round; day-use fee or annual pass; no motorboats, swimming, or wading

Amenities: Toilets at trailhead; pavilion available by reservation; picnic area; nearby campgrounds; services in Woodland Park
Maps: *DeLorme*: Page 50, E2; Trails Illustrated 137: Pikes Peak, Cañon City; USGS Mount Deception
County: Teller
Land status: Pike National Forest, (719) 553-1400; Pikes Peak Ranger District, (719) 636-1602

Finding the trailhead: From Colorado Springs and I-25, take US 24 West for about 17 miles to Woodland Park. Turn right on CO 67 and drive north for 8 miles to Manitou Lake Park on the right. Park in lots west of the lake. Trailhead is opposite restrooms at the first lot (GPS: 39 5.3972, -105 5.9087).

The Hike

This easy loop hike, with 125 feet cumulative elevation gain, strolls around the perimeter of Manitou Lake, offering views south to Pikes Peak, bird-watching with ospreys, warblers, herons, and hummingbirds in wetlands, and sitting by the trout-stocked lake. It's a perfect trail for kids and families. Look for interpretive signs along the trail about natural history.

Start the hike from the trailhead opposite the restrooms at the first parking lot. Hike east and cross a bridge at the north end above a dam. The water spills down into Trout Creek. Continue east on a levee and then thread through pines and tall grass east of the lake. The trail crosses an elevated boardwalk through a marsh on the south end of the lake, with tall cattails providing a perfect refuge for birds. Finish by hiking along the western shore past two accessible docks to the trailhead.

For more adventure, hike North Loop Trail, a lollipop loop that begins at the northwest end of the lake and follows Trout Creek. Another lollipop loop leaves the lake trail at its southeast end and leads to Colorado Campground and adds another mile to the hike. All three trails—Manitou Lake Trail, North Loop Trail, and trail to Colorado Campground—add up to a 2.5-mile, round-trip hike.

Evening clouds reflect in placid Manitou Lake north of Woodland Park.

Pikes Peak towers beyond Manitou Lake and its popular lake hike north of Woodland Park.

The rounded summit of Mount Deception rises behind frozen Manitou Lake and sandstone hoodoos.

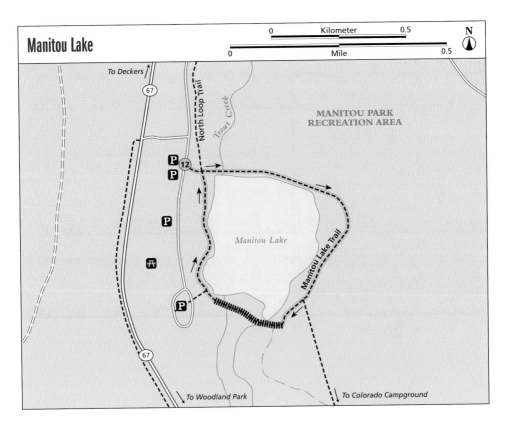

Miles and Directions

0.0 Start at the trailhead east of the first parking lot at the northwest end of the lake. After 160 feet, reach a junction with the return loop on the right and North Loop Trail on the left. Continue east and cross a bridge over the dam at 260 feet.

0.4 Pass a junction with the trail to Colorado Campground and continue southwest on the main trail (GPS: 39 5.2327, −105 5.7241). Walk across a boardwalk on wetlands at the lake's south end.

0.5 End of the boardwalk; continue north on a dirt trail along the lake's western shoreline.

0.8 Arrive back at the trailhead (GPS: 39 5.3972, −105 5.9087).

13 Eleven Mile Canyon Reservoir

This excellent hike, following three trails, follows the northeastern edge of Eleven Mile Canyon Reservoir past rocky islands before swinging inland to meadows and evergreen forests.

Start: Coyote Ridge Trailhead
Difficulty: Easy
Trails: Midland, Black Bear and Coyote Ridge Interpretive Trails (Ponderosa and Aspen Loops)
Hiking time: About 2 hours
Distance: 3.7 miles loop
Elevation trailhead to lake: 8,583 to 8,570 feet at lake; to 8,785 feet at Midland Trail high point (+202 feet)
Restrictions: Fee area; day-use only; swimming, wading, and water contact sports prohibited; leashed dogs allowed

Amenities: Toilets at trailhead; lakeside campground; limited services in Lake George and Florissant
Maps: *DeLorme*: Page 61, A7; Trails Illustrated 152: Elevenmile Canyon, South Park; USGS Elevenmile Canyon
County: Park
Land status: Eleven Mile State Park, (719) 748-3401

Finding the trailhead: From Colorado Springs and I-25, drive west on US 24 to Lake George. Continue 0.8 mile to a left turn on Park CR 92. Drive 9.7 miles on CR 92 to a left turn marked "Coyote Ridge Fishing Access Hiking Trail." Drive 0.5 mile south to the parking lot and trailhead (GPS: 38 55.6835, -105 29.8016).

The Hike

This scenic hike loops across peninsulas jutting into Eleven Mile Canyon Reservoir and traverses along the base of the Puma Hills. Lying in Eleven Mile State Park, the hike has easy grades and spectacular views across the lake toward the Mosquito Range. The reservoir, part of Denver's water supply, is one of Colorado's busiest lakes for recreationists. A dam, built in 1932 at the head of Elevenmile Canyon, blocks the South Platte River, forming the 3,300-acre lake at the southeast corner of South Park.

Start on the east side of Coyote Ridge parking lot. Hike east on the Ponderosa Loop of Coyote Ridge Interpretive Trail to the Midland Trail on the north side of a bay. Follow the Midland Trail along the shoreline to Black Bear Trail. This scenic path weaves through granite cliffs along a rocky peninsula, passing backcountry campsites and views of mountains beyond the lake. Black Bear Trail ends at Midland Trail, which is followed to another rocky peninsula and viewpoint before turning north. The trail crosses grasslands and pine and fir forests before bending west to Coyote Ridge Interpretive Trail's Aspen Loop. The hike threads through rock formations, meadows, and aspen groves back to the trailhead.

Granite islands rise above Eleven Mile Canyon Reservoir on the eastern edge of South Park.

Reflecting in Eleven Mile Canyon Reservoir, summer clouds build over the Puma Hills.

Bulky Thirtynine Mile Mountain towers beyond granite outcrops and islands on the Black Bear Trail.

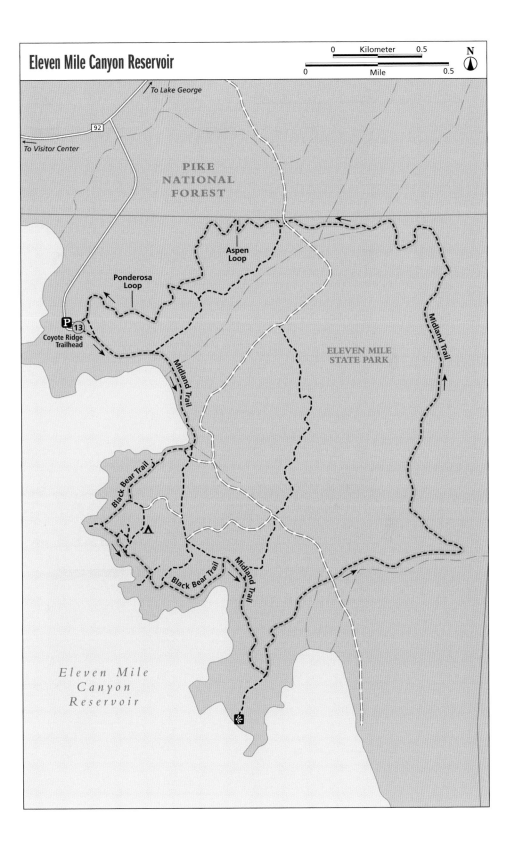

Eleven Mile Canyon Reservoir

0   Kilometer   0.5
0   Mile   0.5

N

To Lake George

92

To Visitor Center

PIKE
NATIONAL
FOREST

Aspen
Loop

Ponderosa
Loop

P
13

Coyote Ridge
Trailhead

Midland Trail

ELEVEN MILE
STATE PARK

Midland Trail

Black Bear Trail

Black Bear Trail

Midland Trail

Eleven Mile
Canyon
Reservoir

Miles and Directions

0.0   Start at trailhead by restrooms. Hike southeast on Coyote Ridge Interpretive Trail's Ponderosa Loop. Beware of social trails for fishing access.

0.15 Reach a junction with Midland Trail on the west side of a bay (GPS: 38 55.6274, –105 29.6485). Go right on Midland Trail.

0.4   Junction on right with Black Bear Trail (GPS: 38 55.4688, –105 29.5602). The Midland Trail goes left. Go right on Black Bear Trail and follow the shoreline of a peninsula, passing campsites.

0.8   Reach a junction at toilets with Midland Trail, a service road (GPS: 38 55.2379, –105 29.6207). Go right on Midland Trail and hike southeast.

1.0   Junction with a trail on left. Keep right.

1.5   Arrive at a junction on a peninsula (GPS: 38 55.0823, –105 29.3961). Go left on Midland Trail. For a viewpoint, go south for 500 feet on side trail to the peninsula's end above lake.

2.6   Reach old road. Continue straight on main trail and hike north along west base of mountains.

3.0   After crossing a grassy valley, reach a junction with service road (GPS: 38 55.8457, –105 29.3488). Continue west on Midland Trail.

3.05 Reach end of Midland Trail at junction with Aspen Loop of Coyote Ridge trail. Go right on Aspen Loop.

3.4   Meet Ponderosa Loop at end of Aspen Loop (GPS: 38 55.7368, –105 29.5873). Go straight on Ponderosa Loop and hike southwest past rock formations.

3.7   Arrive back at the trailhead (GPS: 38 55.6835, –105 29.8016).

Morning mist clears off Eleven Mile Canyon Reservoir and the Puma Hills.

Central Colorado

Aspen, Twin Lakes, Leadville, Frisco, Breckenridge, and Buena Vista

Viewed from the top of Lost Man Pass, the blue-velvet waters of Lost Man Lake are a stunning sight.

14 Maroon Lake

Two 14,000-foot mountains, Maroon Peak and North Maroon Peak or the "Maroon Bells," provide a dramatic backdrop at Maroon Lake in Aspen's Maroon Bells Scenic Area.

Start: Maroon Lake Trailhead
Difficulty: Very easy
Trail: Maroon Lake Scenic Trail #2197
Hiking time: 1 to 2 hours
Distance: 1.9 miles lollipop loop
Elevation trailhead to lakes: 9,565 to 9,585 feet at Maroon Lake (+20 feet)
Restrictions: Mandatory fee area; vehicle access restricted in summer from 8 a.m. to 5 p.m.; Maroon Creek Road open to vehicles before 8 a.m. and after 5 p.m. for a fee; hikers take paid shuttle from Aspen Highlands to the trailhead from 8 a.m. to 5 p.m.; free RFTA shuttle from Ruby Park in Aspen to Aspen Highlands parking lot; parking and shuttle reservations required from mid-May to end of Oct; for reservation info, call (970) 930-6442

or write info@visitmaroonbells.com; make advance shuttle reservations at aspenchamber .org/plan-trip/trip-highlights/maroon-bells/ reservations; no reservations from Nov 1 until road closes for winter; no swimming, wading, or boating in Maroon Lake; leashed dogs only
Amenities: Toilets at trailhead; interpretive signs; services in Aspen
Maps: *DeLorme:* Page 46, E2; Trails Illustrated 128: Maroon Bells, Redstone, Marble; USGS Maroon Bells
County: Pitkin
Land status: White River National Forest, (970) 945-2521; Aspen-Sopris Ranger District, (970) 963-2266; Maroon Bells Hotline: (970) 945-3319

Finding the trailhead: From downtown Aspen, drive 1.0 mile west on CO 82 to the Maroon Creek Road exit at the roundabout on the town's west side. Follow Maroon Creek Road/CR 13 for 4.7 miles to the Maroon Bells Welcome Center. Park at the nearby Aspen Highlands parking lot and ride the RFTA bus to the Maroon Lake shuttle stop. If you have parking reservations for off-hour entry, continue up Maroon Creek Road for 7.8 miles to the parking lot and trailhead (GPS: 39 5.9131, -106 56.4389). The parking, shuttle schedule, and drive-in entry to the trailhead may change. Call the Maroon Bells Hotline for updated information at (970) 945-3319.

The Hike

The Maroon Bells tower above Maroon Lake, forming one of Colorado's most famous mountain vistas, especially in late September when the snow-clad peaks and golden aspens reflect in the calm lake. The marvelous view is considered to be Colorado's most photographed place. Maroon Lake, a popular tourist destination, fills the floor of a deep, glaciated valley below 14,156-foot Maroon Peak and 14,014-foot North Maroon Peak to the west and the jagged profile of 14,025-foot Pyramid Peak to the south. The lake formed after huge mud and debris slides swept down a steep gully on Sievers Mountain to the north, damming West Maroon Creek.

The popularity of Maroon Lake and its classic view of the Maroon Bells led to the US Forest Service restricting access to the lake, trailhead, and parking lot to keep the fragile mountain environment from being loved to death. From mid-May to the end of October, hikers need to take a shuttle bus from a parking lot at Aspen Highlands Ski Area to Maroon Lake. Make reservations ahead of your visit to ensure you get a shuttle ticket. Limited tickets are sold each day, depending on cancellations. Hikers can drive to the lake early in the morning or in the evening and park at the trailhead for a fee. Check the above Restrictions information and contact the Maroon Bells Hotline for updated travel and parking information.

The hike starts from the Maroon Lake Trailhead at the west end of the parking lot or from the shuttle stop at the top of a loop at the end of Maroon Creek Road. Signed, paved trails lead from each trailhead to the lake. The classic lake and peak view is from the east end of Maroon Lake. Plan on elbow-to-elbow company, even early in the morning, if you're grabbing a photo of the iconic scene in September. The Maroon Lake Trail offers several scenic viewpoints, including a stop at the inlet stream at the lake's west end. Most hikers turn around here and return to the trailhead. For full-value fun, continue on the trail, signed "Scenic Loop Trail," to get away from the crowds and enjoy the tumult of West Maroon Creek, wildflowers, and quiet aspen groves.

The Maroon Bells lift tilted rock layers high above Maroon Lake near Aspen.

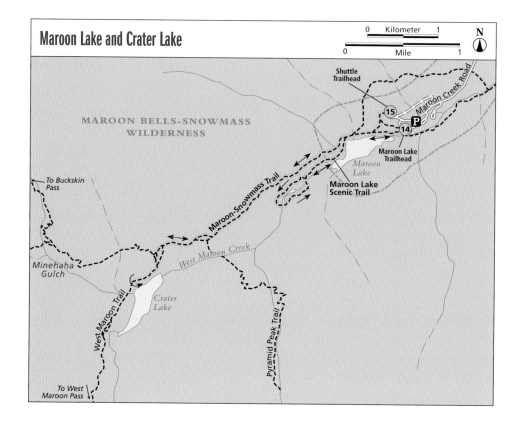

Maroon Lake and Crater Lake

MAROON BELLS-SNOWMASS WILDERNESS

Shuttle Trailhead

Maroon Creek Road

Maroon Lake Trailhead

Maroon Lake

Maroon Lake Scenic Trail

To Buckskin Pass

Maroon-Snowmass Trail

West Maroon Creek

Minehaha Gulch

West Maroon Trail

Crater Lake

Pyramid Peak Trail

To West Maroon Pass

Miles and Directions

0.0 Start at the Maroon Lake Trailhead at the parking lot or an alternative trailhead at the shuttle stop at the road's end. From the trailhead, walk west on paved Maroon Lake Scenic Trail along the northern edge of the lake. A dirt side trail follows the lakeshore, offering stellar views and photo ops of the lake and the Maroon Bells. From the shuttle trailhead, walk 0.1 mile on the paved path and go right at a junction and walk another 0.1 mile toward the lake.

0.2 Reach a junction on the right with the paved trail from the shuttle stop. Continue west on the trail.

0.3 Arrive at a junction with the Maroon-Snowmass Trail (GPS: 39 5.8875, –105 56.7501), which goes west to Crater Lake. A lake viewpoint is to the left. Continue straight on the paved trail along the north and west shoreline of Maroon Lake.

0.4 Stop at a viewpoint that looks east across Maroon Lake.

0.5 Reach a junction with a side trail on the left that goes 200 feet to overlooks on the north and south sides of the lake's inlet stream, Maroon Creek. A footbridge connects the overlooks. After enjoying the views, return to the main trail and go left. Hike along the rushing creek's north bank. Many visitors turn around at the lake's west side and return to the trailhead for a 1.0-mile, out-and-back walk, but the loop section offers fun hiking.

The Maroon Bells and Maroon Lake, one of Colorado's most beloved scenes, rise beyond a clump of asters.

0.7 Reach a junction on the north side of a footbridge with the return section of the loop trail (GPS: 39 5.6878, –105 57.0451). Continue west on the trail along the creek.

0.9 Cross a footbridge over Maroon Creek and bend east on the creek's south side, passing through open meadows and aspen groves.

1.2 Go left and cross the bridge over the creek and reach the junction at the start of the loop. Go right and hike east along the north side of Maroon Lake.

1.9 Arrive back at the trailhead (GPS: 39 5.9131, –106 56.4389). If you are going to the shuttle stop, turn left at the last junction and hike 0.2 mile on the paved trail to the stop.

15 Crater Lake

Crater Lake, tucked against the feet of the Maroon Bells, is a rippled glacial tarn with astounding views, alpine serenity, and breathtaking mountain views that you will never forget.

See map on page 58.
Start: Maroon Lake Trailhead
Difficulty: Moderate
Trails: Maroon Lake Scenic Trail #2197, Maroon-Snowmass Trail #1975, West Maroon Trail #1970
Hiking time: About 3 hours
Distance: 3.8 miles out-and-back
Elevation trailhead to lakes: 9,565 to 10,076 feet at Crater Lake (+520 feet)
Restrictions: Mandatory fee area; vehicle access restricted in summer from 8 a.m. to 5 p.m.; Maroon Creek Road open to vehicles before 8 a.m. and after 5 p.m. for a fee; hikers take paid shuttle from Aspen Highlands to the trailhead from 8 a.m. to 5 p.m.; free RFTA shuttle from Ruby Park in Aspen to Aspen Highlands parking lot; parking and shuttle reservations required from mid-May to end of Oct; for reservation info, call (970) 930-6442 or write info@visitmaroonbells.com; make advance shuttle reservations at aspenchamber .org/plan-trip/trip-highlights/maroon-bells/ reservations; no reservations from Nov 1 until road closes for winter; dogs not allowed at the lake or campsites
Amenities: Toilets at trailhead; interpretive signs; services in Aspen
Maps: *DeLorme*: Page 46, E2; Trails Illustrated 128: Maroon Bells, Redstone, Marble; USGS Maroon Bells
County: Pitkin
Land status: White River National Forest, (970) 945-2521; Aspen-Sopris Ranger District, (970) 963-2266; Maroon Bells Hotline: (970) 945-3319

Finding the trailhead: From downtown Aspen, drive 1.0 mile west on CO 82 to the Maroon Creek Road exit at the roundabout on the town's west side. Follow Maroon Creek Road/CR 13 for 4.7 miles to the Maroon Bells Welcome Center. Park at the nearby Aspen Highlands parking lot and ride the RFTA bus to the Maroon Lake shuttle stop. If you have parking reservations for off-hour entry, continue up Maroon Creek Road for 7.8 miles to the parking lot and trailhead (GPS: 39 5.9131, -106 56.4389). The parking, shuttle schedule, and drive-in entry to the trailhead may change. Call the Maroon Bells Hotline for updated information at (970) 945-3319.

The Hike

Crater Lake lies in a timberline hollow below the Maroon Bells, striking twin peaks that rise sheer above the glassy lake. Reach the alpine tarn, fringed with meadows, willows, and talus, by hiking up a rocky trail from Maroon Lake. The long, narrow lake, fed by West Maroon Creek and a tumbling waterfall in Minehaha Gulch, is one of those amazing places that offers beauty and serenity. It is a worthy destination lake after enjoying the stroll past Maroon Lake near the trailhead and shuttle stop.

The popularity of Maroon Lake and its famous view of the Maroon Bells led to the US Forest Service restricting access to the lake, trailhead, and parking lot to protect the fragile mountain environment from being overrun by visitors. From mid-May to the end of October, hikers need to ride a shuttle bus from a parking lot at Aspen Highlands Ski Area to Maroon Lake. Make reservations ahead of time to ensure you get a shuttle ticket. Limited tickets are sold each day, depending on cancellations. Hikers can drive to the lake early in the morning or in the evening and park at the trailhead for a fee. Check the above Restrictions information and contact the Maroon Bells Hotline for updated travel and parking information.

Start at the Maroon Lake Trailhead or the shuttle stop trailhead and hike west on the paved Maroon Lake Scenic Trail on the north side of the lake to a junction. The hike goes right on Maroon-Snowmass Trail and climbs through aspen glades and conifer forest along slopes north of West Maroon Creek. The rocky trail has few steep sections, but gradually gains elevation to the upper cirque. Cross open terrain with stunning views of the Maroon Bells looming overhead to a junction with West Maroon Trail, which heads left across a meadow to the rim of Crater Lake. Enjoy majestic lake views and ruggedly handsome peaks like 14,025-foot Pyramid Peak and its 13,932-foot neighbor Thunder Pyramid, as well as iconic 14,156-foot Maroon Peak and 14,014-foot North Maroon Peak. From the lake, intrepid hikers trek over Buckskin Pass or head up West Maroon Creek's valley for extended backpacking trips into the wild.

The twin Maroon Bells, among Colorado's most difficult Fourteener hikes, tower above Crater Lake.

Looking south from Crater Lake up West Maroon Creek's glaciated valley to the Maroon Bells and Len Shoemaker Ridge.

Miles and Directions

0.0   Start at the Maroon Lake Trailhead at the parking lot or an alternative trailhead at the shuttle stop at the road's end. From the trailhead, walk west on paved Maroon Lake Scenic Trail along the northern edge of the lake. A dirt side trail follows the lakeshore, offering stellar views and photo ops of the lake and the Maroon Bells. From the shuttle trailhead, walk 0.1 mile on the paved path and go right at a junction and walk another 0.1 mile toward the lake.

0.2   Reach a junction on the right with the paved trail from the shuttle stop. Continue west on the trail.

0.3   Arrive at a junction with the Maroon-Snowmass Trail (GPS: 39 5.8875, –106 56.7501), which goes west to Crater Lake. Go right and then left on the trail, hiking west through forest and talus to a steeper climb into the upper basin.

1.7   Reach a junction with West Maroon Trail on the left (GPS: 39 5.3281, –106 57.9629). Go left on it and hike south for 500 feet through a meadow to the north side of Crater Lake and splendid views south to West Maroon Creek's upper drainage with towering rock peaks lining the valley. Continue south along the lake's west side.

1.9   Reach the west end of Crater Lake near the base of Minehaha Gulch (GPS: 39 5.1908, –106 58.1078). Enjoy the stunning natural beauty, munch a snack, and look west up the gulch to a long, cascading waterfall. Return back down the trail to Maroon Lake.

3.8   Arrive back at the trailhead (GPS: 39 5.9131, –106 56.4389).

16 Linkins Lake

Pull over and stretch your legs on a short, steep hike to Linkins Lake, a lovely shelf lake northwest of Independence Pass.

Start: Independence Lake Trailhead
Difficulty: Moderate
Trails: Lost Man Trail #1996.1, Linkins Lake Trail #1979
Hiking time: About 1 hour
Distance: 1.2 miles out-and-back
Elevation trailhead to lake: 11,506 to 12,008 feet at lake (+502 feet)
Restrictions: Wilderness regulations apply; seasonal access only, Independence Pass closes from early Nov until late May; no toilets at trailhead; no campfires; leashed dogs only;

properly dispose of human waste; camping not recommended to protect fragile plants
Amenities: Services in Twin Lakes and Aspen
Maps: *DeLorme*: Page 47, D5 and D6; Trails Illustrated 127: Aspen, Independence Pass; USGS Independence Pass
County: Pitkin
Land status: White River National Forest, (970) 945-2521; Aspen-Sopris Ranger District, (970) 925-3445; Carbondale office, (970) 963-2266

Finding the trailhead: From US 24 between Buena Vista and Leadville, drive west on CO 82 for 25.4 miles, passing through Twin Lakes and over Independence Pass, to the first hairpin turn on the west side of the pass. Park in a gravel lot on the outside of the turn. The trailhead is on the left side of the parking strip (GPS: 39 7.482, –106 34.909).

The Hike

A stiff hike climbs steep slopes above the upper, U-shaped valley of the Roaring Fork River to Linkins Lake, a glassy pond perched at 12,008 feet in a hanging cirque. Unranked peaks, smoothed by ageless glaciation, surround the lake, with 13,301-foot West Geissler Mountain and its long south ridge scraping the ragged horizon. The popular Linkins Lake Trail, starting from a hairpin turn on the west side of Independence Pass, gains 500 feet in a little more than a half mile. After reaching the crystal-clear lake, catch your breath and hike north along the lakeshore to enjoy views south of the Continental Divide, the twisting spine of North America, and 13,711-foot Twining Peak.

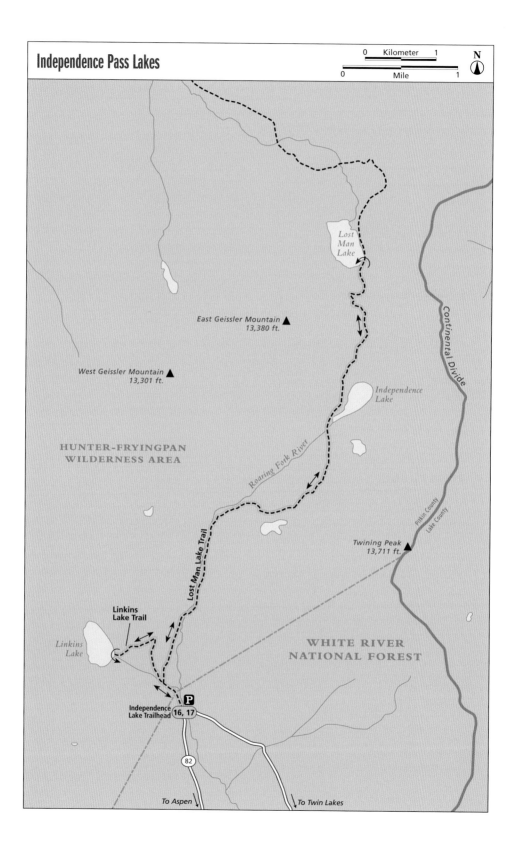

Independence Pass Lakes

0 Kilometer 1
0 Mile 1

N

Lost Man Lake

East Geissler Mountain ▲
13,380 ft.

West Geissler Mountain ▲
13,301 ft.

Independence Lake

Continental Divide

HUNTER–FRYINGPAN
WILDERNESS AREA

Roaring Fork River

Pitkin County
Lake County

Twining Peak ▲
13,711 ft.

Lost Man Lake Trail

Linkins
Lake Trail

WHITE RIVER
NATIONAL FOREST

*Linkins
Lake*

Independence
Lake Trailhead

P

16, 17

82

To Aspen

To Twin Lakes

The short, steep hike to Linkins Lake shares a trailhead with the more popular Independence Lake and Lost Man Lake.

Miles and Directions

0.0 Start at the Independence Lake Trailhead. Hike north on Lost Man Trail alongside the upper Roaring Fork River and cross a footbridge.

0.2 At a signed junction with Linkins Lake Trail, go left on it and enter the Hunter-Fryingpan Wilderness Area (GPS: 39 7.574, –106 34.997). Hike northwest through trees in a shallow valley.

0.3 Reach a junction with an informal trail on the left. Keep right and hike up the main trail (GPS: 39 7.62, –106 35.039). Several braided social trails leave Linkins Lake Trail. Avoid hiking on them to protect the fragile ecosystem.

0.6 Arrive at the southeast side of Linkins Lake (GPS: 39 7.677, –106 35.239). After enjoying the views, hike back down the trail.

1.2 Arrive back at the trailhead (GPS: 39 7.482, –106 34.909).

17 Independence Lake and Lost Man Lake

Reaching two sparkling alpine lakes high above treeline, this Independence Pass hike climbs a glaciated valley below the Continental Divide in the Sawatch Range near Aspen.

See map on page 64.
Start: Independence Lake Trailhead
Difficulty: Moderate
Trail: Lost Man Lake Trail #1996.1
Hiking time: 3 to 4 hours
Distance: 5.4 miles out-and-back
Elevation trailhead to lakes: 11,506 to 12,450 feet at Lost Man Lake; 12,490 feet at Independence Lake; 12,800 feet at Lost Man Pass (+1,294 feet)
Restrictions: Wilderness regulations apply; seasonal access only; Independence Pass closes from early Nov until late May; no toilets at trailhead; no campfires; leashed dogs only; properly dispose of human waste; camping not recommended to protect fragile plants
Amenities: Services in Twin Lakes and Aspen
Maps: *DeLorme*: Page 47, D6; Trails Illustrated 127: Aspen, Independence Pass; USGS Independence Pass
County: Pitkin
Land status: Hunter-Fryingpan Wilderness Area; White River National Forest, (970) 945-2521; Aspen-Sopris Ranger District, (970) 925-3445; Carbondale office, (970) 963-2266

Finding the trailhead: From US 24 between Buena Vista and Leadville, drive west on CO 82 for 25.4 miles, passing through Twin Lakes and over Independence Pass, to the first hairpin turn on the west side of the pass. Park in a gravel lot on the outside of the turn. The trailhead is on the left side of the parking strip (GPS: 39 7.482, -106 34.909).

The Hike

Independence and Lost Man Lakes, glacial lakes in separate cirques west of the Continental Divide, lie along the Lost Man Lake Trail, which climbs north from the Independence Pass highway. Traversing the Sawatch Range, the rooftop of Colorado, the hike passes high peaks, including twin-summited Geissler Mountain on the west and the Continental Divide on the east. The hike, lying entirely above timberline, begins at 11,506 feet and climbs north to a 12,800-foot pass between the lakes, and then drops 350 feet to Lost Man Lake. Independence Lake, named for a ghost town down the valley, is the source of the Roaring Fork River.

Following the trickling river, the trail threads up a wide valley to glistening Independence Lake. The few creek crossings are easily navigable by rock-hopping or stepping across in low water. Use caution in June when snowmelt fills the creek. Past the lake, the trail steepens, climbing slopes covered with tundra and talus to the broad saddle. Enjoy wildflowers along the trail in midsummer. The last section descends switchbacks on rock and talus to Lost Lake, a beautiful tarn with spectacular mountain views.

At the foot of Twining Peak, placid Independence Lake is the source of the mighty Roaring Fork River.

For a longer hike or backpacking trip, do a car shuttle, parking a vehicle at Lost Man Reservoir Trailhead located on CO 82 4 miles west of Independence Lake Trailhead. Do the 9-mile trek by doing the described hike, and then following Lost Man Trail down a gorgeous alpine valley to the lower trailhead.

Miles and Directions

0.0 Start at the Independence Lake Trailhead. Hike north on Lost Man Trail alongside the upper Roaring Fork River and cross a footbridge.

0.2 At a signed junction with Linkins Lake Trail, keep right on the main trail and enter the Hunter-Fryingpan Wilderness Area (GPS: 39 7.574, −106 34.997). Hike north on open slopes west of the Roaring Fork River to a creek crossing. Continue north on the east side of the creek.

1.7 At the second creek crossing, bear right on the west side of the creek and hike north across talus.

1.8 Arrive at the south end of Independence Lake (GPS: 39 8.543, −106 34.199). Continue north on the trail past the lake and climb a steep section up grassy slopes toward the top of the pass.

2.3 Reach the summit of Lost Man Pass (GPS: 39 8.918, −106 34.037), a broad, 12,800-foot pass between 13,380-foot East Geissler Mountain on the left and an unnamed Point 13,366-foot peak on the Continental Divide to the right. Lost Man Lake lies in the cirque to the north. Descend north on the steep, rocky trail, crossing loose boulders and talus to a grassy apron.

2.7 Arrive at the southern shoreline of Lost Man Lake (GPS: 39 9.116, −106 34.049), the hike's turnaround point. To see more of the lake, follow the trail north along the lake's east side. Plenty of rocky outcrops offer superb vistas of Lost Lake. After enjoying lunch and views, return on the trail over Lost Man Pass.

5.4 Arrive back at the trailhead (GPS: 39 7.482, −106 34.909).

18 Windsor Lake

Cradled in a glacier-sculpted cirque below the Continental Divide, Windsor Lake offers stunning views, summer wildflowers, backcountry camping, and the call of the wild.

Start: Windsor Lake Trailhead
Difficulty: Moderate
Trail: Windsor Lake Trail
Hiking time: 2 to 3 hours
Distance: 2.2 miles out-and-back
Elevation trailhead to lake: 10,790 to 11,630 feet at lake (+840 feet)
Restrictions: Observe wilderness regulations; no camping within 100 feet of lakes, streams, and trails; no motorized vehicles or equipment;

dogs must be under control; properly dispose of human and pet waste
Amenities: None at trailhead; services in Leadville
Maps: *DeLorme*: Page 47, C6; Trails Illustrated 126: Holy Cross, Ruedi Reservoir; USGS Mount Massive
County: Lake
Land status: Mount Massive Wilderness Area; San Isabel National Forest, (719) 553-1400; Leadville Ranger District, (719) 486-0749

Finding the trailhead: From Harrison Avenue/US 24 and West 6th Street in Leadville, drive west on West 6th for 0.8 mile to a T-junction with McWethy Drive/CR 4. Go right on CR 4 and drive 2.4 miles to a three-way junction. Keep right on CR 4 and drive 4.3 miles past Turquoise Lake to a Y-junction with CR 9. Keep left on dirt FR 105/Hagerman Pass Road and drive 3.7 miles to the end of the two-wheel-drive road, a parking lot, and the trailhead (GPS: 39 14.8942, -106 28.2277).

The Hike

Windsor Lake snugs against the Continental Divide in a rugged bowl north of 14,429-foot Mount Massive, the second-highest mountain in Colorado. The lovely lake, reached by a short, steep trail, sprawls across a cirque below timberline, its shoreline rimmed by boulders and gleaming cliffs scattered across mountainsides above the lake. A small, unnamed tarn is a bonus lake along the trail before the main event. Look for occasional moose wading in the pond. Lying in 30,540-acre Mount Massive Wilderness Area, Windsor Lake is a popular hiking destination when August wildflowers fill grassy meadows and cloud shadows trail across tall peaks.

The hike begins at a trailhead on the south side of a parking area at the end of the two-wheel-drive section of the Hagerman Pass Road. Beyond this point, the road requires a four-wheel-drive vehicle to climb over Hagerman Pass and descend to Ivanhoe Lake and the Frying Pan River drainage. The trail gains 840 feet between trailhead and lake, so take your time on the lung-busting ascent. Trekking poles are useful, especially when descending steep, gravelly sections. Windsor

The Continental Divide north of 14,429-foot Mount Massive, Colorado's second-highest peak, looms above Windsor Lake's rocky shoreline.

The Continental Divide, the spine of North America, rises beyond Windsor Lake in the Mount Massive Wilderness Area.

Lake is a springboard to more high-country adventures, like hiking up 12,334-foot Busk-Ivanhoe Benchmark, the peak directly north of the lake, or hiking south up a steep drainage to a higher cirque floored by more lakes, including Notch Lake, Pear Lake, and Three Lakes, all above 12,000 feet.

Afternoon clouds drift above Windsor Lake in the Mount Massive Wilderness Area.

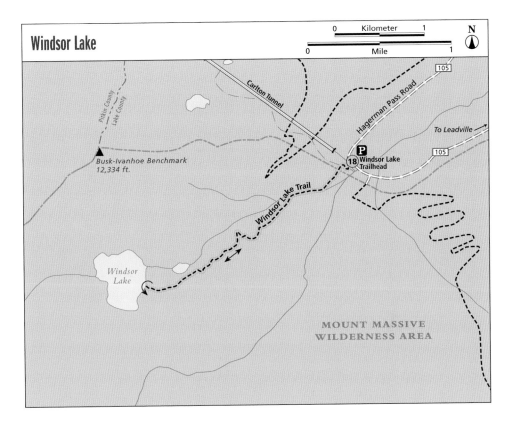

Miles and Directions

0.0 Start at the Windsor Lake Trailhead on the south side of the parking lot and road. Cross a footbridge over a drainage channel from the Busk Ivanhoe Tunnel (an 1897 railroad tunnel converted for autos in 1922 as the Carlton Tunnel) and follow the trail up right into forest.

0.1 Enter Mount Massive Wilderness Area. Hike up the steadily rising trail to a creek crossing. Continue to a steep section, passing a mine adit.

0.7 After gaining 450 feet in 0.3 mile, reach a viewpoint of the Continental Divide to the west, including Busk-Ivanhoe Benchmark (GPS: 39 14.5911, -106 28.8203). Continue on the trail to end of the steep section and gently descend southwest.

0.9 Reach meadows above a smaller tarn below the trail.

1.1 Arrive at the eastern shore of Windsor Lake (GPS: 39 14.5085, -106 29.0926). Return back down the trail.

2.2 Arrive back at the trailhead (GPS: 39 14.8942, -106 28.2277).

19 Timberline Lake

One of the prettiest lakes in the Leadville area, Timberline Lake lies in a spacious alpine cirque surrounded by four peaks on the Continental Divide.

Start: Timberline Lake Trailhead
Difficulty: Moderate
Trails: Colorado Trail #1776, Timberline Lake Trail #1495
Hiking time: About 3 hours
Distance: 4.3 miles out-and-back
Elevation trailhead to lake: 10,035 to 10,860 feet at lake (+825 feet)
Restrictions: Observe wilderness regulations; no camping within 100 feet of lakes, streams, and trails; no motorized vehicles or equipment; leashed dogs only; properly dispose of human and pet waste
Amenities: None at trailhead; services in Leadville
Maps: *DeLorme*: Page 47, C6 and C7; Trails Illustrated 126: Holy Cross, Ruedi Reservoir; USGS Homestake Reservoir
County: Lake
Land status: Holy Cross Wilderness Area; San Isabel National Forest, (719) 553-1400; Leadville Ranger District, (719) 486-0749

Finding the trailhead: From Harrison Avenue/US 24 and West 6th Street in Leadville, drive west on West 6th for 0.8 mile to a T-junction with McWethy Drive/CR 4. Go right on CR 4 and drive 2.4 miles to a three-way junction. Keep right on CR 4 and drive 4.3 miles past Turquoise Lake to a Y-junction with FR 105/Hagerman Pass Road. Stay right on CR 9/Turquoise Lake Road and drive 2.0 miles to a left turn on FR 104E. Drive 325 feet to a parking lot and the trailhead (GPS: 39 17.0924, -106 26.815). The parking lot often fills in summer so park on the road's shoulder.

The Hike

Filling the floor of a broad alpine basin, tree-lined Timberline Lake offers spacious views of an upper, glacier-carved cirque and the Continental Divide, which separates the Atlantic and Pacific watersheds. Four unnamed, 12,000-foot peaks on the Divide scrape the skyline above the lake. Well-traveled Timberline Lake Trail, beginning west of Leadville, follows the Lake Fork, a rushing creek that begins on the Divide and flows east into gleaming Turquoise Lake and then the Arkansas River.

Located in 122,797-acre Holy Cross Wilderness Area, the trail branches off the famed Colorado Trail just west of the trailhead and then follows the Lake Fork up to Timberline Lake. Except for the trail's last sustained half-mile to the lake, the grades are mostly gentle as the footpath ambles across meadows and through dark woods. The two crossings of the Lake Fork can be problematic in early summer when snowmelt fills the creek. Bring trekking poles for balance and prepare for wet feet or bring sandals to wade across. The trail is busy on weekends, so plan a weekday hike for more privacy. For a two-lake day, hike both Timberline Lake and Windsor Lake to the south.

An unnamed, 12,453-foot peak looms beyond Timberline Lake in the Holy Cross Wilderness Area.

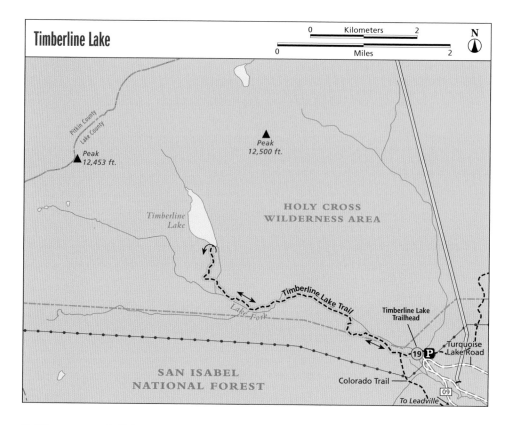

Miles and Directions

0.0 Start at the Timberline Lake Trailhead on the west side of the parking lot. Go left on the Colorado Trail, a 554-mile trail from Denver to Durango, and cross a bridge over Lake Fork creek.

0.08 After 450 feet, reach a junction with Timberline Lake Trail (GPS: 39 17.0884, –106 26.8495) and keep right on the signed trail. The trail climbs and then levels out.

0.3 Enter the Holy Cross Wilderness Area and continue straight on the trail through woods and meadows.

1.2 Reach the first crossing of Lake Fork (GPS: 39 17.3978, –106 27.9307). The water may be high, especially early in summer, so use caution when crossing on rocks and logs.

1.8 Reach the second crossing of Lake Fork, the outlet stream for Timberline Lake. Past the creek, the trail steepens all the way to the lake.

2.15 Arrive at the south shore of Timberline Lake (GPS: 39 17.7301, –106 28.4501). A side trail leads up the left side of the lake, passing backcountry campsites. After a lakeside lunch, return back down the trail.

4.3 Arrive back at the trailhead (GPS: 39 17.0924, –106 26.815).

20 Lily Pad Lake

Lily Pad Lake, nestled on a wooded bench below the Gore Range, is a magical spot for enjoying floating lily pads with boisterous yellow flowers and spectacular mountain views.

Start: Meadow Creek Trailhead
Difficulty: Easy
Trails: Meadow Creek Trail #33, Lily Pad Lake Trail #50
Hiking time: About 2 hours
Distance: 3.0 miles out-and-back
Elevation trailhead to lake: 9,155 to 9,910 feet at lake (+755 feet)
Restrictions: Trail closed to motorized vehicles; leashed dogs only; no campfires within quarter-mile of lake

Amenities: Services in Frisco and Silverthorne
Maps: *DeLorme*: Page 38, E1 and E2; Trails Illustrated 607: Dillon, Silverthorne, 605: Frisco [Local Trails]; USGS Frisco
County: Summit
Land status: Eagles Nest Wilderness Area; Arapaho National Forest, (970) 295-6600; Dillon Ranger District, (970) 468-5400

Finding the trailhead: From I-70 on the north side of Frisco, take exit 203 for Frisco/Breckenridge to a roundabout traffic circle on the north side of the highway. Go through the roundabout and take the gravel road on the northwest side and right of the westbound entrance ramp to I-70. Drive 0.6 mile on dirt FR 1231, a frontage road paralleling the interstate, to a parking lot and trailhead at the road's end (GPS: 39 35.3377, -106 6.3572). The signed Meadow Creek Trailhead is on the north side of the lot.

Option: Alternatively, the north Lily Pad Lake Trailhead, which follows Lily Pad Lake Trail southeast to the lake (not described here), is reached from I-70's exit 205 at Silverthorne. Drive north on CO 9 and go left on Wildernest Road, which becomes Ryan Gulch Road. Drive 3.5 miles through the subdivision to the trailhead and parking lot.

The Hike

One of the best easy hikes near Frisco and Silverthorne in Summit County ends at lovely Lily Pad Lake, a forest-fringed pond on the eastern flank of the Gore Range. A popular trail threads through a dense forest of fir, spruce, and lodgepole pine, glades of quaking aspen, past shiny beaver ponds, and ends at a round lake filled with lily pads in midsummer. The family-friendly hike climbs from a trailhead off I-70 into Eagles Nest Wilderness Area. The trail yields views west of bulky Buffalo Mountain, a local landmark, and south across Lake Dillon to the upper Blue River valley.

The described hike begins at the Meadow Creek Trailhead, which offers ample parking, and gradually ascends north to the lake. An alternative trailhead is northeast of the lake in a Silverthorne neighborhood. Limited parking at this trailhead means

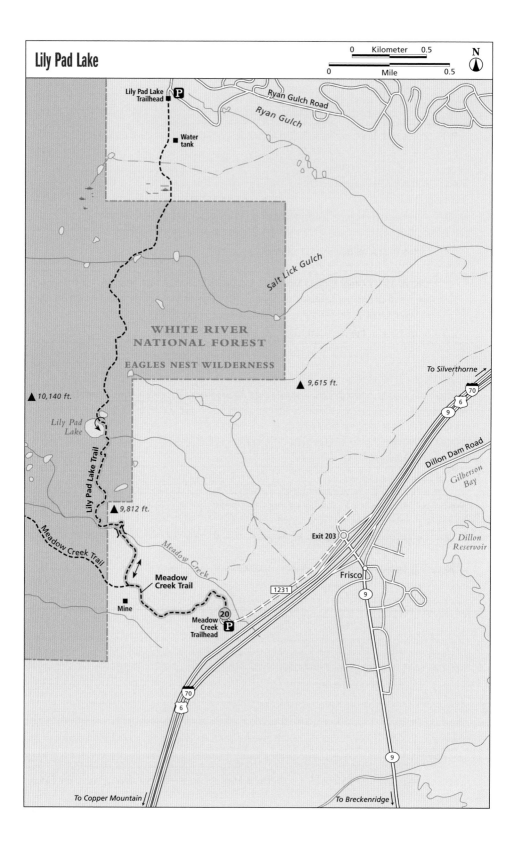

Lily Pad Lake

Lily Pad Lake Trailhead

Ryan Gulch Road

Ryan Gulch

Water tank

Salt Lick Gulch

To Silverthorne

70

6

9

WHITE RIVER
NATIONAL FOREST

EAGLES NEST WILDERNESS

▲ 9,615 ft.

Dillon Dam Road

Gilberson Bay

▲ 10,140 ft.

Lily Pad Lake

Lily Pad Lake Trail

Exit 203

Dillon Reservoir

▲ 9,812 ft.

Meadow Creek

Meadow Creek Trail

Frisco

9

1231

Meadow Creek Trail

Mine

20

Meadow Creek Trailhead

70

6

9

To Copper Mountain

To Breckenridge

N

that the lot is usually jammed. If you start here, it is best to avoid parking hassles by taking the free Summit Stage bus from Frisco to the trailhead.

Miles and Directions

0.0   Start at the Meadow Creek Trailhead and hike north on the well-traveled Meadow Creek Trail with Meadow Creek to the right. The trail bends left and edges along the north edge of a meadow with deadfall.

0.2   Reach a fork and keep right on the main trail.

0.5   Reach a junction with Lily Pad Lake Trail (GPS: 39 35.4459, –106 6.7956). Go right on it. The trail levels out and then begins rising again.

0.8   The trail nears Meadow Creek and enters Eagles Nest Wilderness Area. Continue north across meadows and clumps of trees.

1.5   Reach the east bank of Lily Pad Lake (GPS: 39 35.9763, –106 6.9262) and enjoy views west of 12,777-foot Buffalo Mountain. Return south on the trail. (**Option:** The trail continues north to another trailhead on Ryan Gulch Road on the west side of a neighborhood in Silverthorne. A car shuttle is required to hike to that trailhead.)

3.0   Arrive back at the trailhead (GPS: 39 35.3377, –106 6.3572).

The view from Lily Pad Lake includes Buffalo Mountain on the eastern slope of the Gore Range.

21 Mayflower Lakes

The compact Mayflower Lakes nestle among trees and talus below rugged Mount Helen in central Colorado's Tenmile Range.

Start: Spruce Creek Trailhead
Difficulty: Moderate
Trails: Spruce Creek Trail #58, Mayflower Lakes Trail #58 1A
Hiking time: About 3 hours
Distance: 4.9 miles out-and-back
Elevation trailhead to lakes: 10,380 to 11,315 feet at first lake (+935 feet)
Restrictions: Trail closed to motorized vehicles; leashed dogs only

Amenities: Services in Breckenridge, Alma, and Fairplay
Maps: *DeLorme*: Page 48, A2; Trails Illustrated 606: Breckenridge; USGS Breckenridge
County: Summit
Land status: Arapaho National Forest, (970) 295-6600; Dillon Ranger District, (970) 468-5400

Finding the trailhead: From Fairplay, drive north on CO 9 for 19.3 miles and turn left on unpaved Spruce Creek Road/CR 800. From Breckenridge, drive south on CO 9 for 2.4 miles and turn right on Spruce Creek Road/CR 800. Go 0.1 mile to a T-junction with Crown Drive. Keep left on Spruce Creek Road and drive 1.1 miles to parking on both sides of the road at the trailhead (GPS: N 39 26.221, -106 03.035).

The Hike

The Mayflower Lakes, a collection of two tarns and several smaller ponds, scatter across a bench below the southeast flank of 13,164-foot Mount Helen in the Tenmile Range south of Breckenridge. The lakes make a good addition to the harder hike up to the Mohawk Lakes in the basin above, or hikers who don't want the elevation gain to the upper lakes can do an out-and-back or loop hike to the Mayflower Lakes.

Most of the Mayflower hike follows Spruce Creek Trail from the trailhead to a point where it goes left and begins switchbacking up a steep slope to the higher basin. The signed Mayflower Lakes Trail heads right here and quickly reaches the first and largest lake. Most folks turn around here, but for full-lake value, continue north on the trail to the willow-fringed second pond. From here, return back to the Spruce Creek Trail junction and head east to the trailhead; continue north on Mayflower Lakes Trail to a junction with the Wheeler Trail, which is hiked back to Spruce Creek Trail; or follow Spruce Creek Trail from the junction for a short distance to old mine buildings and a side path that leads to the lower leaps of noisy Continental Falls, a multitiered waterfall that drains the upper basin.

Mohawk Lakes and Mayflower Lakes

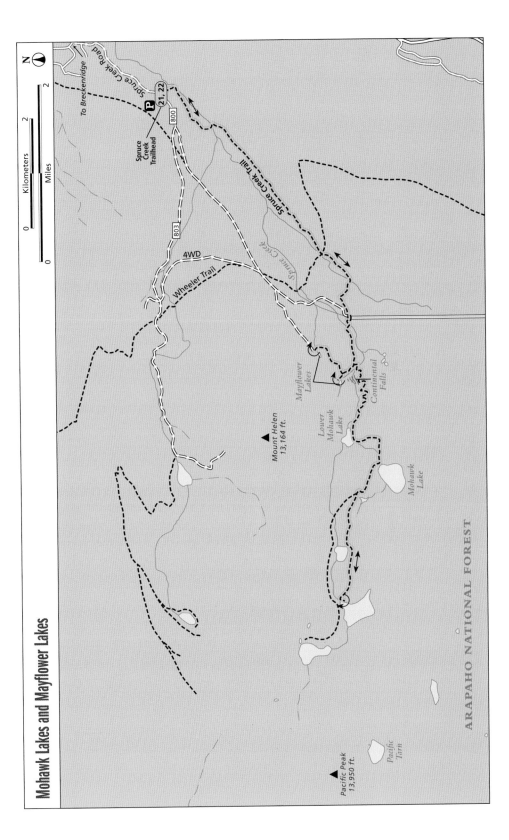

The Mayflower Lakes tuck against the southeastern flank of 13,164-foot Mount Helen.

Miles and Directions

0.0 Begin at the Spruce Creek Trailhead on the south side of road. Follow the trail, marked with blue, diamond-shaped blazes, southwest through a thick conifer forest.

0.4 Cross Spruce Creek on a footbridge.

1.5 Reach the junction with Wheeler Trail #39. Go straight on Spruce Creek Trail into woods. Enjoy views west on the eastern edge of a wide wetland meadow and beaver ponds of Continental Falls and Pacific Peak.

2.0 Pass sign for Spruce Creek Trail and meet a closed road (GPS: 39 25.2953, –106 4.4561). Follow the road past a diversion dam on the left.

2.1 Rejoin Spruce Creek Trail past the dam (GPS:39 25.2895, –106 4.50780).

2.3 Reach a signed junction with Mayflower Lakes Trail #58 1A on the right (GPS: 39 25.2662, –106 4.7579). Keep right on the Mayflower Lakes Trail. A left turn climbs to Continental Falls and the Mohawk Lakes.

2.45 Reach the northeast corner of the main Mayflower Lake as well as nearby small ponds (GPS: 39 25.3462, –106 4.8554).

4.9 Arrive back at the trailhead (GPS: 39 26.221, –106 03.035).

EXTRA CREDIT: UPPER MAYFLOWER LAKE

To visit the northern Mayflower Lake, take the Mayflower Lakes Trail, which goes right at the first lake's outlet stream (GPS: 39 25.3215, –106 4.8179). Hike north for 0.25 mile through forest and over rocks to the small lake. Return back to the first Mayflower Lake for a 0.5-mile round-trip, side excursion.

For a loop hike, the trail continues north from the second lake to a junction with the Wheeler Trail. Go right on it and hike southeast to Spruce Creek Trail, which is followed back to the trailhead.

22 Mohawk Lakes

The twin Mohawk Lakes and four higher, unnamed lakes scatter like a string of glistening pearls in a deep valley below Pacific Peak, the sixty-first-highest mountain in Colorado.

See map on page 79.
Start: Spruce Creek Trailhead
Difficulty: Moderate
Trail: Spruce Creek Trail #58
Hiking time: About 6 hours
Distance: 6.2 miles out-and-back to Mohawk Lake; 8.2 miles out-and-back to highest unnamed lake
Elevation trailhead to lake: 10,380 to 12,090 feet at Mohawk Lake (+1,710 feet); 12,450 feet at highest unnamed lake (+2,070 feet)

Restrictions: Trail closed to motorized vehicles; dogs must be leashed
Amenities: Services in Breckenridge, Alma, and Fairplay
Maps: *DeLorme*: Page 48, A2; Trails Illustrated 606: Breckenridge; USGS Breckenridge
County: Summit
Land status: Arapaho National Forest, (970) 295-6600; Dillon Ranger District, (970) 468-5400

Finding the trailhead: From Fairplay, drive north on CO 9 for 19.3 miles and turn left on unpaved Spruce Creek Road/CR 800. From Breckenridge, drive south on CO 9 for 2.4 miles and turn right on Spruce Creek Road/CR 800. Go 0.1 mile to a T-junction with Crown Drive. Keep left on Spruce Creek Road and drive 1.1 miles to parking on both sides of the road at the trailhead (GPS: N 39 26.221, -106 03.035).

The Hike

Originating from melting snowfields on the northeast face of 13,950-foot Pacific Peak, Spruce Creek dashes down a glaciated valley, pooling in six alpine lakes before plunging down multitiered Continental Falls. From the trailhead south of Breckenridge, hikers ascend Spruce Creek Trail, winding through spruce and fir woods and then scrambling alongside the waterfall to Lower Mohawk Lake, a sparkling tarn below 13,164-foot Mount Helen. Larger Mohawk Lake, flanked by tundra, talus, and cliffs, nestles 261 feet higher in a round bowl. Most hikers turn around here, content with a 6.2-mile hike, but for full value, continue up the less-traveled trail for another 0.9 mile past a couple small tarns to a kite-shaped lake tucked against a cliffed ridge. This is the hike's turnaround point, although a higher lake sits at the head of the cirque. This is reached by a rarely used faint trail.

Plan an early start to do the six-lake hike, especially in summer when afternoon thunderstorms occur almost daily. Bring plenty of water, sports drinks, extra clothing, rain gear, and trekking poles if any snowbanks linger above timberline. The trail is easy to follow to Mohawk Lake but pay attention on the higher path to avoid walking off trail and damaging fragile alpine tundra grasses and plants. The parking areas at the trailhead fill quickly in summer, so arrive early to snag a spot.

The long east ridge of Pacific Peak rises beyond Lower Mohawk Lake in the Tenmile Range.

Mount Helen dominates the northern skyline above Lower Mohawk Lake.

Miles and Directions

0.0 Begin at Spruce Creek Trailhead on the south side of road. Follow the trail, marked with blue-diamond-shaped blazes, southwest through a thick conifer forest.

0.4 Cross Spruce Creek on footbridge.

1.5 Reach the junction with Wheeler Trail #39. Go straight on Spruce Creek Trail into woods. Enjoy views west on eastern edge of a wide wetland meadow and beaver ponds of Continental Falls and Pacific Peak.

2.0 Pass sign for Spruce Creek Trail and meet a closed road (GPS: 39 25.2953, –106 4.4561). Follow the road past a diversion dam on the left.

2.1 Rejoin Spruce Creek Trail past the dam (GPS: 39 25.2895, –106 4.50780).

2.3 Reach a signed junction with Mayflower Lakes Trail #58 1A on the right (GPS: 39 25.2662, –106 4.7579). Stay left toward Continental Falls and Mohawk Lakes. Hike past cabin ruins on the right, cross a creek on a footbridge, and continue past more ruins. Climb a steep slope, passing a mine ruin. Look right for side trails for views of Continental Falls.

2.5 Reach top of Continental Falls to the right (GPS: 39 25.2619, –106 5.0772). Hike west through willows.

2.8 Arrive at south shore of Lower Mohawk Lake. Grab a boulder for lunch and note a waterfall above the lake. Continue south on the trail, climbing over bedrock and through clumps of trees.

3.2 After gaining 261 feet, arrive at east shore of Mohawk Lake. This is a good turnaround point for a 6.2-mile, round-trip hike. Hike northwest on the trail across rocky slopes.

3.5 Reach a small, unnamed tarn on a bedrock shelf. Continue west up rock and tundra slopes.

3.7 Reach the east side of a larger, unnamed tarn. Continue west on gentle tundra slopes.

4.1 Arrive at the northeast edge of an unnamed lake at 12,091 feet below Pacific Peak's rugged east ridge. This gorgeous tarn is the end of the hike. Follow the trail back down. (***Option:*** Reach the highest unnamed lake at 12,450 feet in the cirque by following a faint trail on the north end of lake for 0.1 mile and then hiking 0.2 mile up tundra slopes to it. Walk carefully and don't damage tundra plants.)

8.2 Arrive back at the trailhead (GPS: 39 26.221, –106 03.035).

23 Kroenke Lake

The aqua-green waters of Kroenke Lake fill a high basin below 12,730-foot Birthday Peak and the Continental Divide in the Collegiate Peaks Wilderness Area near Buena Vista.

Start: North Cottonwood Trailhead
Difficulty: Moderate
Trails: Horn Fork Basin Trail #1449, North Cottonwood Trail #1448
Hiking time: About 6 hours
Distance: 8.6 miles out-and-back
Elevation trailhead to lake: 9,886 to 11,500 feet at lake (+1,614 feet)
Restrictions: Wilderness regulations apply; permits at trailhead; no toilets at trailhead; no camping at trailhead; no bikes or motorized

vehicles allowed; leashed dogs only; winter road closure may be in effect
Amenities: Services in Buena Vista
Maps: *DeLorme:* Page 59, B8; Trails Illustrated 129: Buena Vista, Collegiate Peaks, 148: Collegiate Peaks Wilderness Area; USGS Mount Yale
County: Chaffee
Land status: Collegiate Peaks Wilderness Area; San Isabel National Forest, (719) 553-1400; Salida Ranger District, (719) 539-3591

Finding the trailhead: From the junction of US 24 and Main Street in Buena Vista, drive north on US 24 for 0.4 mile and turn left (west) on Crossman Avenue/CR 350 and drive 2.1 miles to a T-junction. Turn right on CR 361 and drive 0.9 mile to a junction with CR 365 (North Cottonwood Road) on the left. Turn left on this unpaved road, which becomes FR 365, and drive 5.1 miles to a parking area on a counterclockwise loop. The trailhead is on the parking lot's west side (GPS: 38 52.259, –106 15.988). *Note:* FR 365 is narrow, rutted, rocky, and exposed in places and a high-clearance, four-wheel-drive vehicle is recommended but may not be required, depending on weather and road conditions. The trailhead may be closed by snow from fall through spring. Parking is limited to twenty vehicles. It is crowded on weekends with hikers trekking up nearby Fourteeners.

The Hike

Forest-fringed Kroenke Lake lies at the head of a cirque below Birthday Peak and two unnamed, 12,000-foot peaks on the Continental Divide in the Collegiate Peaks Wilderness Area. The lake hides in the Sawatch Range, which is topped by fifteen 14,000-foot peaks. The hike's start at North Cottonwood Trailhead is popular with peakbaggers intent on climbing 14,423-foot Mount Harvard and 14,078-foot Mount Columbia. Their route follows the trail toward Kroenke Lake, then veers right on the Horn Fork Basin Trail, which heads north to Mount Harvard. As a lake lover, you'll enjoy the shorter and easier track west to Kroenke Lake.

Fed by North Cottonwood Creek, the lake is reached by a good trail that follows the creek, with the 1,500-foot elevation gain evenly distributed so that there are not

A stiff wind ruffles the waters of Kroenke Lake in the Collegiate Peaks Wilderness Area.

any steep sections. Bring trekking poles for balance for a few creek crossings, especially in early summer when snowmelt fills the creek. The trail leaves the woods as it nears the lake, offering vistas of peaks on the Continental Divide and a glimpse of lofty Mount Columbia to the northeast. Look for moose in the wetlands along the creek south of the lake.

EXTRA CREDIT: BROWNS PASS

For a longer hike and higher views of the lake, continue on the trail toward Browns Pass, along the lake's south shore and then up through trees for a half-mile to rock outcrops at a switchback. To reach Browns Pass, continue on the trail for another mile, passing four small lakelets and climbing over a 12,480-foot, unnamed pass on the Divide. If you have a car shuttle, do a backpacking trip from the lake by hiking up to Browns Pass and then south on Browns Pass Trail to the Denny Creek Trailhead with a jaunt to Hartenstein Lake along the way.

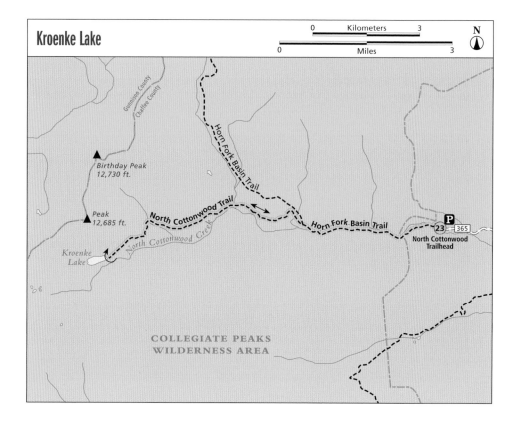

Kroenke Lake

Miles and Directions

0.0 From the North Cottonwood Trailhead, hike west on Horn Fork Basin Trail and after 500 feet cross a footbridge over Horn Fork Creek.

0.6 Enter the Collegiate Peaks Wilderness Area.

1.6 Cross a footbridge over North Cottonwood Creek (GPS: 38 52.227, –106 17.508).

1.7 At a signed trail junction with Horn Fork Basin Trail and Bear Lake to the right, bear left on North Cottonwood Trail toward Browns Pass and Kroenke Lake (GPS: 38 52.268, –106 17.589).

2.6 Cross Horn Fork Creek on a split log (GPS: 38 52.444, –106 18.395).

3.6 Cross North Cottonwood Creek on rocks and logs (GPS: 38 52.305, –106 19.395).

4.3 Arrive at Kroenke Lake to the right (north) of the trail (GPS: 38 51.969, –106 19.898). Return the way you came.

8.6 Arrive back at the trailhead (GPS: 38 52.259, –106 15.988).

24 Hartenstein Lake

Turner Peak and 14,199-foot Mount Yale provide the backdrop for Hartenstein Lake, an alpine lake nestled high in a cirque in the Sawatch Range near Cottonwood Pass.

Start: Denny Creek Trailhead
Difficulty: Moderate
Trails: Browns Pass Trail #1442, Hartenstein Lake Trail #1443
Hiking time: About 3 hours
Distance: 6.0 miles out-and-back
Elevation trailhead to lake: 9,965 to 11,451 feet at lake (+1,486 feet)
Restrictions: Wilderness regulations apply; no camping at trailhead; no bikes or motorized vehicles allowed; leashed dogs only; winter road closure may be in effect

Amenities: Toilets at trailhead; services in Buena Vista
Maps: *DeLorme*: Page 59, B7 and B8; Trails Illustrated 129: Buena Vista, Collegiate Peaks, 148: Collegiate Peaks Wilderness Area; USGS Mount Yale
County: Chaffee
Land status: Collegiate Peaks Wilderness Area; San Isabel National Forest, (719) 553-1400; Salida Ranger District, (719) 539-3591

Finding the trailhead: From US 24 and Main Street in Buena Vista, drive west on West Main Street/CR 306 (Cottonwood Pass Road) for 12 miles to the signed Denny Creek Trailhead parking lot on the road's right side. The paved lot has thirty-eight spots with overflow parking on both sides of the lot. The trailhead is in the middle of the parking lot's north side (GPS: 38 48.899, –106 20.067).

The Hike

Cradled in a glaciated cirque, Hartenstein Lake is a picture-perfect tarn surrounded by forest and deadfall. Fed by two streams originating on the northeast flank of 13,233-foot Turner Peak, the lake is the headwaters for Denny Creek. The lake is a popular destination for hikers and backpackers, who find stunning views of resident Fourteener Mount Yale.

Besides being the trailhead for Hartenstein Lake and Browns Pass, the Denny Creek Trailhead is also the main access point for hikers heading up Mount Yale. Expect a busy parking area, especially during the summer and on weekends and holidays. You'll share the rocky Browns Pass Trail and a couple of creek crossings for the first mile and a half to its junction with the Mount Yale Trail, so bring trekking poles for balance. After branching left off the Browns Pass Trail, the footpath improves near the lake, following open slopes north of Denny Creek. At the lake, enjoy spacious vistas of Mount Yale and Mascot Peak to the east and Turner Peak to the southwest. The trail ends at Hartenstein Lake.

Fourteener Mount Yale brushes the eastern sky above Hartenstein Lake.

The east ridge of an unnamed 12,739-foot peak looms above Hartenstein Lake.

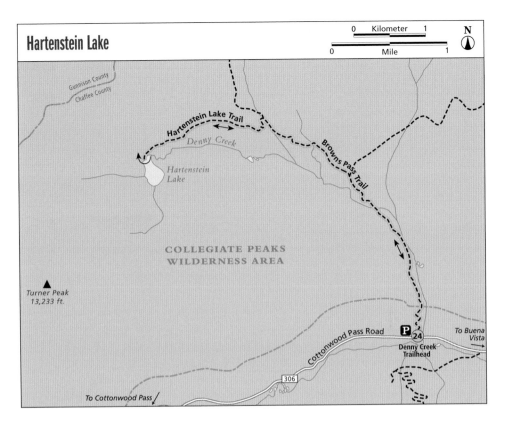

Hartenstein Lake

Miles and Directions

0.0 Begin at the Denny Creek Trailhead on the north side of the parking lot. Climb stone steps and hike north on Browns Pass Trail.

0.3 Enter the Collegiate Peaks Wilderness Area.

1.0 Cross Denny Creek on rocks and tree branches or a log if it's in place (GPS: 38 49.570, –106 20.338).

1.1 Cross Denny Creek again on rocks and branches or through scrub oak and marshes to the trail's left (GPS: 38 49.650, –106 20.450).

1.3 At a signed trail junction with the Mount Yale Trail to the right, stay straight toward Browns Pass and Hartenstein Lake (GPS: 38 49.785, –106 20.550).

1.95 Cross several smaller creeks and an open area and reach a signed trail junction for Browns Pass. Turn left on Hartenstein Lake Trail (GPS: 38 50.088, –106 21.154).

2.0 Cross the North Fork of Denny Creek on logs (GPS: 38 50.085, –106 21.169). The trail curves to the left past boulders and descends into a forest to a small clearing.

3.0 Arrive at the north shoreline of Hartenstein Lake (GPS: 38 49.876, –106 22.011). Return the way you came.

6.0 Arrive back at the trailhead (GPS: 38 48.899, –106 20.067).

25 Ptarmigan Lake

The Ptarmigan Lake Trail offers a spectacular 6.8-mile, round-trip hike from the Cottonwood Pass Road to broad Ptarmigan Lake, an alpine lake in the heart of the rugged Sawatch Range west of Buena Vista.

Start: Ptarmigan Lake Trailhead
Difficulty: Moderate
Trail: Ptarmigan Lake Trail #1444
Hiking time: 3 to 4 hours
Distance: 6.8 miles out-and-back
Elevation trailhead to lake: 10,660 to 12,132 feet at lake (+1,472 feet)
Restrictions: Limited parking at trailhead; bikes and motorized vehicles not allowed; leashed dogs only; winter road closure may be in effect

Amenities: Toilet at trailhead; services in Buena Vista
Maps: *DeLorme*: Page 59, B7 and C7; Trails Illustrated 129: Buena Vista, Collegiate Peaks; USGS Mount Yale, Tincup
County: Chaffee
Land status: San Isabel National Forest, (719) 553-1400; Salida Ranger District, (719) 539-3591

Finding the trailhead: From the stoplight at the intersection of US 24 and Main Street in Buena Vista, drive west on Chaffee CR 306/Cottonwood Pass Road for 14.5 miles, which becomes FR 306, toward Cottonwood Pass. Turn left or south on a marked road that leads 0.1 mile south to a parking lot and the Ptarmigan Lake Trailhead (GPS: 38 48.2059, -106 22.4905). The ten-car parking lot fills quickly, especially on weekends. Extra parking spots are off the access road and overflow parking is on the shoulder of the Cottonwood Pass Road.

The Hike

This gorgeous alpine lake is tucked into a glacier-carved cirque below the north face of 13,218-foot Jones Mountain. The moderate trail, gaining 1,472 feet in elevation, climbs through a thick forest of spruce and fir to the gleaming 11-acre lake at timberline. The trail also passes four smaller unnamed lakes, their still waters reflecting peaks, clouds, and sky. The upper trail section climbs through open meadows strewn with colorful wildflowers from mid-July to early August. The singletrack trail is easy to follow and offers good footing on its dirt and rock bed. Expect plenty of company on the trail on summer weekends or plan your hike midweek to avoid crowds.

Ptarmigan Lake fills a high cirque surrounded by towering peaks, including three 14,000-foot mountains.

An unnamed alpine tarn reflects sky and 13,233-foot Turner Peak along the Ptarmigan Lake Trail.

Hikers pause for a view across Ptarmigan Lake to Mount Yale.

EXTRA CREDIT: JONES MOUNTAIN

For extra credit and great views of Ptarmigan Lake, follow the trail past the lake and climb to a 12,283-foot saddle between Gladstone Ridge to the east and Jones Mountain to the west. Follow the grassy east ridge of Jones Mountain to its rocky summit and spacious views across the central Sawatch Range. This 0.7-mile ascent gains 1,086 feet from lake to summit.

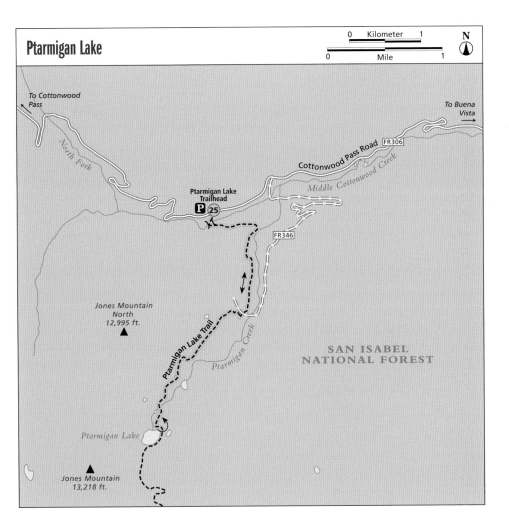

Miles and Directions

0.0 Start at the Ptarmigan Lake Trailhead off the Cottonwood Pass Road. Hike south on the trail and cross Middle Cottonwood Creek.

0.2 Cross a talus slope with views of 14,199-foot Mount Yale to the northeast.

0.5 Bend right onto the western side of Ptarmigan Creek's valley.

1.4 Reach a junction with a closed forest road (GPS: 38 47.5259, –106 22.2003). Continue straight on the marked trail.

2.4 Reach a small creek beside the trail.

2.7 Reach a wide bench with a shallow tarn on the right and an unnamed lake in the valley to the left (GPS: 38 47.0584, –106 22.8118).

3.4 The hike ends at the northeast side of Ptarmigan Lake below Jones Mountain (GPS: 38 46.678, –106 22.9706). The trail continues for 0.25 mile along the east shore of the lake and then climbs south to a pass east of Jones Mountain. Return the way you came.

6.8 Arrive back at the trailhead (GPS: 38 48.2058, –106 22.4905).

26 Lost Lake (Cottonwood Pass)

Cupped in a glaciated sink, Lost Lake is an alpine charmer reached by a short trail south of Cottonwood Pass in the Sawatch Range.

Start: Lost Lake Trailhead
Difficulty: Easy
Trail: Lost Lake Trail
Hiking time: About 2 hours
Distance: 2.4 miles out-and-back
Elevation trailhead to lake: 10,660 to 11,880 feet at Lost Lake (+1,220 feet)
Restrictions: Limited roadside parking at trailhead; no bikes or motorized vehicles; leashed dogs only; road closed in winter

Amenities: Services in Buena Vista; campgrounds east of trailhead
Maps: *DeLorme*: Page 59, B7; Trails Illustrated 129: Buena Vista, Collegiate Peaks; USGS Tincup
County: Chaffee
Land status: San Isabel National Forest, (719) 553-1400; Salida Ranger District, (719) 539-3591

Finding the trailhead: From the stoplight at the intersection of US 24 and Main Street in Buena Vista, drive west on Chaffee CR 306/Cottonwood Pass Road for 17.8 miles toward Cottonwood Pass. Limited parking is on the right side of the paved road, 1.4 miles east of the pass summit. If roadside strip is full, park on the road shoulder and watch for traffic. The unsigned trailhead is on the road's south side (GPS: 38 49.0739, -106 24.3555).

The Hike

Nestled in a bowl below the eastern flank of the Continental Divide, teal-colored Lost Lake is a gorgeous tarn surrounded by talus slopes, rocky outcrops, and glacier-smoothed hills at timberline. A bedrock island, clad with sparse, scrubby trees, punctuates the middle of the lake. A short trail reaches this hidden beauty spot, winding through meadows and marshes, passing a small tarn, and hiking past a boulderfield to the lake's edge. An intermittent trail follows the shoreline but is difficult to navigate across talus on the west side.

The popular trail, gaining about 1,200 feet of elevation to the lake, is best from July to mid-October, since snowdrifts often blanket parts of the trail and snowmelt fills muddy marshes in early summer. Parking is a problem at the trailhead on summer days. Park on the road's shoulder, making sure your vehicle is well off the road. The trailhead is unsigned but look for a trail climbing into a conifer forest. The hike offers splendid views of high peaks in the Sawatch Range, including 13,218-foot Jones Mountain to the southeast and 14,199-foot Mount Yale on the eastern horizon.

Reflecting sky and clouds, quiet Lost Lake tucks against the Continental Divide south of Cottonwood Pass.

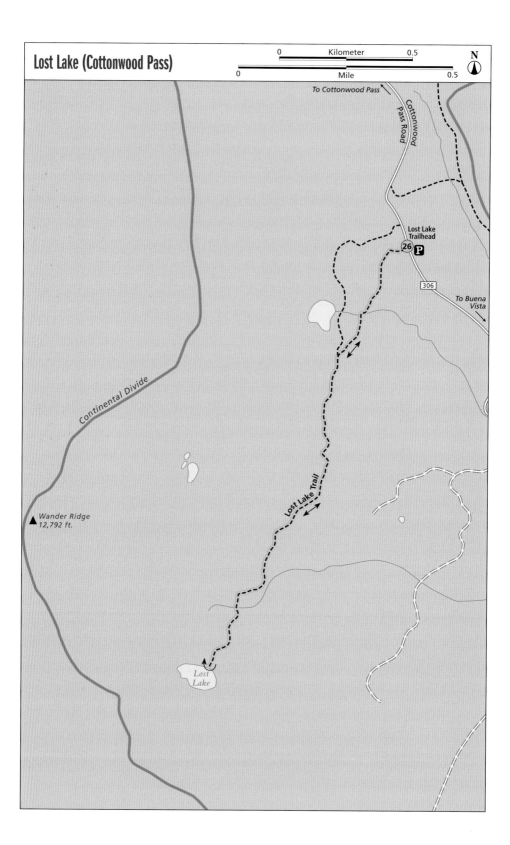

Lost Lake (Cottonwood Pass)

0   Kilometer   0.5

0   Mile   0.5

N

To Cottonwood Pass

Cottonwood Pass Road

Lost Lake Trailhead

26 P

306

To Buena Vista

Continental Divide

Lost Lake Trail

▲ Wander Ridge
12,792 ft.

Lost
Lake

Lost Lake and its rock island lie below Wander Ridge, a 12,792-foot point on the Continental Divide.

Miles and Directions

0.0 Start at the unsigned Lost Lake Trailhead on the south side of the Cottonwood Pass Road. Look for a trail heading south into woods. Hike through trees to open meadows.

0.3 Pass a cutoff trail that leads 350 feet right to an unnamed pond tucked in a hollow beneath the Continental Divide (GPS: 38 48.8766, -106 24.5102). Continue south on the main trail, hiking through meadows and clumps of trees, and then descend and skirt the western edge of a wetland.

1.0 The trail turns left and slogs through a muddy section in the wetland. This is very wet early in the summer. Plan on wet shoes. Continue through trees and climb past a boulderfield on the left.

1.2 Reach the northeast corner of Lost Lake and enjoy a perfect lake view. Side trails go along the north and east sides of the lake to a large talus field. Follow the trail back north.

2.4 Arrive back at the trailhead (GPS: 38 49.0739, -106 24.3555).

Southern Colorado

Pueblo, Westcliffe, Walsenburg, Trinidad, Alamosa, Coaldale, and Crestone

Pyramid-shaped Spread Eagle Peak dominates the western skyline above the lowest of the Lakes of the Clouds.

27 Stout Creek Lakes

The Stout Creek Lakes, two large lakes and a tiny tarn, nestle in a rock-walled basin filled with silence and rugged vistas on the eastern flank of the Sangre de Cristo Mountains.

Start: Rainbow Trailhead at Hayden Creek Campground, Bushnell Lakes Trailhead
Difficulty: Very strenuous
Trails: Rainbow Trail #1336, Stout Creek Lakes Trail #1403
Hiking time: About 11 hours for "Middle Stout Creek Lake"
Distance: 16.4 miles out-and-back to "Middle Stout Creek Lake"
Elevation trailhead to lake: 7,600 to 11,761 feet at "Middle Stout Creek Lake" (+4,161 feet)

Restrictions: Trail closed to motor vehicles; observe wilderness regulations
Amenities: Backcountry camping; services in Coaldale
Maps: *DeLorme*: Page 70, B3 and B4; Trails Illustrated 138: Sangre de Cristo Mountains [Great Sand Dunes National Park and Preserve]; USGS Coaldale, Howard, Bushnell Peak
County: Fremont
Land status: Sangre de Cristo Wilderness Area; San Isabel National Forest, (719) 553-1400; San Carlos Ranger District, (719) 269-8500

Finding the trailhead: From US 50 in Coaldale, take Hayden Creek Road (CR 6) south for 4.7 miles and park at a pullout on the left (GPS: 38 19.79, −105 49.029). The Rainbow Trail is on the road's right side, between Coaldale Campground and Hayden Creek Campground, across from parking pullout and marked with a sign. If pullout is full, go 0.4 mile farther to Hayden Creek Campground, pay a fee to park, and start from a trailhead there.

The Hike

The Twin Sisters, two rugged peaks on the crest of the northern Sangre de Cristo Mountains, loom above the Stout Creek Lakes, three alpine tarns at the head of a glacier-carved cirque. The Stout Creek Lakes Trail, the hardest hike in this book, offers a challenging round-trip excursion with over 5,300 feet of elevation gain, loss, and regain. Get an early start to walk to the remote lakes and back in a day or carry a tent and camp in the lonely upper basin. Plan ahead and carry enough food and water for a full hiking day. If you are uncertain about how much liquid you need, carry a water filter to refill water bottles from the creek.

The hike's first section follows the same route as the Bushnell Lakes hike. Climb the Rainbow Trail to its junction with Bushnell Lakes Trail but continue on the middle fork to stay on Rainbow Trail. The trail descends to a narrow traverse, then turns rocky and disappears into thick forest before rising again. The trail passes through dense scrub oak before it finally opens to sunshine. After 4 miles the route switches back to the southwest and passes the junction with Kerr Gulch Trail and then meets the signed Stout Creek Lakes Trail.

Set below the Twin Sisters, the remote Stout Creek Lakes are reached by a long, steep hike.

The trail heads west up the sunny side of the tight valley, passing through shady woods, occasional meadows, and stepping over deadfall. Stout Creek rumbles over many waterfalls and cascades below the trail. Look for side trails that lead down to the falls. Consult *Hiking Waterfalls Colorado* (second edition, FalconGuides) for more info. A short side trail leads to small "Lower Stout Creek Lake." Above it is "Stout Creek Falls." The trail climbs above the rocky valley floor and traverses down to "Middle Stout Creek Lake," a large lake that reflects sky, clouds, and peaks. Turn around here or continue around the lake to the upper lake, another alpine pool nestled below the Twin Sisters. Be sure to rest on the lakeshore before starting the return hike—it's a long way back to the trailhead!

Bushnell Lakes and Stout Creek Lakes

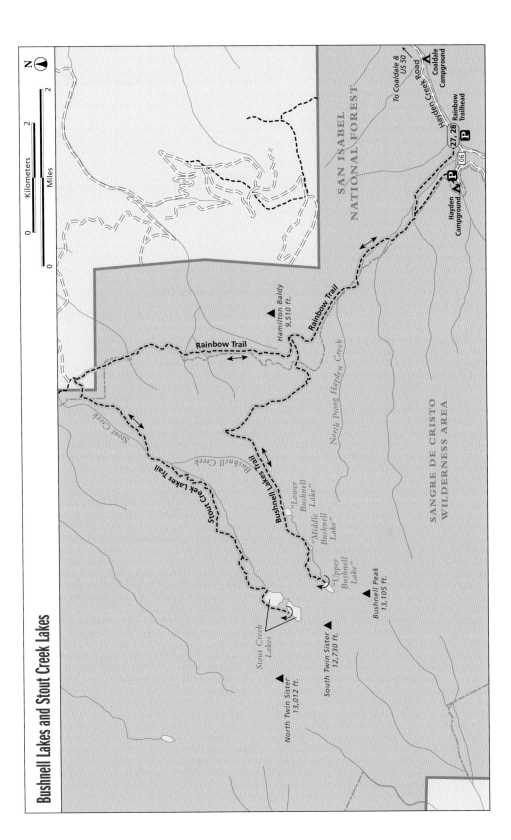

North Twin Sister
13,012 ft.

South Twin Sister
12,730 ft.

Stout Creek Lakes

Bushnell Peak
13,105 ft.

"Upper Bushnell Lake"

"Middle Bushnell Lake"

"Lower Bushnell Lake"

Stout Creek Lakes Trail

Stout Creek

Bushnell Creek

Bushnell Lakes Trail

Rainbow Trail

Hamilton Baldy
9,510 ft.

North Prong Hayden Creek

Rainbow Trail

SANGRE DE CRISTO WILDERNESS AREA

SAN ISABEL NATIONAL FOREST

To Coaldale & US 50

Hayden Creek Road

Coaldale Campground

Rainbow Trailhead

27, 28

P

06

P

Hayden Campground

N

0   2   Kilometers   2
0   2   Miles

Miles and Directions

0.0 Begin at the Rainbow Trailhead across the road from a parking pullout. Hike northwest on the Rainbow Trail along the North Prong of Hayden Creek.

0.7 Cross the North Prong of Hayden Creek on logs.

0.8 Pass the junction with the Hayden Creek Campground trail on the left. Continue straight (watch for this junction on the way back so you take the correct fork to the trailhead). Cross the creek and its tributaries six more times.

2.8 Reach a three-way trail junction at a saddle. Take the middle fork to stay on the Rainbow Trail. The left trail is Bushnell Lakes Trail.

4.8 Reach a junction with Kerr Gulch Trail on the right. Continue straight on Rainbow Trail.

5.0 Reach the junction with Stout Creek Lakes Trail on the left. Leave the Rainbow Trail and hike west on Stout Creek Lakes Trail.

5.1 Reach the Sangre De Cristo Wilderness Area boundary and sign a trail register. Continue up the trail, cross the creek on a log bridge, and pass through deadfall.

7.6 Pass "Lower Stout Creek Falls" on the left. Cut off the main trail on side trails to view the waterfall. Continue west on the main trail.

7.7 Pass "Middle Stout Creek Falls" (GPS: 38 21.428, –105 52.934). Cut off the main trail to view it.

7.8 Continue up the main trail to a junction. Go left for 0.1 mile to 11,280-foot "Lower Stout Creek Lake" (GPS: 38 21.3844, –105 52.9937) and views west of "Stout Creek Falls" above the lake. Return to the junction and go left. Hike up left across the mountainside and then traverse down across talus and grassy slopes.

8.2 Reach the eastern shore of 11,761-foot "Stout Creek Lake" (GPS: 38 21.2287, –105 53.2896). Note the waterfalls and cascades below the lake to the east. Turn around here and return to the trailhead.

16.4 Arrive back at the trailhead (GPS: 38 19.799, –105 49.029).

EXTRA CREDIT: "UPPER STOUT CREEK LAKE"

Follow a 0.5-mile trail around the north and west sides of the lake and climb to the eastern edge of 11,860-foot "Upper Stout Creek Lake" (GPS: 38 21.0677, –105 53.5081). This increases the total distance to 17.4 miles.

28 Bushnell Lakes

Tucked into a narrow cirque in the northern Sangre de Cristo Mountains, the three Bushnell Lakes are remote, pristine ponds that make a difficult hike into a worthwhile journey.

See map on page 101.
Start: Rainbow Trail at Hayden Creek Campground, Bushnell Lakes Trailhead
Difficulty: Very strenuous
Trails: Rainbow Trail #1336, Bushnell Lakes Trail #1402
Hiking time: About 7 hours for "Lower Bushnell Lake"; about 8 hours for "Middle Bushnell Lake" and "Upper Bushnell Lake"
Distance: 10.2 miles out-and-back for "Lower Bushnell Lake"; 11.6 miles out-and-back to "Middle Bushnell Lakes"; 12.2 miles out-and-back to "Upper Bushnell Lake"
Elevation trailhead to lake: 7,600 to 11,140 feet at "Lower Bushnell Lake" (+3,540 feet);

11,905 feet at "Upper Bushnell Lake" (+4,305 feet)
Restrictions: Trail closed to motor vehicles; observe wilderness regulations
Amenities: Backcountry camping; services in Coaldale
Maps: *DeLorme*: Page 70, B3 and B4; Trails Illustrated 138: Sangre de Cristo Mountains [Great Sand Dunes National Park and Preserve]; USGS Coaldale, Bushnell Peak
County: Fremont
Land status: Sangre de Cristo Wilderness Area; San Isabel National Forest, (719) 553-1400; San Carlos Ranger District, (719) 269-8500

Finding the trailhead: From US 50 in Coaldale, take Hayden Creek Road (CR 6) south for 4.7 miles and park at a pullout on the left. The Rainbow Trail is on the road's right side, between Coaldale Campground and Hayden Creek Campground, across from a parking pullout and marked with a sign (GPS: 38 19.79, –105 49.029). If pullout is full, go 0.4 mile farther to Hayden Creek Campground, pay a fee to park, and start from a trailhead there.

The Hike

The hike to the triple Bushnell Lakes, hidden in a high cirque in the Sangre de Cristo Mountains, is one of the toughest lake hikes in this book. The Bushnell Lakes Trail, ending at the upper lake below 13,105-foot Bushnell Peak, is a full-value adventure with over 4,000 feet of elevation gain. The payday is three glassy, alpine lakes and three gorgeous waterfalls between the lakes. Expect a long day of hard hiking or plan on hauling a tent and staying overnight at the lower lake. The basin is wild, scenic, and rarely visited, so expect few people to interrupt your solitude.

The last mile of road to the trailhead is unmaintained in winter, so park at a pullout at a barrier at Coaldale Campground and hike up the road if it's closed. Be sure to get on the Rainbow Trail on the right (north) side of the road opposite the parking area, or you will head in the wrong direction.

Ice glazes "Middle Bushnell Lake" below a snowy ridge in the Sangre de Cristo Mountains.

"Bushnell Lakes Falls" tumbles down a cliff into "Lower Bushnell Lake."

The first trail section follows the North Prong of Hayden Creek, crossing the creek seven times before its junction with Bushnell Lakes Trail. At the junction, take the left fork, sign the wilderness register, and enter the Sangre de Cristo Wilderness Area. The trail steepens here, crossing talus fields and climbing switchbacks until it swings into a long valley. A shaded, north-facing section is often covered with dangerous snow and ice. Bring MICROspikes and an ice axe for safety. The trail climbs to "Lower Bushnell Lake," a lovely tarn surrounded by forest. A frothy waterfall gushes down cliffs above the lake. This is the end of the hike for most people.

Beyond here, the trail has become faint, overgrown, and is hard to follow. Pay attention to the terrain and follow your map to stay on course to the middle and upper lakes. Also, enjoy more waterfalls below each of the lakes. Trekking poles are handy for creek crossings and help on steep, rocky sections.

Miles and Directions

0.0 Begin at Rainbow Trailhead across the road from the parking pullout. Hike northwest on Rainbow Trail along the North Prong of Hayden Creek.

0.7 Cross the North Prong of Hayden Creek on logs.

0.8 Pass the junction with Hayden Creek Campground trail on the left. Continue straight (watch for this junction on the way back so you take the correct fork to the trailhead). Cross the creek and its tributaries six more times.

2.8 Reach a three-way trail junction at a saddle. Take the left (southwest) fork on Bushnell Lakes Trail. Sign register, enter Sangre de Cristo Wilderness Area, and begin ascending a long, steep slope, crossing several talus fields, and gaining over 1,500 feet of elevation before bending into Bushnell Creek's valley.

4.7 Traverse a steep slope with a long valley below. If snowfields or ice exist, use MICROspikes and an ice axe for safety. Follow the trail past cliffs to the left and through forest. Reach a social trail to the right but keep left and climb a steep trail to the first lake.

5.1 Reach the east side of "Lower Bushnell Lake" (GPS: 38 21.1104, –105 52.5117) and views of dramatic "Bushnell Lakes Falls" tumbling down cliffs above the lake. Return to the trailhead here or continue to the upper lakes for more adventure. From here, the trail is hard to follow at times and overgrown in places. Walk around the north side of the lake for 300 feet to a wetland, then head left up brushy slopes.

5.6 Pass above "Middle Bushnell Lakes Falls" below the middle lake. Continue up the faint trail.

5.8 Arrive at "Middle Bushnell Lake" (GPS: 38 20.9222, –105 52.8673). Walk around the north side of the lake for 300 feet to a wetland. Continue on a brushy trail up left from the lake to benches that lead west on the north side of the valley.

5.9 Pass above "Upper Bushnell Lake Falls" between the middle and upper lakes. Continue up the faint trail on slopes above the creek to the upper lake. Again, the trail is overgrown and hard to find.

6.1 Reach the rocky east shore of "Upper Bushnell Lake" (GPS: 38 20.7987, –105 53.2134). Turn around here and hike down the trails.

12.2 Arrive back at the trailhead (GPS: 38 19.79, –105 49.029).

29 Lakes of the Clouds

The triple Lakes of the Clouds hide in a glaciated cirque below elegant Spread Eagle Peak in the Sangre de Cristo Wilderness Area near Westcliffe.

Start: Gibson Creek Trailhead
Difficulty: Strenuous
Trails: Rainbow Trail #1336, Swift Creek Trail #1351, Lakes of the Clouds Trail #1349
Hiking time: About 6 hours
Distance: 10.8 miles loop
Elevation trailhead to lakes: 9,195 to 11,630 feet at upper lake (+2,435 feet)
Restrictions: Observe wilderness regulations; trail closed to motor vehicles; dogs must be under control; camp 300 feet from water sources

Amenities: Backcountry camping; services in Coaldale
Maps: *DeLorme*: Page 71, D5 and D6; Trails Illustrated 138: Sangre de Cristo Mountains [Great Sand Dunes National Park and Preserve]; USGS Beckwith Mountain, Electric Peak
County: Fremont
Land status: Sangre de Cristo Wilderness Area; San Isabel National Forest, (719) 553-1400; San Carlos Ranger District, (719) 269-8500

Finding the trailhead: From the junction of Main Street and 3rd Street/CO 69 in Westcliffe, drive north on CO 69 for 0.6 mile and turn left on CR 170/Hemenway Road, which becomes Pines Road. Drive 4.4 miles to a Y-junction. Go left on CR 171 and drive southwest for 1.3 miles to a junction. Turn right on CR 172/North Taylor Road and drive west for 2.2 miles to a parking lot and the Gibson Creek Trailhead (GPS: 38 8.2972, -105 36.0394). A connector trail (#1360) goes 530 feet west to the Rainbow Trail from the north end of the parking lot.

The Hike

The three Lakes of the Clouds scatter across an alpine basin surrounded by towering mountains, including 13,423-foot Spread Eagle Peak on the south, 13,524-foot Peak of the Clouds on the southwest, and 13,513-foot Silver Peak at the head of the cirque in the Sangre de Cristo Mountains. The shining lakes, lying at timberline, are a popular hiking and backpacking destination reached by two trails that offer stunning views and campsites used as basecamps for peakbagging adventures.

It is best to do the hike clockwise from the Rainbow Trail, getting the steep, rocky section of the Swift Creek Trail done with fresh legs in the morning. The trail continues ascending to join the Lakes of the Clouds Trail, which is followed to the lakes. The return leg is down the longer, gentler, and more scenic Lakes of the Clouds Trail. Look up the valley to stunning views of pyramid-shaped Spread Eagle Peak.

When driving to the trailhead, the last road section turns narrow, rough, and rutted. A passenger car may not be able to navigate it, so park before the rough section and walk the road to the trailhead. Also, a confusing sign at the edge of the parking

Pyramid-shaped Spread Eagle Peak dominates the western skyline above the lowest of the Lakes of the Clouds.

lot says the Gibson Trailhead is another 0.1 mile away. Walk up the trail from the parking lot on the first leg of the hike to the "official" Gibson Trailhead.

Miles and Directions

0.0 Start on the north side of the parking lot and hike west on an old road.

0.1 Reach the Gibson Creek Trailhead and a T-junction. Go right onto the Rainbow Trail and hike north through forest and open grassland to scattered trees.

0.6 Reach a junction with Swift Creek Trail. Go left and hike west, steadily gaining over 400 feet on the rocky trail until the angle eases.

2.2 Cross to Swift Creek's north bank (GPS: 38 8.54, –105 37.641). Continue west up wooded slopes.

3.0 Reach a T-junction with the Lakes of the Clouds Trail (GPS: 38 8.542, –105 38.317) at 10,750 feet. Go left (straight) on Lakes of the Clouds Trail, cross a drainage, and bend southwest.

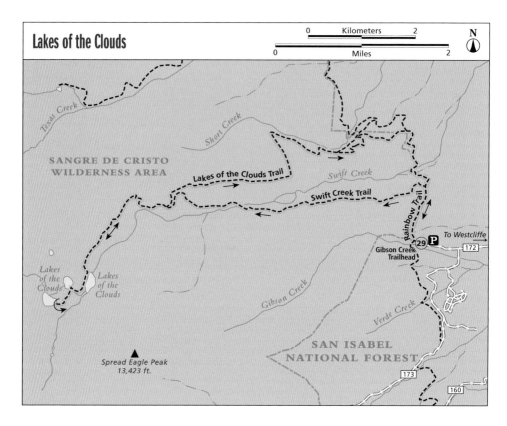

Lakes of the Clouds

4.2 Arrive at the north end of the first lake (GPS: 38 8.076, –105 39.018). Continue southwest on the trail on the lake's west side, then bend west and climb slopes.

4.4 Reach the southeast shore of the second lake (GPS: 38 7.982, –105 39.17). Backtrack on the trail and cross the lake's outlet creek to the right, below the trail, on branches. On the other side, follow the trail that contours southwest, to the left, across wooded slopes (do not follow a social trail that goes straight up).

4.7 Arrive at the east edge of the third and highest Lakes of the Clouds at timberline (GPS: 38 7.8657, –105 39.3127). After enjoying the views, return to the main trail and hike east on the trail you came up (do not return to the second lake), passing the first lake at 5.2 miles.

6.4 Reach the junction with the Swift Creek Trail (GPS: 38 8.542, –105 38.317). The return loop starts here. Continue straight (bear left) on Lakes of the Clouds Trail.

9.0 Reach a T-junction with the Rainbow Trail (GPS: 38 9.02, –105 36.614). Go right on it, hiking east downhill and then bending south and crossing Swift Creek.

10.1 Reach the junction with the start of Swift Creek Trail. Continue hiking straight south.

10.7 Reach a junction with the Gibson Access Trail, the short connector to the parking lot. Go left and hike east on it.

10.8 Arrive back at the trailhead (GPS: 38 8.2972, –105 36.0394).

30 Comanche Lake

Comanche Lake, lying on the fabled Venable-Comanche loop hike, reflects sky, clouds, and the rugged northeast wall of Comanche Peak on the crest of the Sangre de Cristo Mountains in Hiltman Creek's upper alpine valley.

Start: Comanche Trailhead
Difficulty: Moderate
Trail: Comanche Trail #1345
Hiking time: About 5 hours
Distance: 8.0 miles out-and-back
Elevation trailhead to lake: 9,050 to 11,650 feet at lake (+2,600 feet)
Restrictions: Observe wilderness regulations; no bicycles or motorized vehicles in wilderness area; dogs must be leashed; dispose of human waste properly

Amenities: Vault toilets at trailhead; backcountry camping; services in Westcliffe
Maps: *DeLorme*: Page 71, E6; Trails Illustrated 138: Sangre de Cristo Mountains [Great Sand Dunes National Park and Preserve]; USGS Horn Peak
County: Custer
Land status: Sangre de Cristo Wilderness Area; San Isabel National Forest, (719) 553-1400; San Carlos Ranger District, (719) 269-8500

Finding the trailhead: From Westcliffe, take CO 69 South for 3.3 miles, then turn right (west) on CR 140 (Schoolfield Road), following signs to Alvarado Campground. Drive 4.6 miles and turn left on CR 141 (Schoolfield Road/Willow Lane). Go 0.2 mile and turn right to get back on CR 140 (Schoolfield Road). Drive 1.6 miles and bear right on CR 148, then go 0.4 mile to parking at the trailhead and the road's end (GPS: 38 4.9315, –105 33.8824).

The Hike

Comanche Lake perches on a shelf at 11,650 feet in a narrow, glacier-chiseled cirque below 13,277-foot Comanche Peak and 13,244-foot Spring Mountain in the Sangre de Cristo Mountains. The gorgeous alpine lake, surrounded by tundra meadows, willow thickets, and windswept trees, is reached by the Comanche Trail, which steadily climbs a wooded valley along Alvarado and Hiltman Creeks. The popular trail, busy on summer weekends, is part of the renowned 11.7-mile Venable-Comanche loop hike, which passes both Venable Lakes and Comanche Lake, climbs over two passes above 12,700 feet, and crosses the exposed Phantom Terrace. Check out a description of this extra credit hike in the Venable Lakes chapter.

Comanche Trail, beginning near Alvarado Campground, is well signed, easy to follow, and alternates between shady forest and sunny slopes. The jewel-like lake, unseen until the final hill, fills a deep hollow. Beyond towers the northeast face of Comanche Peak cleaved with rock ribs and sheer cliffs. A shallow, unnamed tarn hides above Comanche Lake. For higher lake views, continue up the trail another 2.3 miles to Comanche Pass and then scamper left up the easy north ridge of Comanche Peak to its summit and forever views south to Kit Carson Peak, Challenger Point, and

Comanche Lake and its unnamed twin straddle a deep, glacier-carved valley in the Sangre de Cristo Wilderness Area.

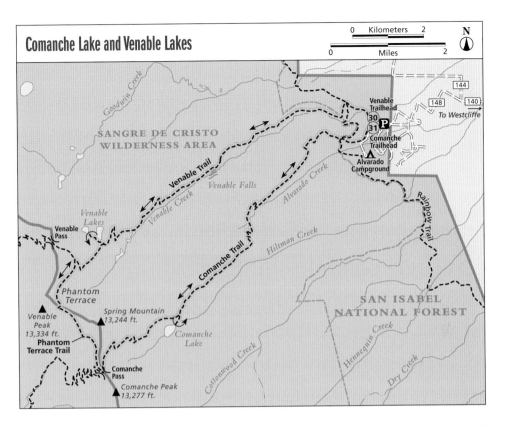

Crestone Peak and Needle. Don't forget to look east at Comanche Lake, its crystal waters reflecting sky blue.

Miles and Directions

0.0 Start at the Comanche Trailhead left of the toilets at the parking lot. Hike southwest parallel to the road to Alvarado Trailhead, then head west.

0.5 Reach a four-way signed junction with the Rainbow Trail (GPS: 38 4.8204, –105 34.2867). Continue straight on the Comanche Trail, hiking uphill before bending left and climbing west above Alvarado Creek.

2.3 Start up a steep north-facing slope (GPS: 38 4.0828, –105 35.3254), making thirteen switchbacks through thick forest.

2.8 Reach the top of the switchbacks and a ridgeline. Bend west and contour up a sunny slope above Hiltman Creek, crossing open slopes and talus north of the creek.

3.9 Reach a Y-junction with a side trail to Comanche Lake (GPS: 38 3.2567, –105 36.1511). Head left and gently descend.

4.0 Arrive at the northeast edge of Comanche Lake and enjoy views of Comanche Peak at the head of the cirque (GPS: 38 3.1818, –105 36.1853). Return back down the trail.

8.0 Arrive back at the trailhead (GPS: 38 4.9315, –105 33.8824).

31 Venable Lakes

The two Venable Lakes nestle on a high bench below skyscraping Venable Peak, a pyramid-shaped peak on the crest of the Sangre de Cristo Range southwest of Westcliffe.

See map on page 111.
Start: Venable Trailhead
Difficulty: Moderate
Trail: Venable Trail #1347
Hiking time: About 5 hours
Distance: 9.0 miles out-and-back
Elevation trailhead to lakes: 9,055 to 11,990 feet at lower lake; 12,065 feet at upper lake (+3,010 feet)
Restrictions: Observe wilderness regulations; no bicycles or motorized vehicles in wilderness area; leashed dogs only; dispose of human waste properly
Amenities: Vault toilets at trailhead; backcountry camping; services in Westcliffe
Maps: *DeLorme*: Page 71, E6; Trails Illustrated 138: Sangre de Cristo Mountains [Great Sand Dunes National Park and Preserve]; USGS Horn Peak
County: Custer
Land status: Sangre de Cristo Wilderness Area; San Isabel National Forest, (719) 553-1400; San Carlos Ranger District, (719) 269-8500

Finding the trailhead: From Westcliffe, take CO 69 South for 3.3 miles, then turn right (west) on CR 140 (Schoolfield Road), following signs to Alvarado Campground. Go 4.6 miles and turn left on CR 141 (Schoolfield Road/Willow Lane) and go 0.2 mile and turn right to get back on CR 140 (Schoolfield Road). Drive 1.6 miles and bear right on CR 148, then go 0.4 mile to parking at the trailhead and the end of the road (GPS: 38 04.950, –105 33.885).

The Hike

The twin Venable Lakes perch on the eastern edge of a wide shelf above a deep glaciated gorge below 13,334-foot Venable Peak and 13,244-foot Spring Mountain. The lower oblong lake fills a depression below a scree slope, while the smaller, teardrop-shaped upper lake sits on a higher bench. Reach the lakes by the well-trod Venable Trail, which follows Venable Creek up a long valley, passing Venable Falls, to Venable Basin, a spectacular valley floored with a lush wetland and flanked by soaring peaks and ridges. Small ponds dot the valley floor. These were once large lakes but have since filled with sediment and debris. The trail climbs out of the basin to the shelf lakes above timberline.

The well-traveled trail is popular on summer weekends so plan a weekday excursion for privacy. It is easy to follow with well-signed junctions and few steep grades. Plan on a long trail day by bringing snacks, lunch, and drinks. Bring trekking poles and MICROspikes for early summer and late autumn hikes. Backpackers find the best campsites in the lower basin rather than at the lakes or car camp at Alvarado Campground near the trailhead.

The Venable Lakes lie high above timberline below Venable Peak and the Phantom Terrace.

"Upper Venable Lake" nestles in a basin below an unnamed 12,873-foot peak.

Past the lakes, the Venable Trail climbs to a high junction with the Phantom Terrace Trail (#359), the middle section of the fabled Venable-Comanche loop hike, which combines the Venable, Phantom Terrace, and Comanche Trails into an 11.7-mile adventure. Venable Trail heads up right from the junction to 12,920-foot Venable Pass and drops down the range's west side to the North Fork of Crestone Creek. The left trail traverses across the upper southeast face of Venable Peak on the infamous Phantom Terrace, an airy, scary trail that contours above sheer cliffs on a hidden ledge system to an unnamed pass. The hike continues across the west face of Spring Mountain to Comanche Pass, then follows Comanche Trail east to Comanche Lake and back to the trailhead. See the Extra Credit sidebar to do this iconic hike.

Miles and Directions

0.0 Begin at the Venable Trailhead and follow signs for Venable Trail on the north end of the parking lot. Hike northwest on Venable Trail on an old four-wheel-drive road.

0.5 Reach a junction with the Rainbow Trail. Go right to stay on Venable Trail.

0.6 Reach a junction with the signed Venable Trail on the left. Go left on it toward Venable Lakes. Hike west on slopes north of Venable Creek, passing through aspen groves and conifer woods.

2.3 Reach a signed junction for Venable Falls (GPS: 38 04.553, -105 35.690). To see the waterfall, go left on the side trail that switchbacks 0.1 mile down to the falls in a rocky gorge, then return to the junction and go left on Venable Trail. Hike through forest above the creek to a wetland area with beaver ponds. Hike up open slopes to timberline.

4.3 Arrive at the south end of "Lower Venable Lake" (GPS: 38 3.9187, -105 37.0396). Continue around the lake's southwest side and northwest up slopes.

4.5 Reach the southeast corner of "Upper Venable Lake" (GPS: 38 3.9899, -105 37.1853). Continue up the Venable-Comanche loop hike by following Venable Trail west or turn around here and follow the trail down the valley.

9.0 Arrive back at the trailhead (GPS: 38 4.9526, -105 33.8801).

EXTRA CREDIT: VENABLE-COMANCHE LOOP

Combine the Venable and Comanche Trails with the Phantom Terrace Trail to make a loop hike between two mountain valleys by passing three lakes, crossing two high passes, and traversing below three 13,000-foot peaks. Be prepared for a full day so remember a headlamp to light the trail at night. The Phantom Terrace Trail section is exposed and dangerous, and a fall would be fatal. Watch for trail damage on the Terrace and use caution on the last steep section at the end. That shaded section as well as other parts of the upper trail hold snow and ice for much of the year, so MICROspikes or crampons are essential. Also, bring an ice axe and trekking poles if you see snow on the peaks. It is best to do the hike counterclockwise by hiking to Venable Lakes first, then doing the Phantom Traverse and descending down the Comanche Trail.

0.0 Begin at the Venable Trailhead and follow the above Miles and Directions to Venable Lakes.

4.3 Arrive at a junction on the left about 250 feet from "Lower Venable Lake" (GPS: 38 3.8933, –105 36.9927). Go left on Venable Trail and hike up grassy slopes.

4.8 Reach a junction marked by a post with Phantom Terrace Trail on the left. Go left on it. Venable Trail heads up right to Venable Pass. Angle up left on the trail, slowly climbing steepening grass slopes.

5.2 Trail begins traversing across broken cliff bands.

5.3 Start across the Phantom Terrace section (GPS: 38 3.4285, –105 37.5744). Step carefully on the exposed trail and use caution on snow or ice. At the end of the Terrace is a steep 35-foot section that tops out on the ridgeline. This is often icy.

5.4 Reach a 12,730-foot saddle, the hike's highest point, on the ridge (GPS: 38 3.3559, –105 37.5227). To climb 13,334-foot Venable Peak, hike 100 feet west on the trail and scramble 0.25 mile up grassy slopes to the summit. The next trail section is spectacular with amazing views south to Crestone Peak and Needle, Kit Carson Peak, and Challenger Point. Traverse south below the range crest on good trail, passing below 13,244-foot Spring Mountain, which is easily climbed.

6.3 Arrive at 12,700-foot Comanche Pass and the end of Phantom Terrace Trail (GPS: 38 2.7794, –105 37.0465). It is a quick 0.3-mile hike that gains almost 600 feet from the pass to the summit of 13,277-foot Comanche Peak. From the pass and ridge, begin descending northeast across tundra and rock slopes on the Comanche Trail.

6.6 Reach the start of switchbacks that descend northeast on grassy slopes. The angle eases as the trail passes timberline and heads east across a bench above Comanche Lake.

7.7 Reach a junction with the 0.1-mile trail that goes right to Comanche Lake (GPS: 38 3.2567, –105 36.1511). Following the Miles and Directions in the Comanche Lake chapter, continue east on Comanche Trail and descend the valley.

11.2 Reach a four-way signed junction with the Rainbow Trail (GPS: 38 4.8204, –105 34.2867). Continue east toward the trailhead.

11.7 Arrive back at the trailhead (GPS: 38 4.9315, –105 33.8824).

32 Macey Lakes

The triple Macey Lakes, glassy tarns in double alpine cirques on the eastern flank of the Sangre de Cristo Mountains, are the watery reward at the end of an arduous hike up Macey Creek from the Wet Mountain Valley.

Start: Horn Creek Trailhead
Difficulty: Strenuous
Trails: Horn Creek Trail #1342, Rainbow Trail #1336, Macey Trail #1341
Hiking time: About 8 hours
Distance: 12.4 miles out-and-back to lower lake
Elevation trailhead to lakes: 9,140 to 11,506 feet at lower lake (+2,366 feet); 11,643 feet at middle lake (+2,503 feet); 11,865 feet at upper lake (+2,735 feet)
Restrictions: Observe wilderness regulations; no bicycles or motorized vehicles; leashed dogs only

Amenities: Vault toilets; backcountry camping; services in Westcliffe
Maps: *DeLorme*: Page 71, E6; Trails Illustrated 138: Sangre de Cristo Mountains [Great Sand Dunes National Park and Preserve]; USGS Horn Peak
County: Custer
Land status: Sangre de Cristo Wilderness Area; San Isabel National Forest, (719) 553-1400; San Carlos Ranger District, (719) 269-8500

Finding the trailhead: From Westcliffe, take CO 69 South for 3.3 miles, then turn right (west) on CR 140 (Schoolfield Road). Drive 1.8 miles and turn left on CR 129 (Macey Lane), then go 2.0 miles and turn right on CR 130 (Horn Creek Road). Drive 2.4 miles to Horn Creek Ranch, passing a small trailhead for Rainbow Trail (which also accesses the lakes, but adds 0.2 mile to the hike in each direction), then turn right and drive 0.5 mile to the parking lot and trailhead (GPS: 38 03.112, -105 32.159).

The Hike

The three Macey Lakes sit in twin glacial cirques below the crest of the rugged Sangre de Cristo Mountains, with an unnamed 13,541-foot peak towering above the upper lake, 12,982-foot Little Baldy Mountain flanking the valley's northern edge, and 13,705-foot Colony Baldy rimming the southern sky. Reach the gorgeous lakes, fed by springs and snowmelt, by a challenging hike that begins at Horn Creek Trailhead and follows the Rainbow Trail to the Macey Trail, which climbs a long valley to the string of alpine tarns above 11,000 feet. An added bonus is Macey Falls, which splashes over bedrock into a punchbowl in a cliff-lined gorge below the trail.

Plan on a full day of hiking to visit the lakes or tote a tent and camp at the lower lake for starry skies and time to explore or climb the surrounding peaks. This trail description reaches Macey Lake, the turnaround point for most hikers. Be prepared for a major creek crossing on the trail, so bring trekking poles, especially in spring

Macey Lake lies below twin cirques that hold the two upper lakes in the Sangre de Cristo Wilderness Area.

Macey Lake fills a cliff-lined cirque on the east flank of the Sangre de Cristo Mountains.

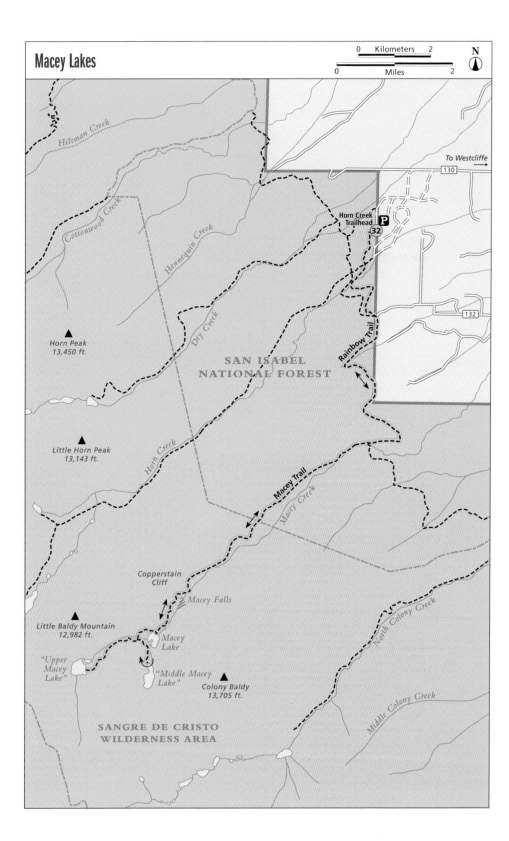

Macey Lakes

To Westcliffe

130

Hiltman Creek

Cottonwood Creek

Henneguin Creek

Horn Creek
Trailhead

P
32

Dry Creek

SAN ISABEL
NATIONAL FOREST

Rainbow Trail

132

Horn Peak
13,450 ft.

Little Horn Peak
13,143 ft.

Horn Creek

Macey Trail

Macey Creek

North Colony Creek

Copperstain
Cliff

Macey Falls

Little Baldy Mountain
12,982 ft.

Macey
Lake

"Upper
Macey
Lake"

"Middle Macey
Lake"

Colony Baldy
13,705 ft.

Middle Colony Creek

SANGRE DE CRISTO
WILDERNESS AREA

and early summer. There are campsites near the lake but do not set up a tent under dead snags. Also, practice Leave No Trace principles.

More directions and mileages are included for those who want to trek to the two other lakes. However, the trails are not as well traveled as the lower trail, so pay attention to stay on course and look for signs of previous hikers. Deadfall is encountered on the trail and snowdrifts cover the upper trail until late June. The hike to "Upper Macey Lake" is worth the effort though, with spectacular mountain views from a pristine pond.

Miles and Directions

0.0 Begin at the Horn Creek Trailhead on the west side of a parking lot and circular road. Hike southwest on the Horn Creek Trail to the Rainbow Trail.

0.6 Reach a junction with the Rainbow Trail (GPS: 38 2.7216, –105 32.3627). Go left and cross a footbridge over Horn Creek. Head south toward signed Macey Trail.

3.2 Reach the junction with Macey Trail (GPS: 38 1.5066, –105 32.1832). Go right on Macey Trail and hike southwest up the creek's right side.

4.1 Cross into Sangre de Cristo Wilderness Area (GPS: 38 1.078, –105 33.042).

5.3 Copperstain Cliff is to the right and a ribbon falls from high cliffs is to the left on Colony Baldy's north face.

5.5 Reach a junction on the left with a side trail that goes to Macey Falls in a gorge below. Hike to Macey Falls (GPS: 38 00.339, –105 34.002) and return back to the main trail and go left. Look for a creek crossing farther west. It usually requires rock hopping but use caution if the creek is high.

6.2 Arrive at a rocky peninsula jutting into the east side of Macey Lake (GPS: 38 0.0449, –105 34.2902). Enjoy the alpine views, then head back down the trail. Alternatively, continue to the two higher lakes.

12.4 Arrive back at the trailhead (GPS: 38 03.112, –105 32.159).

EXTRA CREDIT: MIDDLE AND UPPER LAKES

After enjoying Macey Lake, head up rough trails to the middle and upper lakes. Round trip mileage to the upper lake and back to the trailhead is 14.2 miles. Round-trip mileage to both lakes is 14.8 miles. To reach "Upper Macey Lake," follow a trail around the north side of Macey Lake to the Macey Spur Trail, which goes left to "Middle Macey Lake." Continue through woods above a creek, then cross it and climb southwest across open slopes to "Upper Macey Lake" (GPS: 38 59.7971, –105 34.9977) after 0.9 mile. To reach "Middle Macey Lake," return down the trail from the upper lake to the spur path on the right. Follow it for 0.3 mile up steep slopes to "Middle Macey Lake" (GPS: 37 59.8271, –105 34.3305).

33 Lake Pueblo

The Arkansas River flows southeast into Pueblo West, filling Lake Pueblo, a reservoir for the City of Pueblo's water supply and a prime southern Colorado recreation area.

Start: North Shore Trailhead
Difficulty: Easy
Trails: North Shore Trail, Sky Line Trail
Hiking time: 30 to 45 minutes
Distance: 1.6 miles lollipop loop
Elevation trailhead to lake: 4,928 to 4,945 feet on bluff (+17 feet) to 4,830 feet at lake (depending on water level)
Restrictions: Fee area; open for hiking 5 a.m. to 10 p.m. year-round; leashed pets allowed; no fireworks or open fires; no collecting of natural resources

Amenities: Vault toilet at trailhead; picnic tables and ramadas at trailhead; park campgrounds; visitor center at south side of park; services in Pueblo West
Maps: *DeLorme*: Page 73, C5; Trails Illustrated none: USGS Swallows; Lake Pueblo State Park trail map
County: Pueblo
Land status: Lake Pueblo State Park, (719) 561-9320

Finding the trailhead: From I-25 on the north side of Pueblo, take exit 108 toward Pueblo West and drive west on East Purcell Boulevard. Drive 6.1 miles and at a traffic circle, take the first exit onto East Platteville Boulevard. Go 0.6 mile and turn left onto North McCulloch Boulevard; then 7.3 miles and turn left onto South Nichols Road; then 0.8 mile on Pueblo Reservoir Road. Continue 0.3 mile through the north entrance and pay gate and take the first right on North Marina Road. Go 0.5 mile and turn right on West Fishing Road. Continue 0.7 mile to a parking area and the trailhead at the north end of the lot (GPS: 38 16.6284, -104 47.5463).

The Hike

This hike in Lake Pueblo State Park follows a segment at the north end of the 4.71-mile North Shore Trail and adds a detour on the Sky Line Trail for an easy and scenic lollipop loop. There's no shade on the route, but Pueblo's warm climate makes it a perfect winter hike for the whole family.

Broken sandstone lines the trail, bordered by river rock, ancient juniper trees, cholla cactus, yucca, sagebrush, and driftwood. Take plenty of photos but leave the rocks, driftwood, and plant life behind for others to enjoy. On the bluff, stay away from loose edges that can crumble away.

With more than 400 campsites and many miles of hiking and biking trails, Lake Pueblo State Park is the most popular state park in Colorado. If you live in the area, consider an annual state park pass to take full advantage of the park year-round.

The North Shore Trail skirts a shallow cove along Lake Pueblo's rocky shoreline.

A thousand-year-old juniper along the Sky Line Trail overlooks Lake Pueblo.

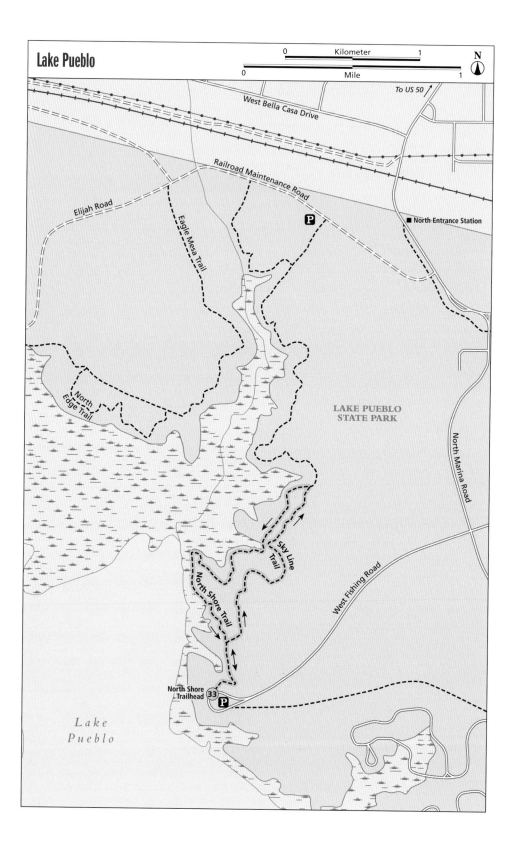

Kilometer

Mile

N

To US 50

West Bella Casa Drive

Railroad Maintenance Road

Elijah Road

Eagle Mesa Trail

North Entrance Station

North Edge Trail

LAKE PUEBLO STATE PARK

North Marina Road

Sky Line Trail

North Shore Trail

West Fishing Road

North Shore Trailhead

33

Lake Pueblo

The North Shore Trail twists across eroded hills above Lake Pueblo.

Miles and Directions

0.0 From the trailhead, hike northeast on North Shore Trail. This is not the trail on the left that goes west to the lake, but the one on the right that skirts the lake's shore.

0.15 At trail junction, bear right onto the Sky Line Trail (GPS: 38 16.7216, -104 47.5126).

0.25 The trail ascends and crosses a bluff with views west of the lake. From this vantage point, the Spanish Peaks appear to the south, while the Wet Mountains—including Pueblo County high point Greenhorn Mountain—line the sky from southwest to northwest. Pikes Peak is visible to the north.

0.65 The trail descends north.

0.7 At trail junction, turn left onto the North Shore Trail to loop south along the lake (GPS: 38 17.0303, -104 47.306). Note that continuing north on the North Shore Trail leads to a small parking lot on Railroad Maintenance Road, an alternate trailhead for this hike. Continue hiking south.

1.45 At the trail junction, continue south to the trailhead.

1.6 Arrive back at the trailhead (GPS: 38 16.6284, -104 47.5463).

34 Martin Lake

West of Walsenburg, a paved trail, accessible for wheelchairs, encircles Martin Lake, passing picnic areas and a swim beach, and with scenic views of the Spanish Peaks.

Start: Cuerno Verde Trailhead
Difficulty: Easy
Trails: Cuerno Verde Trail, Hogback Nature Trail
Hiking time: About 1 hour
Distance: 2.7 miles loop
Elevation trailhead to lake: 6,420 to 6,410 feet at lake
Restrictions: Fee area; day-use only; open 5 a.m. to 10 p.m.

Amenities: Paved surface; ADA wheelchair accessible; swim beach; leashed dogs and bikes allowed; restrooms and water at trailhead
Maps: *DeLorme*: Page 82, D4; Trails Illustrated none; USGS Walsenburg South; Lathrop State Park trail map
County: Huerfano
Land status: Lathrop State Park, (719) 738-2376

Finding the trailhead: From Walsenburg and I-25, drive 3 miles west on US 160 to a marked turn on the right to Lathrop State Park. Drive north on CR 502 past the entrance station and turn right to the visitor center and parking lot. The trailhead is on the lot's east side (GPS: 37 36.1699, –104 49.9397).

For the Hogback Nature Trail, continue past the visitor center to a three-way junction. Turn right on CR 502 and drive 1 mile to a Y-junction. Keep left and drive to a right turn past the campground. Drive 275 feet north to a parking lot and the trailhead (GPS: 37 36.9602, –104 50.1627).

The Hike

Martin Lake and Horseshoe Lake are two reservoirs in Lathrop State Park west of Walsenburg. The state park, established in 1962 as Colorado's first, is a great getaway with swim beaches, trails, two campgrounds, and lakeside picnic areas. Martin Lake offers a wheelchair-accessible trail that circumnavigates the broad lake, yielding spectacular mountain views. Horseshoe Lake, seen from a park road on its west shore, and a wetland area to the west are hot spots for birding, including raptors, waterfowl, and shorebirds. Bring binoculars to identify rare species like brown pelicans, Pacific loons, and tundra swans. The Hogback Nature Trail north of Martin Lake is a hidden gem hike with gorgeous views across the lakes to the twin Spanish Peaks, called *Huajatolla* or "breasts of the earth" by the Utes.

Start Cuerno Verde Trail around Martin Lake from a trailhead at the visitor center. The concrete path heads north to a junction. Keep left and hike along the southern lakeshore past picnic tables, a boat ramp, and a swim beach. Head north along the trail, shaded by cottonwoods, on the lake's western edge to the north side of Martin Lake. The trail bends east along the lake and dips south to a social trail that jogs to a marvelous viewpoint above ruddy sandstone boulders. The rest of the trail follows the lake's eastern edge, crossing a dam and returning to the trailhead.

The Spanish Peaks etch the horizon above a sandstone boulder that sits on the north shore of Martin Lake at Lathrop State Park.

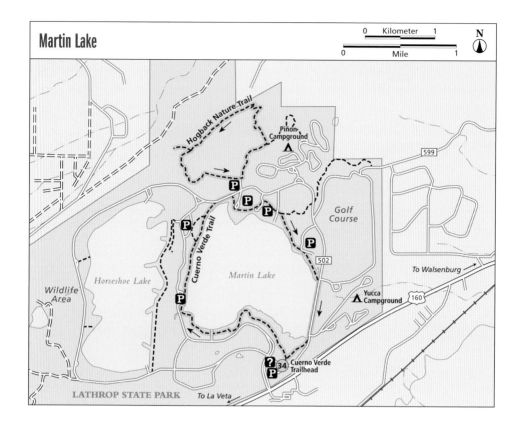

Miles and Directions

0.0 Start at the marked Cuerno Verde Trailhead on the east side of the visitor center parking lot and hike north.

0.05 Cross Road 502 and walk to a Y-junction (GPS: 37 36.1987, –104 49.9136). Go left on the paved trail. The right fork is the return trail.

0.5 Hike northwest south of the lake. Past a picnic pavilion and restrooms, angle right to the east edge of a parking lot by the lake (GPS: 37 36.3201, –104 50.2148).

0.6 Walk west along the parking lot edge to the paved trail and restrooms by a swim beach. Hike northwest to a bridge and then north along the lake's western edge, passing picnic tables and restrooms.

1.4 Reach a paved road north of the lake and hike east on a sidewalk on the road's south side (GPS: 37 36.8596, –104 50.281).

1.5 Reach the sidewalk's east end and turn right on the concrete trail.

1.6 Turn left at the south end of a parking area. A social trail goes south from here for 300 feet to a scenic overlook above cliffs on Martin Lake's north shore. Return to the trail and head east and then south along the lake's eastern shoreline.

2.6 Reach the first trail junction southeast of the lake. Continue straight toward the visitor center.

2.7 Arrive back at the trailhead (GPS: 37 36.9602, –104 50.1627).

EXTRA CREDIT HIKE: HOGBACK NATURE TRAIL

After a picnic lunch, drive to the park's north side and hike the Hogback Nature Trail. This 1.5-mile loop swings through a pygmy forest of junipers and piñon pines to the crest of The Hogback, a long volcanic dike with spacious views southwest to the Spanish Peaks and Culebra Range and north to Greenhorn Mountain. A short side trail climbs to the site of pioneer photographer William Henry Jackson's famed circa-1890 photograph of the two lakes and the snowcapped Spanish Peaks.

Miles and Directions

- **0.0** Start at trailhead on north side of parking lot (GPS: 37 36.9596, –104 50.1611). Hike northeast on the trail.
- **0.25** Reach a junction at sandstone boulders (GPS: 37 37.1039, –104 50.0159). Keep left on Hogback Nature Trail. A right turn leads to Piñon Campground.
- **0.5** Reach the top of the hogback and views of the lakes and Spanish Peaks.
- **0.7** Junction with William Henry Jackson Trail (GPS: 37 37.071, –104 50.4305). Go right to visit the site of Jackson's photograph of the lakes and peaks.
- **0.8** Descend south from the hogback and bend southeast on the trail.
- **1.5** Arrive back at the trailhead.

The twin Spanish Peaks rise beyond a boulder-strewn beach at Martin Lake in Lathrop State Park.

35 Trinidad Lake

Trinidad Lake drowns a broad valley west of Trinidad, forming a reservoir filled with snowmelt-laden water from the Culebra Range. Explore the lake on a long hike through hills on the north shore.

Start: Levsa and Reilly Canyon Trailhead in Carpios Ridge Campground
Difficulty: Moderate
Trails: Levsa Canyon Trail, Reilly Canyon Trail
Hiking time: 2.5 to 5 hours
Distance: 4.9 miles one way with car shuttle, 9.4 miles out-and-back
Elevation trailhead to hike end: 6,347 to 6,244 feet at trail's end

Restrictions: Fee area; leashed dogs allowed; trail closed to motorized vehicles and horses
Amenities: Restrooms and water at trailhead; park campground; services in Trinidad
Maps: *DeLorme*: Page 93, D6 and D7; Trails Illustrated none; USGS Trinidad West; Trinidad State Park map
County: Las Animas
Land status: Trinidad Lake State Park, (719) 846-6951

Finding the trailhead: From I-25 in Trinidad, take exit 13 and go east on West Main Street. At a four-way stop, turn left on Nevada Avenue. Pass through a roundabout and drive west for 3.5 miles following signs for CO 12 on several streets—University, Prospect, Stonewall, and Robinson—through west Trinidad. Continue past the first park entrance and turn left at the second entrance to the visitor center and Carpios Ridge Campground. Drive south for 0.6 mile to the trailhead and parking lot on the west side of the Camper Services building (GPS: 37 8.6601, -104 34.207).

The Hike

Trinidad Lake, a 3-mile-long lake created by a dam built for flood control and irrigation, fills the historic Purgatoire River valley west of Trinidad. Protected as a Colorado state park, the lake is surrounded by ridges and rounded hills covered with piñon pine and juniper trees. The remote Culebra Range, topped by 14,069-foot Culebra Peak, stretches across the western horizon while angular Fishers Peak dominates the southern skyline. Trinidad Lake offers plenty of recreation, including a campground and seven trails.

The best hike follows the Levsa Canyon Trail to Reilly Canyon Trail across dry hills and valleys north of the lake from the campground to Reilly Canyon. The well-signed trail is rated strenuous with a rocky surface, lots of ups and downs, and almost 1,500 feet of round-trip elevation gain. It is recommended to do the hike one way with a car shuttle at Reilly Canyon Trailhead but check first to make sure the road to the trailhead is accessible.

Bulky Fishers Peak rises beyond Trinidad Lake and broken rimrock boulders.

The Levsa Canyon Trail offers marvelous views across Trinidad Lake to scrubby hills.

Begin west of the Camper Services building at the Carpio Ridge Campground and walk to a junction with Carpios Cove Trail. Keep right on scenic Levsa Canyon Trail. The trail heads west along rimrock with picturesque views across Trinidad Lake to Fishers Peak. Continue to the Reilly Canyon Trail at the next junction. The next section crosses flat-topped hills and dips into sharp canyons with occasional lake views. End at a trailhead and parking area in Reilly Canyon. Get picked up here or return on the trail to the campground.

Miles and Directions

0.0 Start at Levsa and Reilly Canyon Trailhead in the campground. Hike south on wide Levsa Canyon Trail.

0.05 Reach junction with 0.5-mile Carpios Ridge Trail. Go right on marked Levsa Canyon Trail and Reilly Canyon Trail.

0.1 Reach junction with Levsa Canyon Trail return loop; also marked Reilly Canyon Trail (GPS: 37 8.5798, –104 34.2653). Keep left on Levsa Canyon Trail and pass views across lake.

0.7 Arrive at junction and signed start of Reilly Canyon Trail (GPS: 37 8.6446, –104 34.4212). Continue straight and ascend to a mesa top. The return Levsa segment to trailhead is to the right.

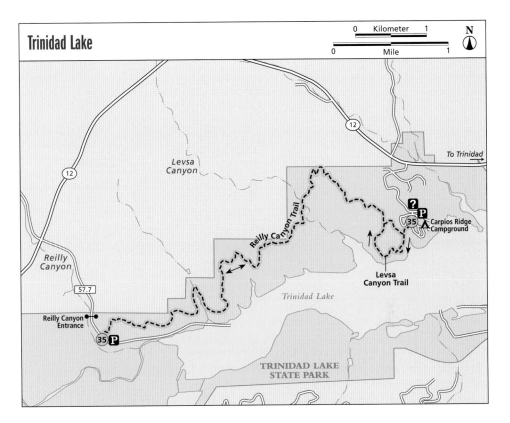

Trinidad Lake

0 Kilometer 1
0 Mile 1

N

Levsa Canyon

To Trinidad

Reilly Canyon Trail

35 Carpios Ridge Campground

Reilly Canyon

Levsa Canyon Trail

57.7

Trinidad Lake

Reilly Canyon Entrance

35 P

TRINIDAD LAKE STATE PARK

1.9 Descend a canyon and reach the dry bottom of Levsa Canyon (GPS: 37 8.7841, –104 35.0437). Continue south and climb onto another mesa.

2.9 Reach floor of a dry wash. Hike southwest across dry hills.

3.7 Descend dry slopes and bend north into a grassy wash north of lake (GPS: 37 8.2773, –104 35.865). Head northwest across rolling hills.

4.9 Arrive at west Reilly Canyon Trailhead and parking lot on dirt CR 57.7 (GPS: 37 7.9869, –104 36.5689). This is the turnaround for round-trip hikers or the pickup point for one-way hikers. Reilly Canyon entrance is 160 feet up the road. Follow directions below for round-trip hike.

9.0 Return east on Reilly Canyon Trail to its end at junction with Levsa Canyon Trail. Go left on marked Levsa Canyon Trail.

9.3 Reach first junction at start of Levsa Canyon Trail loop. Go right.

9.4 Arrive back at the trailhead (GPS: 37 8.6601, –104 34.2074).

36 Willow Lake

Willow Lake Trail ascends a steep valley to a spectacular lake fed by a waterfall below Kit Carson Peak and Challenger Point in the Sangre de Cristo Mountains.

Start: Willow Lake and South Crestone Creek Trailhead
Difficulty: Strenuous
Trail: Willow Lake Trail
Hiking time: 7 to 9 hours
Distance: 9.8 miles out-and-back
Elevation trailhead to lake: 8,890 to 11,564 feet at Willow Lake (+2,674 feet)
Restrictions: Wilderness rules apply; open year-round; no dogs, bikes, or motorized vehicles allowed; parking lot fills in summer; camp 300 feet from water sources
Amenities: Backcountry camping below Willow Lake; services in Crestone
Maps: *DeLorme*: Page 71, E5 and E6; Trails Illustrated 138: Sangre de Cristo Mountains; USGS Crestone, Crestone Peak
County: Saguache
Land status: Sangre de Cristo Wilderness Area; Rio Grande National Forest, (719) 852-5941; Saguache District Office, (719) 655-2502

Finding the trailhead: From US 160 east of Alamosa or US 285 south of Villa Grove, drive to Moffat on CO 17 and turn east on CR T/Crestone Road. Follow the road east for 11.8 miles to a Y-junction south of Crestone. Go left on Birch Street to Crestone. Drive to Galena Avenue and follow signs to the South Crestone Creek Trailhead. Follow dirt Galena Avenue to a two-wheel-drive parking lot and trailhead at 1.5 miles or continue 0.75 mile on a rougher road to the four-wheel-drive parking and trailhead. High-clearance vehicles can drive to the upper trailhead. Trailhead is on the east side of the parking lot (GPS: 37 59.3366, –105 39.7487).

The Hike

The Willow Lake Trail climbs a steep valley to a gorgeous lake in a glacier-sculpted cirque in the heart of the Sangre de Cristo Wilderness Area. Willow Lake, one of Colorado's prettiest alpine tarns, is surrounded by towering peaks, including 14,171-foot Kit Carson Peak and 14,081-foot Challenger Point. Both are popular with peakbaggers who camp below the lake. The trail is easily done as a day hike but plan on spending most of the day hiking up the trail and admiring the atmospheric views at Willow Lake.

Begin at the Willow Lake and South Crestone Creek Trailhead southeast of Crestone on the west side of the Sangres. The first couple of miles thread through meadows and forests before the trail begins climbing steeper slopes broken by cliff bands. Higher the trail follows tumbling Willow Creek and passes several waterfalls including "Lower Willow Creek Falls" and spectacular "Black Slide Falls," a ribbon of water gushing down a black-streaked slab. At 11,100 feet, the trail edges below steep cliffs on Challenger Point and enters meadows in the upper valley. Look for bighorn sheep, elk, and mule deer. The final section scrambles past "Upper Willow Creek Falls" to a terrace and the hike's end above breathtaking Willow Lake. For dramatic

Willow Lake tucks in a rock-walled cirque below Kit Carson Mountain in the Sangre de Cristo Wilderness Area.

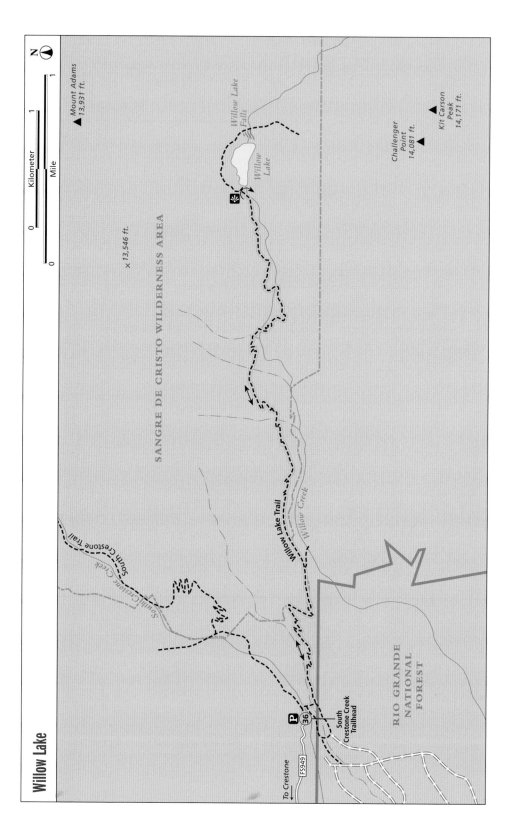

Willow Lake

N

Kilometer
0   1

Mile
0   1

Mount Adams
13,931 ft.

Willow Lake Falls

Willow Lake

SANGRE DE CRISTO WILDERNESS AREA

x 13,546 ft.

Challenger Point
14,081 ft.

Kit Carson Peak
14,171 ft.

South Crestone Creek Trail

South Crestone Creek

Willow Lake Trail

Willow Creek

RIO GRANDE NATIONAL FOREST

P
36

South Crestone Creek Trailhead

To Crestone

FS949

An unnamed 13,541-foot mountain towers above Willow Lake and "Willow Lake Falls."

effect, "Willow Lake Falls" pours 100 feet over a cliff into the placid lake opposite the overlook. For a lakeside view, follow a short trail down to the western shore by the lake's outlet stream. Return down the trail to complete the hike.

Miles and Directions

0.0 Start at the trailhead for South Crestone Creek and Willow Lake Trails. Go straight for 250 feet to a junction. Go right on marked Willow Lake Trail (#865) and cross South Crestone Creek after 300 feet.

0.1 Reach a Y-junction. Go left on Willow Lake Trail.

1.0 Reach the Sangre de Cristo Wilderness Area boundary.

1.4 Reach ridge above Willow Creek Park. Descend east into valley.

3.2 Pass "Hiker's Falls" on the left side of the trail (GPS: 37 59.6059, –105 37.7249).

3.4 Pass "Lower Willow Creek Falls" on the trail's right side (GPS: 37 59.5966, –105 37.5633).

3.5 Cross Willow Creek at 10,850 feet. Hike southeast up wooded slopes.

3.7 Pass "Black Slide Falls" on a black streak on the left side of the trail. Continue up the rocky trail below cliffs.

4.7 Reach forested slopes and meadows north of Willow Creek. This is a designated camping area. Continue 0.1 mile past "Upper Willow Creek Falls" (GPS: 37 59.6293, –105 36.706) to Willow Lake.

4.9 Reach an overlook above Willow Lake (GPS: 37 59.6542, –105 36.6938). To reach "Willow Lake Falls," continue across the trail north of Willow Lake for 0.5 mile to the top of the waterfall, then return.

9.8 Arrive back at the trailhead (GPS: 37 59.3366, –105 39.7487).

Southwestern Colorado

Silverton, Ouray, Dolores, and Mancos

Rocky ridges and scree fields enclose "Lower Blue Lake" below Dallas Peak in the Mount Sneffels Wilderness Area.

37 Highland Mary Lakes, Verde Lake, and Lost Lake

This fabulous hike passes four high-elevation, glacial lakes on a high, rolling upland and an extra-credit lake tucked in a hidden cirque in the scenic heart of the San Juan Mountains southeast of Silverton.

Start: Highland Mary Trailhead
Difficulty: Strenuous
Trails: Highland Mary Trail #606, Whitehead Peak Trail #674
Hiking time: About 4 hours
Distance: 6.2 miles out-and-back
Elevation trailhead to lake: 10,400 to 12,090 feet at third Highland Mary Lake (+981 feet)
Restrictions: Limited parking; wilderness rules apply; no mountain bikes; dogs must be under control

Amenities: Highland Mary primitive campground; services in Silverton
Maps: *DeLorme*: Page 77, C5; Trails Illustrated 141: Telluride, Silverton, Ouray, Lake City; USGS Howardsville
County: San Juan
Land status: Weminuche Wilderness Area; San Juan National Forest, (970) 247-4874; Columbine District, (970) 884-2512

Finding the trailhead: From the junction of US 550 and CR 10 on the south side of Silverton, drive north through Silverton on CR 110/Greene Street to a right turn on Blair Street/CR 2. Drive northeast on CR 2 toward Howardsville for 4.1 miles to a right turn on CR 4/FR 589 and drive south (pass Highland Mary Primitive Campground at 3.3 miles) for 3.7 miles to mine ruins before the road starts switchbacking up slopes to the right. Low-clearance, two-wheel-drive vehicles should park in pullouts on the road here (GPS: 37 47.3148, –107 34.6941) and walk 0.9 mile up the road to the Highland Mary Trailhead. High-clearance, four-wheel-drive vehicles can continue up the rough road for 0.8 mile to a lower parking lot or 0.9 mile to a higher one at the trailhead (GPS: 37 46.8556, –107 34.7826). Parking at the lower, two-wheel-drive trailhead adds an additional 1.8 miles to the hike.

The Hike

The seven Highland Mary Lakes, named for a nearby mine, scatter like gleaming jewels across a 12,000-foot basin atop the San Juan Mountains southeast of Silverton. Nestled among glacier-scraped hills, the three largest lakes are reached by the Highland Mary Trail, which steeply climbs up Cunningham Creek's narrow valley, passing waterfalls and cascades, to the northern edge of the shallow basin. The trail swings past the small first lake, a shallow pond with a small island, to the second lake, a long lake hemmed by bedrock hillsides covered with willows and tundra. The half-mile-long third lake, the largest and deepest of the lakes, fills a wide bowl at 12,090 feet. The trail threads along a humped ridge between the second and third

A wooded island rises from the first Highland Mary Lake in the Weminuche Wilderness Area.
Photo by Geoff Irons

lakes and then traverses rolling hills blanketed with alpine wildflowers to the Verde Lakes, including 12,186-foot Verde Lake. The trail heads left here to the Continental Divide Trail, which twists north to the Canadian border. For extra credit, energetic hikers can visit hidden Lost Lake, a round 12,182-foot tarn tucked beneath cliffs, by following Whitehead Peak Trail down a vale below Verde Lake and then heading west across a high bench to the lake.

The Highland Mary Trail, lying in the Weminuche Wilderness Area, is easy to follow except for a marshy section across the inlet stream at the third lake. The open terrain is exposed to severe storms, so pay attention to the weather and get to a lower elevation before lightning strikes. Large snowdrifts blanket the basin in June. Bring MICROspikes and trekking poles for snow traction. Backpackers often trek up to the lakes. Don't camp on the lake shores. Dispose of human waste by using Wagbags and packing your poop out.

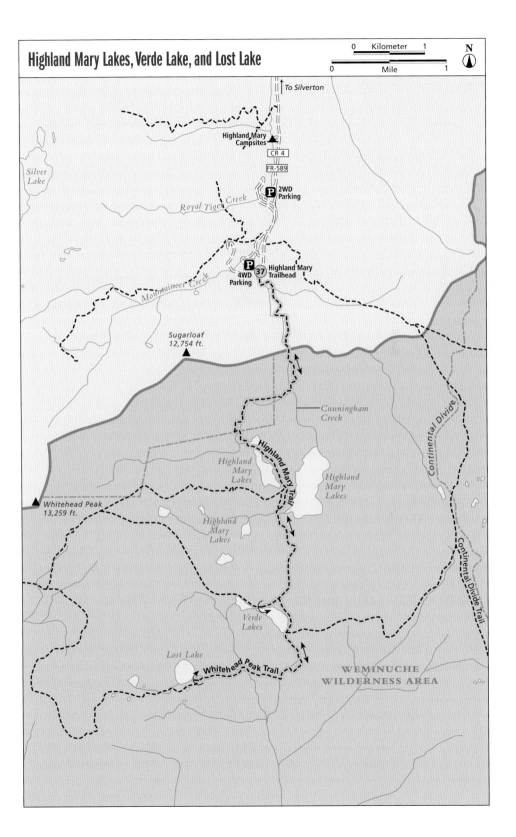

Highland Mary Lakes, Verde Lake, and Lost Lake

0 Kilometer 1

0 Mile 1

N

To Silverton

Highland Mary Campsites

CR 4

FR-589

2WD Parking

Royal Tiger Creek

Silver Lake

4WD Parking

37

Highland Mary Trailhead

Mountaineer Creek

Sugarloaf 12,754 ft.

Cunningham Creek

Highland Mary Trail

Highland Mary Lakes

Highland Mary Lakes

Continental Divide

Whitehead Peak 13,259 ft.

Highland Mary Lakes

Verde Lakes

Continental Divide Trail

Lost Lake

Whitehead Peak Trail

WEMINUCHE WILDERNESS AREA

Miles and Directions

0.0 Start at the Highland Mary Trailhead at the highest parking area (reached by four-wheel-drive vehicles). Hike south through forest along the east side of Cunningham Creek.

0.3 Past a waterfall, reach a junction on the left with a trail that climbs southeast to the Continental Divide; this can be used as the return leg for a loop hike. Keep straight through forest and willows along the creek.

1.0 Cross Cunningham Creek to its west bank (GPS: 37 46.2102, –107 34.5718) and head west up a side drainage, then south up a narrow canyon.

1.5 Reach a junction below a talus field in the canyon. Keep right and hike up around the top of the talus, then drop down and cross a creek.

1.8 Reach the west side of the first Highland Mary Lake at 12,080 feet (GPS: 37 45.9266, –107 34.8883). Continue around its south side.

1.9 Reach the north end of the second lake (GPS: 37 45.8899, –107 34.804). Hike south along its eastern shoreline.

2.2 Reach the south end of the second lake and continue onto a divide above the large third lake to the left.

2.3 Arrive at a viewpoint above the western edge of the third lake (GPS: 37 45.6069, –107 34.6203). A side trail drops down to the lakeshore. Continue hiking south, crossing a marshy area at the inlet creek at the lake's south end. The fourth lake hides directly west behind a rounded rock ridge. Follow the trail south across open meadows to a 12,330-foot crest, then descend gently southwest. Enjoy scenic views south to the rugged Grenadier Range, including 13,864-foot Vestal Peak, 13,803-foot Arrow Peak, and 13,765-foot West Trinity Peak.

3.0 Reach a junction with a side trail (GPS: 37 45.0825, –107 34.6586) that heads east to the Continental Divide Trail and the Whitehead Mountain Trail, which descends southeast to the east end of Verde Lake (take this trail for the option to Lost Lake). Go right and descend southwest to the north shore of Verde Lake.

3.1 Reach the north shore of Verde Lake and the turnaround point (GPS: 37 45.0276, –107 34.7821). Enjoy the views and then retrace the trail back north.

6.2 Arrive back at the trailhead (GPS: 37 46.8556, –107 34.7826).

EXTRA CREDIT: LOST LAKE

From the junction above Verde Lake, hike southeast on Whitehead Peak Trail #674 for 0.3 mile to the east end of Verde Lake. Descend a shallow valley to a wetland with willows. Bend west and continue to a bench after 0.7 mile. Hike west on the trail through willows and arrive at the southeast side of Lost Lake after 1.4 miles. Return back to the junction with Highland Mary Trail for a 2.8-mile hike, making the round-trip distance 9 miles.

38 Ice Lake Basin Lakes

Ice Lake Trail climbs through spruce forests and meadows, passes dramatic waterfalls, and reaches three gorgeous alpine lakes tucked against dramatic, glacier-sculpted mountains.

Start: Ice Lake Trailhead
Difficulty: Strenuous
Trail: Ice Lake Trail #505
Hiking time: About 5 hours
Distance: 7.0 miles out-and-back
Elevation trailhead to falls viewpoints: 9,930 to 12,257 feet at Ice Lake (+2,327 feet)
Restrictions: Limited parking; citations issued for illegal parking; practice Leave No Trace ethic; use Wagbags for human waste; pack out trash; follow existing trails only; check for possible permit system
Amenities: Trailhead vault toilets; services in Silverton
Maps: *DeLorme*: Page 76, B3; Trails Illustrated 141: Telluride, Silverton, Ouray, Lake City; USGS Ophir
County: San Juan
Land status: San Juan National Forest, (970) 247-4874; Columbine Ranger District, (970) 884-2512

Finding the trailhead: From the intersection of US 550 and CO 62 in Ridgway, take US 62 west toward Ouray and Silverton. Drive 59.6 miles and turn right on unpaved CR 7/FR 585, toward South Mineral Campground. From Silverton, drive 2.0 miles on US 550 and turn left on CR 7/FR 585. Continue 4.4 miles to the parking lot and trailhead on the right (GPS: 37 48.4, -107 46.438).

The Hike

Hiding in the heart of the San Juan Mountains, Ice Lake Basin is an alpine wonderland enclosed by a parade of peaks, including Vermilion, Beattie, U. S. Grant, and Fuller Peaks, pointed Golden Horn, and Pilot Knob's rocky fin. Ice Lake, the basin's main attraction at 12,257 feet, is tinted a fluorescent turquoise color, resulting from glacier-grinded rock flour suspended in the icy water. The above-timberline cirque offers two other large lakes—12,605-foot Fuller Lake and 12,392-foot Island Lake—and a handful of small tarns. Lower Ice Lake Basin harbors "Lower Ice Lake."

The basin is reached by Ice Lakes Trail, a popular path that passes eight waterfalls between the trailhead and Ice Lake. Plan on a full day to see the falls and visit the lakes, although many hikers turn around at the lower basin rather than climb the steep last mile to the upper bowl. The reward for that final effort is the broad upper basin, its ring of ragged peaks, tundra meadows filled with wildflowers from late July through August, and the crystalline lakes. Although it adds extra mileage, hike the extra credit trails to Fuller and Island Lakes after visiting Ice Lake for a full-value adventure.

Ice Lake's fluorescent blue comes from glacial rock flour, a fine powder suspended in the water that reflects sunlight. Photo by Ben Loftin

A parade of high peaks, including Vermilion Peak, Golden Horn, and Pilot Knob, reflect in Ice Lake in the San Juan Mountains. Photo by Ben Loftin

Ice Lake Trail is one of the most heavily used footpaths in the San Juans with crowds of people jamming it on weekends. This has led to resource damage, including deterioration of fragile tundra caused by social trails that fan across the high-elevation landscape, campers making fires above treeline, human waste and toilet tissue, and trash. To protect the trail and upper basins, the US Forest Service plans to establish a permit system to limit over-use of the area. Call the ranger station before arriving to see what restrictions are in place.

The trail starts steep, passing through meadows and woods, some burned in the Ice Fire in October 2020. The fire torched almost 600 acres on lower Ice Lake Trail, leaving exposed soils and dead tree snags alongside the trail. As the trail climbs, it passes many waterfalls, including "Clear Creek Falls." Consult *Hiking Waterfalls Colorado* (FalconGuides 2022) for info about all the waterfalls. After climbing to Lower Ice Lake Basin, the trail swings around its northern edge with views south of "Lower Ice Lake." The trail's hardest part ascends steep, exposed slopes to a long traverse above a cliff to upper Ice Lake Basin.

Miles and Directions

0.0 Begin at the Ice Lake Trailhead and hike up switchbacks. Cross Clear Creek at 0.5 mile.

1.1 Arrive at upper leaps of "Clear Creek Falls." Continue up trail.

2.1 Arrive at a viewpoint for "Lower Ice Lake Basin Falls" (GPS: 37 48.642, -107 47.263). Continue up the trail into the lower basin and look for more waterfalls. Hike past "Lower Ice Lake" on the left.

Ice Lake Basin Lakes

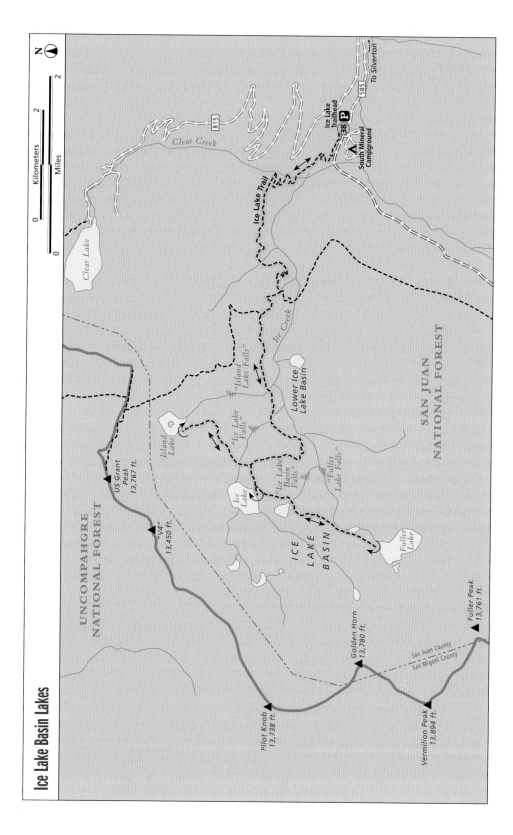

UNCOMPAHGRE
NATIONAL FOREST

SAN JUAN
NATIONAL FOREST

ICE
LAKE
BASIN

Clear Lake

Clear Creek

815

Ice Lake Trail

Ice Lake
Trailhead

38 P

South Mineral
Campground

585

To Silverton

Island Lake

Ice Creek

"Island
Lake Falls"

Lower Ice
Lake Basin

"Ice Lake
Falls"

Ice
Lake

"Ice Lake
Basin Falls"

"Fuller
Lake Falls"

Fuller
Lake

US Grant Peak
13,767 ft.

"V4"
13,450 ft.

Pilot Knob
13,738 ft.

Golden Horn
13,780 ft.

San Juan County
San Miguel County

Vermilion Peak
13,894 ft.

Fuller Peak
13,761 ft.

N

0   2   Kilometers   2

0   Miles   2

Island Lake nestles in a glacier-sculpted cirque below US Grant Peak in Ice Lake Basin.
Photo by Ben Loftin

2.7 Begin climbing switchbacks on steep, rocky slopes to the upper basin.

3.35 Reach Ice Lake Basin and a junction with Island Lake Trail on the right. Continue straight.

3.45 Reach junction with Fuller Lake Trail on the left. Continue straight.

3.5 Arrive at the southeast shoreline of Ice Lake (GPS: 37 48.768, –107 48.521). After admiring the view, return down the trail.

7.0 Arrive back at the trailhead (GPS: 37 48.4, –107 46.438).

EXTRA CREDIT: ISLAND LAKE AND FULLER LAKE

ISLAND LAKE: From the junction at 3.35 miles with the out-and-back Island Lake Trail, go right and hike northeast for 0.5 mile to Island Lake (GPS: 37 49.1171, –107 48.1602). Return to the junction for a 1.0-mile hike and then to the trailhead for an 8.0-mile hike.

FULLER LAKE: From the junction at 3.45 miles with the out-and-back Fuller Lake Trail, go left and hike south for 0.8 mile up to Fuller Lake (GPS: 37 48.2229, –107 48.8133). Return to the junction for a 1.5-mile hike and then to the trailhead for an 8.6-mile hike.

ISLAND AND FULLER LAKES: Follow above directions to both lakes and then return to the trailhead for a 9.6-mile, round-trip hike.

39 Blue Lakes

The iconic Blue Lakes are a string of three alpine tarns in a glaciated basin below the west flank of rugged Mount Sneffels, the twenty-seventh highest mountain in Colorado, between Ouray and Telluride.

Start: Blue Lakes Trailhead
Difficulty: Strenuous
Trail: Blue Lakes Trail #201
Hiking time: About 6 hours
Distance: 8.2 miles out-and-back to upper lake; 6.4 miles out-and-back to lower lake
Elevation trailhead to lake: 9,345 to 10,915 feet at "Lower Blue Lake" (+1,576 feet); 11,750 feet at "Upper Blue Lake" (+2,405 feet)
Restrictions: Limited parking; wilderness rules apply; no mountain bikes; dogs must be under control; no campfires—use a gas stove; follow Leave No Trace ethics; dispose properly of human and pet waste
Amenities: Services in Ridgeway
Maps: DeLorme: Page 66, E3; Trails Illustrated 141: Telluride, Silverton, Ouray, Lake City; USGS Mount Sneffels, Telluride
County: Ouray
Land status: Mount Sneffels Wilderness Area; Uncompahgre National Forest, (970) 874-6600; Ouray Ranger District, (970) 240-5300

Finding the trailhead: From the junction of US 550 and CO 62 in Ridgway, drive 4.8 miles west on CO 62. Turn left (south) on CR 7 (which becomes FR 851.1 at the forest boundary). Drive south on the dirt road for 8.9 miles to the trailhead at the road's end (GPS: 38 2.078, –107 48.4323). Keep right after 2 miles at a junction when CR 71 goes left. The road is passable to cars in dry conditions, although the last 2 miles are rough with potholes. Park near the trailhead and avoid parking along the access road north of the trailhead.

The Hike

The Blue Lakes, three of Colorado's most beautiful lakes, tuck into a lofty cirque surrounded by towering mountains, including 14,157-foot Mount Sneffels and 13,815-foot Dallas Peak in the 16,587-acre Mount Sneffels Wilderness Area. The popular Blue Lakes Trail climbs from the trailhead on the East Fork of Dallas Creek to "Lower Blue Lake" and then scrambles steeply to the two upper lakes. Most hikers turn around at the lower lake, but it is worth the effort to climb the additional 0.9 mile and gain over 800 feet to the upper lakes, both shining tarns snuggled into the upper basin. Cobalt-blue "Lower Blue Lake," the largest of the three, nestles against talus slopes and cliffs below Dallas Peak, Colorado's one-hundredth-highest peak. "Middle Blue Lake" fills a narrow valley below a jagged ridge west of Mount Sneffels, while the highest "Upper Blue Lake," a tundra-fringed tarn, lies below a ragged ridge of unranked points and 13,000-foot Blue Lakes Pass. The trail continues up to the pass and drops into Yankee Boy Basin on the other side.

Rocky ridges and scree fields enclose "Lower Blue Lake" below Dallas Peak in the Mount Sneffels Wilderness Area.

The Blue Lakes basin and trail are very popular with hikers and backpackers, who camp by the lower lake. The area has become degraded by thousands of people who hike the trail during the summer, leaving behind trash, improperly disposing of human and dog waste, and trampling wildflowers and fragile tundra. To save the Blue Lakes, practice a Leave No Trace ethic and follow commonsense rules. Camping is allowed at least 100 feet from the lake in existing sites. Campfires are not allowed; use a stove. Walk only on trails to avoid damaging plants, grass, and trees. Properly dispose of waste by using a Wagbag or bring a toilet kit with sanitary wipes, toilet paper, a trowel, and plastic baggies. Bury your business in a cathole and carry toilet paper out in a plastic bag. In 2017 rangers buried over 300 piles of human excrement in the trail corridor. The trail is busy, especially on weekends, so arrive early to snag a parking space rather than along the road where vegetation is damaged.

Miles and Directions

0.0   Start at the Blue Lakes Trailhead at the south end of the parking lot. Hike south on doubletrack Dallas Trail #200 for 300 feet to a signed junction with Blue Lakes Trail on the right. Go right on it and hike southwest on the singletrack trail. The trail steadily climbs slopes above the East Fork of Dallas Creek, with views east of Mount Sneffels. The grade eases past an open avalanche area and reaches a waterfall to the left.

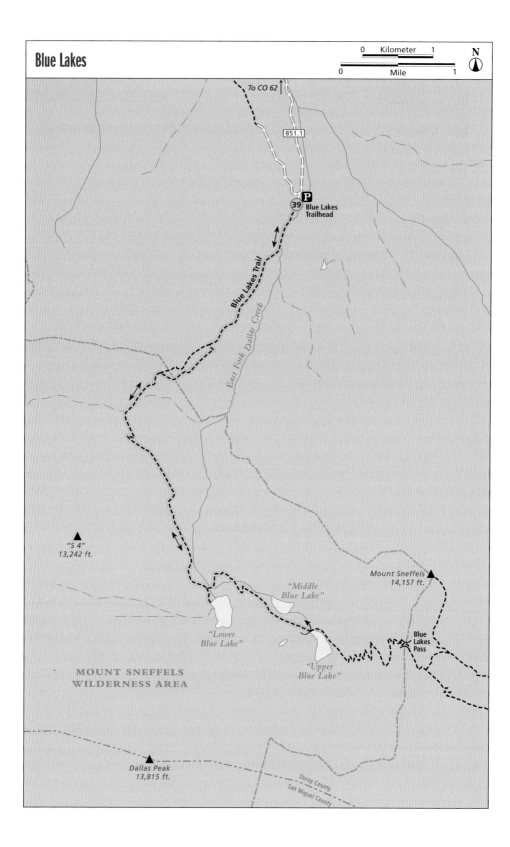

Blue Lakes

0 Kilometer 1
0 Mile 1

N

To CO 62

851.1

P
39 Blue Lakes
Trailhead

Blue Lakes Trail

East Fork Dallas Creek

"S 4"
13,242 ft.

"Middle
Blue Lake"

Mount Sneffels
14,157 ft.

Blue
Lakes
Pass

"Lower
Blue Lake"

"Upper
Blue Lake"

MOUNT SNEFFELS
WILDERNESS AREA

Dallas Peak
13,815 ft.

Ouray County
San Miguel County

Upper Blue Lake reflects jagged peaks in the Mount Sneffels Wilderness Area.

3.1 Reach a junction in thick forest (GPS: 38 0.1601, –107 49.008). Continue straight to the first lake. The left fork is the trail to the upper lakes.

3.2 Arrive at the north shore of "Lower Blue Lake." Enjoy stunning mountain views from a lakeside boulder or hike on a trail around the lake. Most hikers turn around at the lower lake and return to the trailhead for a 6.4-mile hike. To continue the hike, return north to the trail junction.

3.3 At the junction, go right on Blue Lakes Trail. Cross the East Fork of Dallas Creek on logs. Keep left and follow the trail through trees then right across talus slope to another creek crossing. Follow the narrow trail up steep grassy slopes with views of "Lower Blue Lake" to an overlook and side trail to "Middle Blue Lake" at 11,565 feet (GPS: 38 0.1085, –107 48.6441). Continue southeast on the trail above the lake.

4.2 After gaining 829 feet, arrive at the north end of "Upper Blue Lake" (GPS: 37 59.9486, –107 48.3253). After enjoying the upper lake, return the way you came on the main trail.

8.2 Arrive back at the trailhead (GPS: 38 2.078, –107 48.4323).

40 Lake Hope

Tucked into an alpine cirque below San Miguel Peak, Lake Hope is a shining jewel with marvelous views of surrounding high mountains and Trout Lake in southwestern Colorado's San Juan Mountains.

Start: Lake Hope Trailhead
Difficulty: Moderate
Trail: Lake Hope Trail #410
Hiking time: About 3 hours
Distance: 4.6 miles out-and-back
Elevation trailhead to lake: 10,735 to 11,910 feet at lake (+1,175 feet)
Restrictions: Hikers and horseback riders only; no mountain bikes

Amenities: Services in Telluride
Maps: *DeLorme*: Page 76, B3; Trails Illustrated 141: Telluride, Silverton, Ouray, Lake City; USGS: Ophir
County: San Juan
Land status: San Juan National Forest, (970) 247-4874; Columbine Ranger District, (970) 884-2512

Finding the trailhead: From West Colorado Avenue in Telluride, take CO 145 South for 10.1 miles and turn left on CR 63A, signed "Trout Lake." Follow road south for 1.7 miles and turn left on Hope Lake Road/FR 627. Follow rough road for 2.6 miles to the trailhead (GPS: 37 48.2993, –107 51.0938). Depending on conditions, the road may require a high-clearance vehicle. Park at the trailhead, along the road, or at an overflow area down the road.

The Hike

Lake Hope, cupped in an alpine basin below 13,752-foot San Miguel Peak, is a spectacular lake surrounded by cliffs, ridges, and snowfields. The lake, at the headwaters of the Lake Fork of the San Miguel River, is a manmade reservoir that was built in the early 1900s to divert water to the Ames Hydroelectric Generating Plant below Ophir and to maintain Trout Lake's level. A small dam blocks the outlet stream. Officially called Lake Hope on USGS maps, the lake is also called Hope Lake at the trailhead and other sources.

The scenic trail, gaining over 1,000 feet of elevation to the lake, is popular with hikers trekking up its wildflower-festooned meadows in summer. The trail and lake offer spacious views of the San Miguel Range, including three Fourteeners—Mount Wilson, El Diente Peak, and Wilson Peak—and 13,110-foot Lizard Head, considered Colorado's toughest peak to climb. East of the lake towers multicolored, 13,894-foot Vermilion Peak.

The trail is easy to follow with gradual grades up the steep slope to the lake. Look up right from the trail for views of "Lake Hope Falls," a long cascade. The trail is busy in summer, especially on weekends. Arrive early for a parking space and few people at the lake. Pack rain gear for afternoon thunderstorms, extra clothes, snacks, and drinks.

Lake Hope nestles in a hanging cirque below San Miguel Peak, Colorado's 124th-highest mountain, in the San Juan Mountains. Photo by John Kirk

Vermilion Peak towers above small tarns in meadows east of Lake Hope.

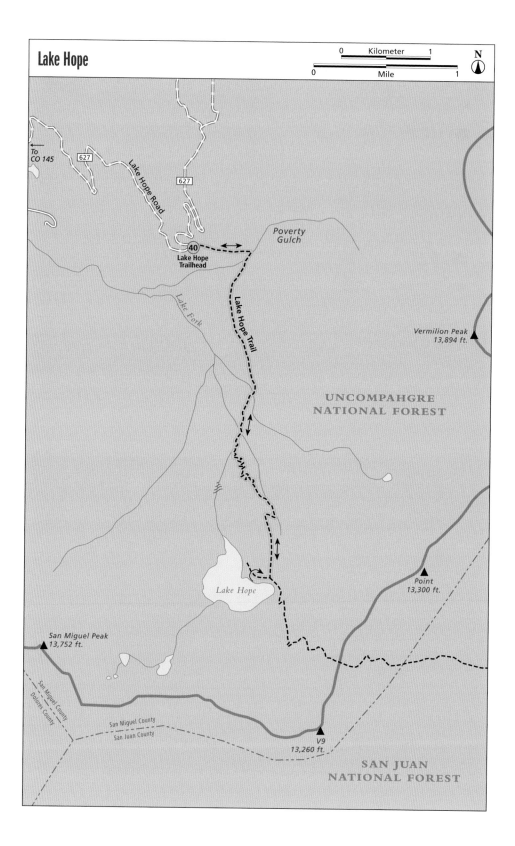

Lake Hope

To
CO 145

627

Lake Hope Road

627

Poverty
Gulch

40
Lake Hope
Trailhead

Lake Fork

Lake Hope Trail

Vermilion Peak
13,894 ft.

UNCOMPAHGRE
NATIONAL FOREST

Lake Hope

Point
13,300 ft.

San Miguel Peak
13,752 ft.

San Miguel County
Dolores County

San Miguel County
San Juan County

V9
13,260 ft.

SAN JUAN
NATIONAL FOREST

Kilometer

Mile

N

A rocky ridge, topped by peak "V9," reflects in Lake Hope on an early June morning.
Photo by John Kirk

Miles and Directions

0.0   Start at the Lake Hope Trailhead on the east side of a hairpin turn. Hike east on the signed trail, contouring across a wooded, south-facing slope.

0.3   Cross a creek in Poverty Gulch (GPS: 37 48.283, –107 50.825). Use caution when the creek is high in June. Bend south and lose elevation, then begin climbing and contouring through forest on west-facing slopes below talus fields. Look for views west toward the San Miguel Range.

1.1   Trail reaches Lake Fork on the right at 10,885 feet and begins climbing, switchbacking through forest to timberline and then up steep grassy slopes. After the angle eases, continue up tundra slopes.

2.2   Reach a Y-junction on the east side of Lake Hope (GPS: 37 47.0327, –107 50.711). The left trail continues southeast, climbing 0.7 mile to a 12,445-foot pass and then dropping into the South Fork of Mineral Creek drainage. Go right and hike above the eastern shore of Lake Hope.

2.3   Arrive at a viewpoint above Lake Hope with views across the lake to San Miguel Peak (GPS: 37 47.0451, –107 50.7977). Return back down the trail.

4.6   Arrive back at the trailhead (GPS: 37 48.2993, –107 51.0938).

41 Navajo Lake

Navajo Trail climbs a lush valley to Navajo Lake, a shimmering lake tucked into an alpine basin surrounded by soaring peaks and ridges in the San Miguel Mountains.

Start: Navajo Lake Trailhead
Difficulty: Strenuous
Trail: Navajo Lake Trail #635
Hiking time: About 7 hours
Distance: 9.0 miles out-and-back
Elevation trailhead to lake: 9,330 to 11,140 feet at Navajo Lake (+1,810 feet)
Restrictions: Wilderness rules apply; no campfires in Navajo Basin; no camping within 100 feet of water sources; dogs must be under control

Amenities: Backcountry camping; services in Rico and Telluride
Maps: *DeLorme*: Page 76, B1; Trails Illustrated 141: Telluride, Silverton, Ouray, Lake City; USGS: Dolores Peak
County: Dolores
Land status: Lizard Head Wilderness Area; San Juan National Forest, (970) 247-4874; Dolores Ranger District, (970) 882-7296

Finding the trailhead: From West Colorado Avenue in Telluride, take CO 145 South for 17.4 miles, over Lizard Head Pass, and turn right on unpaved Dunton Road (CR 38 / FR 535). Drive 7.3 miles, passing Kilpacker Trailhead, to a signed right turn to Navajo Trailhead. Continue 0.1 mile to parking at the trailhead (GPS: 37 48.3062, -108 3.7949).

The Hike

Scenic Navajo Lake, pooling in long, glacier-carved Navajo Basin, lies among mountain giants, including three Fourteeners—14,252-foot Mount Wilson, 14,160-foot El Diente Peak, and 14,016-foot Wilson Peak—in the heart of Lizard Head Wilderness Area. The lake, formed by a glacial moraine, is reached by Navajo Lake Trail, which follows the West Dolores River up a broad valley. The trail threads through dense forest and open meadows blotched with wildflowers, and passes several waterfalls, including "West Dolores River Falls" and dramatic "Navajo Basin Falls." Consult *Hiking Waterfalls Colorado* (FalconGuides 2022) for directions to the falls.

The popular trail is not only used by lake hikers and backpackers but also by mountaineers set on climbing the high peaks, so expect company as you hike. The trail has a good footbed, moderate grades, a steep section that gains almost 1,000 feet in a mile and is well-marked and easy to follow. After arriving at Navajo Lake, enjoy spectacular views up the basin to Wilson Peak, Mount Gladstone, and Mount Wilson while you munch snacks. If you're ambitious, continue around the lake's north shore for more views or follow the trail for a couple more miles to 13,014-foot Rock of Ages saddle below Wilson Peak.

Navajo Lake offers stunning views up a glaciated valley to 13,913-foot Gladstone Peak in the San Miguel Mountains.

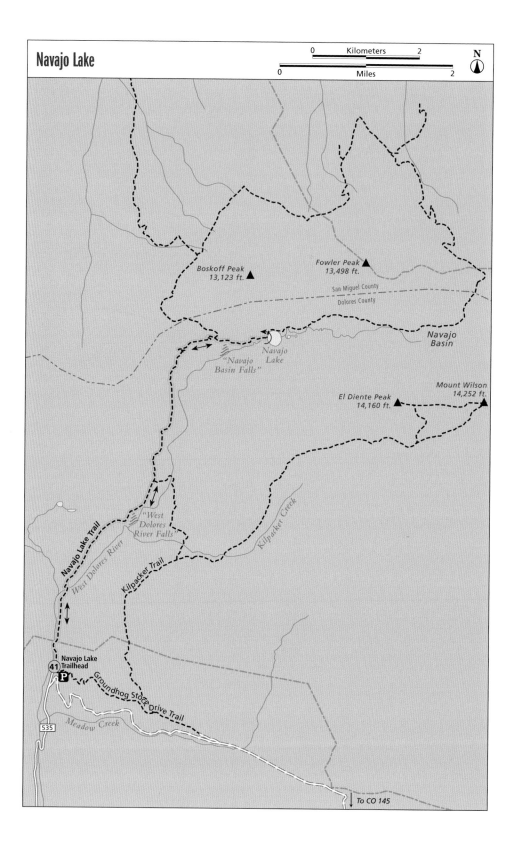

Navajo Lake

Kilometers 0 — 2
Miles 0 — 2

N

Boskoff Peak
13,123 ft. ▲

Fowler Peak
13,498 ft. ▲

San Miguel County
Dolores County

Navajo
Basin

"Navajo
Basin Falls"

Navajo
Lake

Mount Wilson
14,252 ft. ▲

El Diente Peak
14,160 ft. ▲

Kilpacker Creek

"West
Dolores
River Falls"

Navajo Lake Trail

West Dolores River

Kilpacker Trail

Navajo Lake
Trailhead
41
P

Groundhog Stock Drive Trail

535

Meadow Creek

To CO 145

Navajo Lake is a popular base camp for climbers seeking the summits of three Fourteeners in the San Miguel Mountains.

Miles and Directions

0.0 Begin at Navajo Lake Trailhead and hike north. Pass a junction with Groundhog Stock Drive Trail (#534) and continue on Navajo Lake Trail with the river on the left.

0.2 Pass a bridge on left (part of Groundhog Stock Drive Trail) and stay straight on main trail. Enter Lizard Head Wilderness Area.

0.8 Cross bridge to left over West Dolores River and begin climbing through meadows and evergreen forests, with views of El Diente and Dolores Peak.

1.7 Reach junction with a side trail that goes right to "West Dolores River Falls."

2.2 After gaining almost 900 feet, reach a junction with Kilpacker Trail (#203) on right. Stay straight on Navajo Lake Trail.

3.4 Trail begins climbing steeply and switchbacking up open slopes.

4.0 Reach junction with Woods Lake Trail, which goes left for 4.5 miles to Woods Lake. Continue straight on signed main trail and gently descend toward lake.

4.5 Arrive at Navajo Lake's northwest shore (GPS: 37 50.8503, -108 1.6976). Return to trailhead down Navajo Lake Trail.

9.0 Arrive back at the trailhead (GPS: 37 48.3062, -108 3.7949).

42 Jackson Gulch Reservoir

An easy trail crosses open terrain above the eastern shoreline of Jackson Gulch Reservoir, an agricultural-storage lake in Mancos State Park north of the old town of Mancos in southwestern Colorado.

Start: Vista Trailhead
Difficulty: Easy
Trail: Mule Deer Trail
Hiking time: About 1 hour
Distance: 2 miles out-and-back
Elevation trailhead to lake: 8,850 to 8,825 feet at lake (-25 feet; depending on water level)
Restrictions: Fee area; park open 5 a.m. to 10 p.m. year-round; leashed dogs only; dogs not allowed in lake; no swimming, fireworks, or open fires
Amenities: Trailhead vault toilets, picnic tables, and interpretive signs; park campground; services in Mancos
Maps: *DeLorme*: Page 85, A7; Trails Illustrated 144: Durango, Cortez; USGS Millwood
County: Montezuma
Land status: Mancos State Park, (970) 533-7065

Finding the trailhead: From the junction of US 160 and North Main Street/CO 184 in Mancos, drive north on North Main Street/CO 184 for 0.3 mile and turn right (east) on CR 42, signed for Mancos State Park. Follow the road northeast for 4.2 miles to CR N. Turn left on dirt CR N and drive 0.4 mile to the park entrance. Make the first right turn and drive 100 feet to a parking lot and the Vista Trailhead (GPS: 37 24.0569, -108 16.1582).

The Hike

Jackson Gulch Reservoir, the centerpiece of Mancos State Park, lies at the western foot of the La Plata Range, the westernmost extension of the Rocky Mountains in Colorado. The 125-acre reservoir (when it's full) formed in the late 1940s after a 180-foot-high dam was built across Jackson Gulch. Water, diverted from the West Mancos River to the reservoir by an inlet canal, is used for agriculture so the lake is often drawn down by late summer.

The state park, besides offering the usual water-based activities like boating, has two campgrounds and a trail network accessed by three trailheads. For lake views, the Mule Deer Trail is an easy hike along the lake's eastern shore, passing groves of towering cottonwoods, dense scrub oak thickets, and an old quarry that sometimes fills with water. The trail, northwest of Mancos and Mesa Verde National Park, is a fine family-friendly hike in an off-the-beaten-track state parkland.

The La Plata Mountains scrape the clouds beyond Jackson Gulch Reservoir at Mancos State Park.

The Mule Deer Trail winds through cottonwoods and meadows by Jackson Gulch Reservoir.

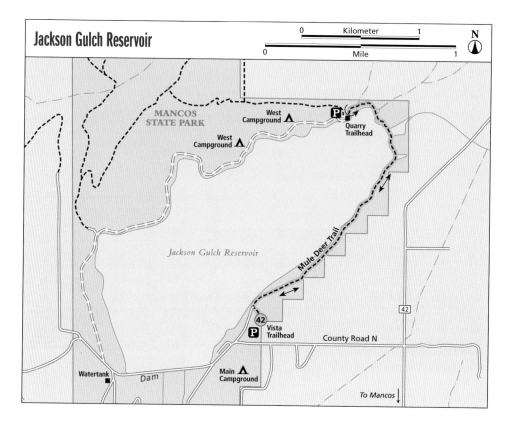

Miles and Directions

0.0   Start at the Vista Trailhead. Hike northwest on signed Mule Deer Trail and descend a hill.

0.05 Reach a junction and go right on the marked trail. Hike northeast on a terrace above the lake's eastern shore until the trail bends northwest. Cross a bridge over the inlet stream to a pond and bend left.

1.0   Reach the Quarry Trailhead at the end of the park road on the lake's north side (GPS: 37 24.5692, –108 15.8795). Turn around here and hike back on the trail.

2.0   Arrive back at the trailhead (GPS: 37 24.0569, –108 16.1582).

Western Colorado

Crested Butte, Cimarron, Cedaredge, and Grand Junction

A singletrack trail runs along the northern edge of Cobbett Lake on Grand Mesa.

43 Copper Lake

High in Copper Basin south of East Maroon Pass, Copper Lake shimmers in a high basin in the Maroon Bells–Snowmass Wilderness Area north of Crested Butte.

Start: (Lower) Copper Creek Trailhead (Judd Falls Trailhead), junction of Gothic Road #317 and Road #317.3A
Difficulty: Strenuous
Trails: Judd Falls Trail, Copper Creek Trail #983
Hiking time: About 6 hours
Distance: 10.5 miles out-and-back
Elevation trailhead to lake: 9,600 to 11,321 feet at Copper Lake (+1,721 feet); +2,091 feet total elevation gain out-and-back
Restrictions: No bicycles; leashed dogs only; wilderness rules apply; backcountry camping

by permit only; bear canisters required for overnight food storage
Amenities: Trailhead toilets; services in Crested Butte
Maps: *DeLorme*: Page 58, A2 and page 46, E2; Trails Illustrated 131: Crested Butte, Pearl Pass, 128: Maroon Bells, Redstone, Marble; USGS Maroon Bells
County: Gunnison
Land status: Gunnison National Forest, (970) 874-6600; Gunnison Ranger District, (970) 641-0471

Finding the trailhead: From CO 135/6th Street in downtown Crested Butte, drive north for about 8.3 miles onto unpaved Gothic Road/FSR 317 and to a parking lot at the junction with four-wheel-drive FR 317.3A. High-clearance four-wheel-drive vehicles can turn right and continue on Road 317.3A for 0.5 mile to the Copper Creek/Trailriders Trailhead. All other vehicles should park at the lower parking area. The hiking trail begins up the four-wheel-drive road, across from the kiosk and toilets (GPS: 38 57.9707, –106 59.6092). Trailhead address: 8000 CR 317, Crested Butte.

The Hike

Copper Lake spreads across the floor of Copper Basin, a glacier-plucked cirque below Precarious Peak, "Cassi Peak," and East Maroon Pass in the southern end of the Elk Mountains, a rocky range that boasts six Fourteeners. The lake, lying just below treeline, offers open mountain views, a willow-fringed shoreline, and shining water. Designated backcountry campsites surround the lake, beckoning backpackers for a quiet lakeside night or a stopover on a longer trek north into the Maroon Bells–Snowmass Wilderness Area.

The hike to Copper Lake follows a well-traveled path through dense forest and across meadows bursting with summer wildflowers until rising gently to the lake in its final half-mile. The hike requires many creek crossings, so bring trekking poles and consider sandals for wading. The creeks run high in June or after heavy rain.

Summer clouds float above unnamed peaks and Copper Lake in Copper Basin.

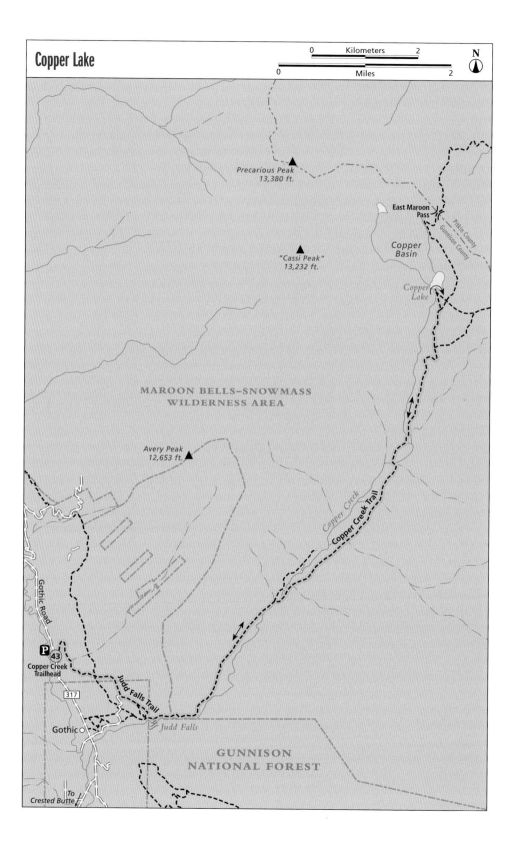

Copper Lake

0   Kilometers   2

0   Miles   2

N

Precarious Peak
13,380 ft.

East Maroon
Pass

Copper
Basin

Pitkin County
Gunnison County

Copper
Lake

"Cassi Peak"
13,232 ft.

MAROON BELLS–SNOWMASS
WILDERNESS AREA

Avery Peak
12,653 ft.

Copper Creek

Copper Creek Trail

Gothic Road

P 43
Copper Creek
Trailhead

317

Judd Falls Trail

Gothic

Judd Falls

GUNNISON
NATIONAL FOREST

To
Crested Butte

Copper Lake sits in Copper Basin below Precarious Peak in the Maroon Bells–Snowmass Wilderness Area.

Miles and Directions

0.0 From the parking area and lower trailhead, get on the trail across from the kiosk and hike east on it. Alternatively, hike up the road, which adds 0.1 mile to the hike one way.

0.1 When the trail meets the rough road, turn right and hike the road, past a small pullout on the right (GPS: 38 57.9542, –106 59.5241).

0.3 At the upper Copper Creek/Trailriders Trailhead and four-wheel-drive parking, continue straight (counterclockwise) around the lot (GPS: 38 57.8439, –106 59.315).

0.4 Pick up the Judd Falls Trail on the lot's east side (GPS: 38 57.8366, –106 59.2831).

0.9 At a signed trail junction, turn left on Copper Creek Trail (GPS: 38 57.58, –106 58.8835). Alternatively, take a short detour to the right to view Judd Falls from an overlook.

1.0 Enter the Maroon Bells–Snowmass Wilderness Area.

2.4 Cross Copper Creek on rocks and tree branches.

3.1 Cross the creek again on rocks and branches.

3.3 The trail contours below a boulder field.

3.8 Cross the creek a third time.

3.9 Cross the creek a fourth time.

4.0 Cross the creek for the fifth and final time.

4.8 At a signed junction with Conundrum Creek Trail, remain straight on Copper Creek Trail, which gets steeper and rockier (38.998064, –106.942551).

5.1 At the next junction with East Maroon Trail, bear left on Copper Creek Trail. The trail levels out before dipping slightly to the lake (GPS: 39 0.1126, –106 56.5055).

5.25 Reach the south shore of Copper Lake (GPS: 39 0.2439, –106 56.5507). After enjoying amazing mountain views, return down the trail.

10.5 Arrive back at the trailhead (GPS: 38 57.9707, –106 59.6092).

44 Blue Lake (Raggeds Wilderness Area)

The Oh-be-joyful Trail threads up a broad valley past waterfalls, meadows, and thick forest to Blue Lake, a dazzling shelf lake perched in a cirque below 12,646-foot Afley Peak in the Ruby Range.

Start: Oh-be-joyful Trailhead
Difficulty: Strenuous
Trail: Oh-be-joyful Trail #836
Hiking time: 6 to 8 hours
Distance: 13 miles out-and-back
Elevation trailhead to lake: 8,965 to 11,062 feet at lake (+2,097 feet)
Restrictions: Wilderness rules apply; dogs must be under control

Amenities: Toilets and campground at trailhead; services in Crested Butte
Maps: *DeLorme*: Page 58, A1 and A2; Trails Illustrated 131: Crested Butte, Pearl Pass; USGS Oh-Be-Joyful
County: Gunnison
Land status: Raggeds Wilderness Area; Gunnison National Forest, (970) 874-6600; Gunnison Ranger District, (970) 641-0471; BLM Gunnison Field Office, (970) 642-4940

Finding the trailhead: From Butte Avenue in Crested Butte, drive north on Gothic Road/CR 317 for 0.6 mile. After crossing the Slate River, turn left on Slate River Road/CR 374. Drive 6 miles to a left turn on marked BLM RD 3220. Pass an upper parking lot and descend the rough and rocky road to the Oh-be-joyful Trailhead, parking lot, and campground. Low-clearance vehicles should park at the upper lot (GPS: 38 54.8827, -107 1.9807).

The Hike

Blue Lake nestles in a high cirque below Afley and Purple Peaks in the heart of the Ruby Range and Raggeds Wilderness Area northwest of Crested Butte. The cupped lake, surrounded by talus fields and high cliffs, is reached by the Oh-be-joyful Trail, which threads through meadows strewn with wildflowers and over a dozen waterfalls in a glaciated, U-shaped valley. The trail, gaining over 2,000 feet of elevation, has mostly gentle grades except for the final steep pull up to the lake. It's easy to follow but watch for the junction signed for "Peeler Basin" and "Daisy Pass." Make sure to head left toward Peeler Basin.

The hike starts at Oh-be-joyful Campground, crosses the Slate River on a footbridge, and heads west along an old, closed road, passing overlooks of several waterfalls including 80-foot "Oh-be-joyful Creek Slide Falls" and "Oh-be-joyful Creek Falls," a horsetail that drops into a rocky cauldron. Higher, the trail passes "Upper Oh-be-joyful Creek Falls" in a gorge to the left. Consult *Hiking Waterfalls Colorado* (FalconGuides 2022) for more waterfall details. The next section slowly ascends a wide, flower-filled valley flanked by high peaks and ridges before scrambling through thick forest into a basin. The final segment zigzags up grassy slopes to the shimmering alpine lake.

Blue Lake reflects clouds, sky, and high mountains, including Afley Peak and Oh-be-joyful Peak in the Ruby Range.

Blue Lake (Raggeds Wilderness Area)

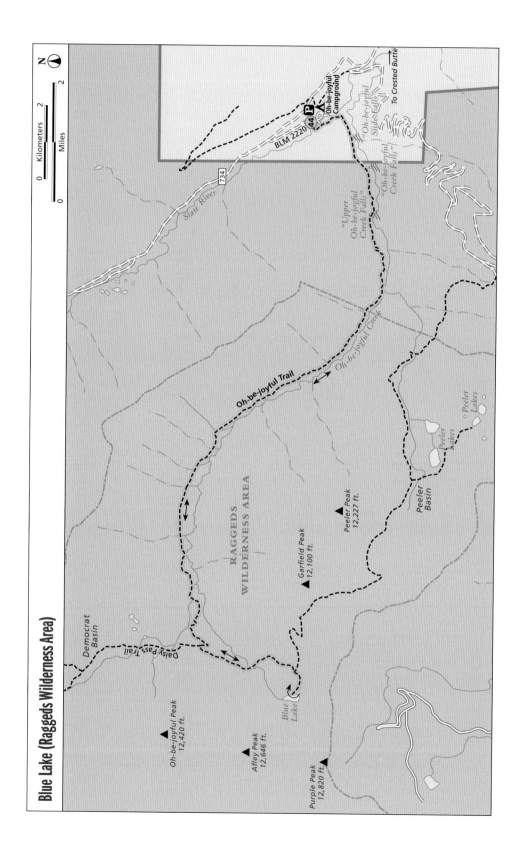

Blue Lake perches on a high bench below Scarf Ridge at the headwaters of Oh-be-joyful Creek.

Miles and Directions

0.0   Start at Oh-be-joyful Trailhead right of restrooms. Descend stairs and follow road to left. Cross bridge over Slate River and bend left. Follow trail south and then west up slope north of creek and waterfalls.

1.10   Arrive at a viewpoint above "Upper Oh-be-joyful Creek Falls" in the gorge on the left (GPS: 38 54.4919, –107 2.7515). Continue on the trail, enter Raggeds Wilderness Area, and follow trail northwest up glaciated valley.

3.5   Pass a large boulder left of the trail (GPS: 38 55.4811, –107 4.5696). This is a good rest stop. Continue up the valley through meadows and woods. The trail climbs out of the valley through thick forest.

5.2   Reach a waterfall and cascade in a ravine right of the trail. Continue uphill on the trail.

5.3   Arrive at a signed junction labeled "Daisy Pass" to the right and "Peeler Basin" to the left (GPS: 38 55.5752, –107 6.2668). Go left on Oh-be-joyful Trail. A right turn climbs to Democrat Basin. The trail bends left and slowly climbs into a basin at treeline.

5.8   Cross Oh-be-joyful Creek and hike up glacier-polished rock. Climb through a grove of spruce trees and reach a clump of trees (GPS: 38 54.9921, –107 6.4253).

6.2   Begin hiking the steep trail up grassy slopes, steadily traversing up right.

6.5   Arrive at the eastern shore of Blue Lake (GPS: 38 54.9787, –107 6.6655). Rest here or follow a rough path around the lake. Return down the trail.

13.0   Arrive back at the trailhead (GPS: 38 54.8827, –107 1.9807).

45 Lost Lake Slough, Lost Lake, and Dollar Lake

The Three Lakes Trail is a loop hike that passes three gorgeous lakes—Lost Lake Slough, Lost Lake, and Dollar Lake—below East Beckwith Peak on the northern edge of the West Elk Mountains.

Start: Three Lakes Trailhead at the parking lot west of Lost Lake Slough
Difficulty: Moderate
Trails: Three Lakes Trail (#843), Dollar Lake Trail
Hiking time: 1.5 to 3 hours
Distance: 3.4 miles loop
Elevation trailhead to lake: 9,612 to 10,030 feet at Dollar Lake (+418 feet)
Restrictions: Open daily; leashed dogs allowed; no mountain bikes; trail is inaccessible in winter since access roads are closed Nov to May; call (970) 641-0044 for closure dates

Amenities: Trailhead toilets; camping at Lost Lake Campground; picnic area at trailhead; services in Crested Butte
Maps: *DeLorme*: Page 57, B8; Trails Illustrated 133: Kebler Pass, Paonia Reservoir; USGS Anthracite Range
County: Gunnison
Land status: Gunnison National Forest, (970) 874-6600; Paonia Ranger District, (970) 527-4131

Finding the trailhead: From Crested Butte, drive west on the Kebler Pass Road/CR 12 for about 16 miles to FR 706. Turn left or south and follow narrow FR 706 for 2 miles to Lost Lake Campground and the road's end. From Paonia, drive east on CO 133 for 15 miles and turn right on the Kebler Pass Road/CR 12. Follow the dirt road east for 14.5 miles to FR #706 and turn right or south and drive 2 miles to Lost Lake Campground. Go right at Lost Lake Slough and follow a dirt road to a hikers' parking lot, picnic area, and the signed trailhead (GPS: 38 52.1412, –107 12.7169).

The Hike

The Three Lakes Trail passes three lakes nestled against the northern flank of 12,432-foot East Beckwith Peak in the West Elk Mountains. The family-friendly hike, gaining 565 feet of elevation, has gentle grades, is easy to follow, and offers spacious views of the Anthracite and Ruby Ranges. West of Crested Butte, the popular trail is best from mid-July to early August when wildflowers splotch meadows and late September when quaking aspen brush gold across the mountainsides.

Start at the signed trailhead on the west side of 9,623-foot Lost Lake Slough, a storage reservoir that reflects clouds and sky, and hike south for 0.6 mile across conifer-clad hillsides to the northeast shore of 9,870-foot Lost Lake. Hike along the lake's east shore and dip into a valley. A short trail goes right for 125 feet to "Lost Lake Falls," a three-tiered waterfall on Middle Creek. Return to the trail and bend

Golden aspens line Lost Lake Slough on the Three Lakes Trail.

Dollar Lake nestles among rocky moraines on the east flank of East Beckwith Peak.

Marcellina Mountain and The Raggeds tower beyond Lost Lake Slough from the Three Lakes Trail.

east across a wooded hillside. An open talus slope offers great views of 11,438-foot Marcellina Mountain to the northwest. Continue to a junction and go right on short Dollar Lake Trail to a lovely spring-fed pond tucked in a wooded hollow at 10,030 feet. It's a good place for a snack stop. Return to the junction and head north on Three Lakes Trail, which descends to the east side of 10-acre Lost Lake Slough. Cross the lake's outlet stream and follow the dirt campground road on its north shore west to the trailhead. This last section offers a perfect photo op of East Beckwith Peak reflected in the still lake.

Miles and Directions

0.0 Start at the Three Lakes Trailhead on the west side of the parking lot west of Lost Lake Campground and Lost Lake Slough. Hike south on the marked Three Lakes Trail (#843).

0.2 Reach a junction. Go straight on the marked trail.

0.6 Reach the northeast shore of Lost Lake (GPS: 38 51.7852, -107 12.5834).

0.9 Reach a junction at a creek. A trail heads right for 125 feet to "Lost Lake Falls."

1.2 Trail crosses a talus slope with views north of Lost Lake Slough and Marcellina Mountain.

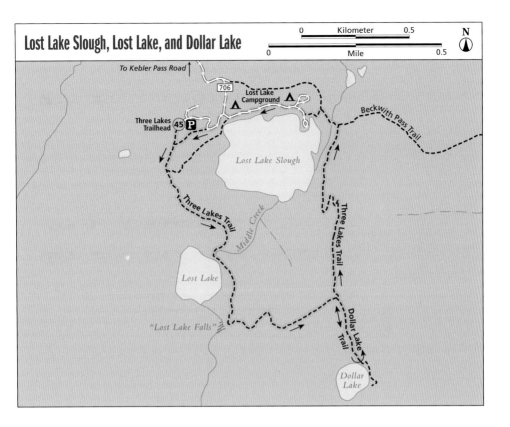

Lost Lake Slough, Lost Lake, and Dollar Lake

1.4 Reach a T-junction with Dollar Lake Trail (GPS: 38 51.679, –107 12.1638). Go right and hike 0.2 mile south to Dollar Lake.

1.6 Reach Dollar Lake (GPS: 38 51.51, –107 12.082). After admiring the view, turn around and hike north on Dollar Lake Trail.

1.8 Reach junction with Three Lakes Trail. Go straight and hike downhill.

2.4 Trail reaches the eastern edge of Lost Lake Slough.

2.6 Junction with Beckwith Pass Trail (#842). Keep left on Three Lakes Trail.

2.8 Reach the east loop road for Lost Lake Campground (GPS: 38 52.1904, –107 12.3039). Go left and hike west on the shoulder of the gravel road alongside the north shore of Lost Lake Slough.

3.1 Go left on the Horse Campground loop road (the road goes to the trailhead).

3.2 When the road bends right, go left on an unmarked trail under a large spruce tree (GPS: 38 52.1298, –107 12.6197) and hike west.

3.3 Reach a T-junction with Three Lakes Trail (GPS: 38 52.0928, –107 12.7308). Go right to return to the trailhead

3.4 Arrive back at the trailhead (GPS: 38 52.1412, –107 12.7169).

46 Crystal Reservoir (Curecanti)

Scenic Mesa Creek Trail crosses a bridge over the Gunnison River below Morrow Point Dam in Curecanti National Recreation Area and threads along the rocky north bank of Crystal Reservoir to high cliffs at trail's end.

Start: Mesa Creek Trailhead
Difficulty: Moderate
Trail: Mesa Creek Trail
Hiking time: About 1 hour
Distance: 1.4 miles out-and-back
Elevation trailhead to lake: 6,800 to 6,755 feet at trail's end (-45 feet)
Restrictions: Fee area; leashed dogs allowed; sudden high water releases from dam; strong currents

Amenities: Trailhead toilets; Cimarron Campground in Cimarron; narrow-gauge railroad exhibit near parking lot; services in Montrose; limited services in Cimarron
Maps: DeLorme: Page 67, A5; Trails Illustrated 245: Black Canyon of the Gunnison National Park Map, Curecanti National Recreation Area; USGS Cimarron
County: Montrose
Land status: Curecanti National Recreation Area, (970) 641-2337 x205

Finding the trailhead: From the junction of Townsend Avenue and Main Street in downtown Montrose, drive east for 19.3 miles to Cimarron. Turn left (north) on Morrow Point Dam Road and drive 1.2 miles to a parking area and the trailhead at road's end (GPS: 38 27.165, -105 32.6683).

The Hike

Crystal Reservoir, lying in 43,095-acre Curecanti National Recreation Area, is a 6-mile-long finger lake hidden in the upper Black Canyon of the Gunnison River. The reservoir, surrounded by steep slopes and cliffs, is part of a ladder of three lakes in the Bureau of Reclamation's Upper Colorado River Storage Project, storing water and providing hydroelectric power.

This short hike on Mesa Creek Trail along the lake's upper section provides dramatic views of the narrow canyon, passes a waterfall, and offers wildlife and solitude. The trail, given a moderate rating for rocky sections, passes the mouths of the Cimarron River and Mesa Creek. The trail ends when it meets a sheer cliff that dives into the lake. After the hike, visit a kiosk with interpretive panels by the parking lot that overlooks 468-foot Morrow Point Dam, a narrow-gauge railroad exhibit beside the access road, and a visitor center in Cimarron. A park campground is also in Cimarron.

Start by descending the wide trail to a service road alongside the river below the dam. Cross a footbridge over the Gunnison River and follow the trail along the river's north bank and the uppermost section of glassy Crystal Reservoir. The trail passes a side path that leads to a tumbling waterfall in a side canyon and a picnic table above

Beginning below Morrow Point Dam, Mesa Creek Trail follows the north bank of Crystal Reservoir.

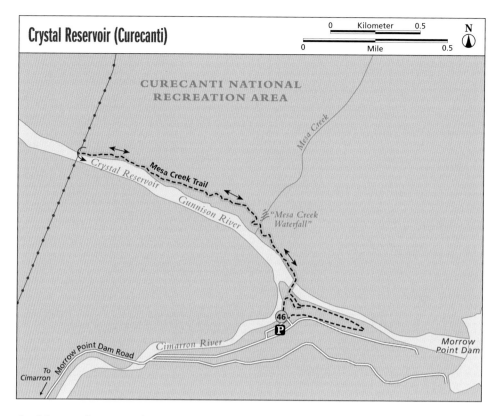

the lake. Farther west the trail passes beneath ponderosa pines and a soaring cliff before gently descending to the hike's turnaround point where water meets granite.

Miles and Directions

0.0 Start at the trailhead on the west side of the parking lot. Descend north on the trail.

0.1 Reach a junction with a service road. Go left on the road.

0.25 Arrive at a bridge across the Gunnison River. Cross bridge to the north bank and hike west.

0.35 Reach a junction on the right for a short trail to "Mesa Creek Falls" (GPS: 38 27.3359, –107 32.7308). Continue west on main trail.

0.7 Reach the trail's end at a cliff that dives into the lake (GPS: 38 27.4339, –107 33.1102). Turn around and retrace trail east.

1.15 Arrive at north side of the bridge. Cross and go left on service road.

1.4 Arrive back at the trailhead (GPS: 38 27.165, –105 32.6683).

47 Cobbett Lake

The family-friendly Cobbett Lake Trail loops around the shoreline of a small lake north of the Grand Mesa Visitor Center.

Start: Cobbett Lake Trailhead
Difficulty: Easy
Trail: Cobbett Lake Trail #747
Hiking time: About 30 minutes
Distance: 0.5 mile loop
Elevation trailhead to lake: 10,210 feet at trailhead and lake
Restrictions: Hikers only; leashed dogs only; do not walk through campsites if occupied

Amenities: Restrooms at visitor center; Cobbett Lake Campground; services in Grand Junction and Cedaredge
Maps: *DeLorme*: Page 44, E2; Trails Illustrated 136: Grand Mesa; USGS Grand Mesa
County: Delta
Land status: Grand Mesa National Forest; Grand Valley Ranger District, (970) 242-8211; Grand Mesa Visitor Center, (970) 856-4153

Finding the trailhead: From I-70, take exit 49 and drive southeast on CO 65/Grand Mesa Scenic Byway for 34.4 miles to the trailhead on Baron Lake Drive/FR 121 at the Grand Mesa Visitor Center (GPS: 39 2.4068, -107 59.1868). The Cobbett Lake Trailhead and parking lot are on the north side of the road across from the visitor center.

From Cedaredge, drive north on CO 65 for 16.1 miles to trailhead and visitor center. Alternatively, park at the visitor center rather than the lakeside lot.

The Hike

The Cobbett Lake Trail circles Cobbett Lake, formerly called Carp Lake, alongside Grand Mesa Scenic Byway and opposite the Grand Mesa Visitor Center. The easy hike is perfect for a scenic stroll after stopping at the visitor center to see interpretive displays.

Start at a parking lot on the south side of Cobbett Lake. This description makes a counterclockwise circuit around the lake. Go right through a picnic area and hike northeast along the eastern shoreline. This section connects Cobbett Lake Campground with the visitor center. At the lake's northeast corner, reach a junction with a trail that connects to Ward Lake. Bend northwest and hike between the lake and campground.

Past the campground, meet FR 120. The hike's second half follows a less-defined trail around the west shoreline. Walk the road's edge and then dip back to the shore. Follow the path along the lakeshore below CO 65 to the parking lot's west side.

Grand Mesa Lakes

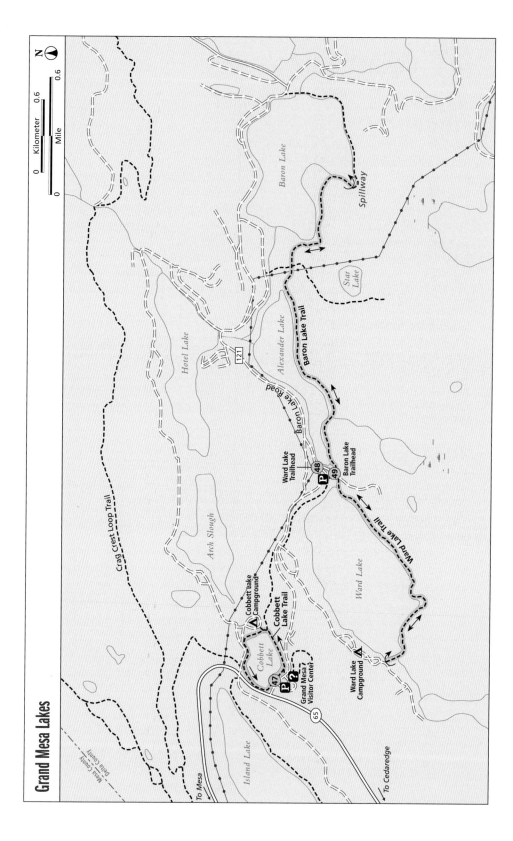

Spruce trees frame Cobbett Lake on Grand Mesa.

Miles and Directions

0.0 Start at the trailhead sign on the east side of the parking lot. The return trailhead is on the lot's west side. Follow the trail east past picnic tables.

0.15 Trail turns northeast and follows the shore of Cobbett Lake.

0.2 Reach junction with Cobbett to Ward Trail (#746) on right (GPS: 39 2.4404, –107 59.0212). Continue left on main trail to campground. Follow the trail close to the lakeshore to avoid walking through campsites.

0.25 Continue northwest along lake to FR 120. Keep on left side of road.

0.3 Leave the road and follow the trail through grass on the lake's northern edge, climb through boulders, and head south on the western shoreline.

0.5 Arrive back at the trailhead on the west side of the parking lot (GPS: 39 2.4286, –107 59.2178).

48 Ward Lake

The Ward Lake Trail, one of Grand Mesa's best wildflower hikes, edges through forest and meadows along the lake's south shore to an earthen dam and campground.

See map on page 178.
Start: Ward Lake Trailhead
Difficulty: Easy
Trail: Ward Lake Trail #744
Hiking time: About 1 hour
Distance: 1.8 miles out-and-back
Elevation trailhead to lake: 10,144 to 10,160 feet at high point (+16 feet); 10,110 feet at lake (-34 feet)
Restrictions: Hikers only; leashed dogs only

Amenities: Vault toilet at trailhead; restrooms at visitor center; Ward Lake Campground at lake's west side; services in Grand Junction and Cedaredge
Maps: *DeLorme*: Page 44, E2; Trails Illustrated 136: Grand Mesa; USGS Grand Mesa
County: Delta
Land status: Grand Mesa National Forest; Grand Valley Ranger District, (970) 242-8211; Grand Mesa Visitor Center, (970) 856-4153

Finding the trailhead: From I-70, take exit 49 and drive east and south on CO 65/Grand Mesa Scenic Byway for 34.4 miles to Baron Lake Drive/FR 121 and the Grand Mesa Visitor Center. Turn east and drive 0.9 mile on the dirt road to a sharp right turn on Ward Way/FR 1211E. Keep right and drive 225 feet to a parking lot and the Ward Way Picnic Area (GPS: 39 2.2685, –107 58.4347). The hike starts here but the trailhead is on closed Ward Way. The Baron Lake Trail (Hike 49) also starts here.

From Cedaredge, drive north on CO 65 for 16.1 miles to the trailhead and visitor center and turn right or east on Baron Lake Road. Follow above directions to the trailhead.

The Hike

The Ward Lake Trail is an out-and-back hike from the lake's east inlet to the north side of its dam to the west. The friendly trail has minimal elevation gain, spacious lake views, and one of Grand Mesa's best wildflower displays. For a longer day hike, combine this trail with the Baron Lake Trail, which begins at the same parking lot, for a 4.4-mile round-trip hike. The best hiking months are July through September.

Begin the hike at the parking lot for Ward Way Picnic Area on the east side of Ward Lake. Walk southeast on Ward Way, a closed road, across the tumbling inlet stream to the signed Ward Lake Trailhead. Head right on the twisting trail along the lake's rocky south shoreline. The trail winds through a mature spruce forest. Stop at occasional breaks in the trees for views north across the glassy lake to Crag Crest, a long ridge that forms the spine of Grand Mesa.

After a half-mile, the trail passes beneath a huge talus slope. Look among the boulders at the base for thickets of elegant columbines, the Colorado state flower. The trail eventually reaches a dam that enlarged the lake for water storage. Stroll

Spruce trees frame Ward Lake, the deepest lake on Grand Mesa, on the Ward Lake Trail.

The Ward Lake Trail follows the lake's south shoreline through a mature forest.

Ward Creek riffles over boulders before emptying into placid Ward Lake on Grand Mesa.

across the earthen dam and end the hike at Ward Lake Campground. Follow the trail back to the trailhead and parking lot to complete the hike.

Miles and Directions

0.0 Start on the east side of the Ward Way Picnic Area parking lot east of the lake. Walk southeast on a closed dirt road between Ward and Baron Lakes, passing a gate, to the signed Ward Lake Trailhead on the right.

0.05 Go right on the singletrack trail and follow it along the lake's south shoreline.

0.5 Reach the northern edge of a talus slope. Look for columbines growing among boulders. Continue west along the shoreline.

0.8 Reach the south end of a dam on the west side of Ward Lake. Turn northwest and walk across the top of the dam.

0.9 Arrive at the north end of the dam and Ward Lake Campground (GPS: 39 2.0875, -107 59.1329). Turn around here for the return leg.

1.8 Arrive back at the trailhead (GPS: 39 2.2685, -107 58.4347).

49 Alexander Lake and Baron Lake

The scenic Baron Lake Trail, edging along the shoreline of Alexander and Baron Lakes, offers excellent lake views, solitude, and plenty of wildflowers.

See map on page 178.
Start: Ward Way Picnic Area parking lot near Baron Lake Trailhead
Difficulty: Easy
Trail: Baron Lake Trail #751
Hiking time: 1 to 2 hours
Distance: 2.6 miles out-and-back
Elevation trailhead to lake: 10,144 to 10,145 feet at Alexander Lake; 10,105 feet at Baron Lake (–39 feet)

Restrictions: Hikers only; leashed dogs only
Amenities: Vault toilet at trailhead; restrooms at visitor center; services in Grand Junction and Cedaredge
Maps: *DeLorme*: Page 44, E2; Trails Illustrated 136: Grand Mesa; USGS Grand Mesa
County: Delta
Land status: Grand Mesa National Forest; Grand Valley Ranger District, (970) 242-8211; Grand Mesa Visitor Center, (970) 856-4153

Finding the trailhead: From I-70, take exit 49 and drive east and south on CO 65/Grand Mesa Scenic Byway for 34.4 miles to Baron Lake Drive/FR 121 and the Grand Mesa Visitor Center. Drive 0.9 mile east on the dirt road to a sharp right turn on Ward Way/FR 1211E. Keep right and drive 225 feet to a parking lot and the Ward Way Picnic Area (GPS: 39 2.2685, –107 58.4347). The hike starts here but the trailhead is on closed Ward Way. The Ward Lake Trail (Hike 48) also starts here.

From Cedaredge, drive north on CO 65 for 16.1 miles to the trailhead and visitor center and turn right or east on Baron Lake Road. Follow above directions to trailhead.

The Hike

This hike, following Baron Lake Trail, follows the south and west shorelines of Alexander Lake and Baron Lake to Baron's spillway and an unnamed outlet creek. It's a family-friendly hike with little elevation gain, scenic lake views, and wildflower-strewn meadows in summer. Beginning at a common parking lot, the hike is easily combined with Ward Lake Trail for a 4.4-mile excursion. Best months for hiking are July through September.

Start the hike at the Ward Way Picnic Area's parking lot between Ward and Alexander Lakes. Head southwest on Ward Way, a closed forest road, for 325 feet to the signed Baron Lake Trailhead on the left. Walk east on the narrow path through a mature spruce forest along the south shoreline of long Alexander Lake. A forest road and scattered cabins and Alexander Lake Lodge lie along the lake's northeastern edge and beyond rises rocky Crag Crest. Past the lake, the trail climbs past tall trees to a junction with an old road. Continue southeast across gentle slopes to a broad meadow overlooking Baron Lake.

The next section threads across a wooded peninsula on Baron's western shore before dipping down to meadows along the lake's edge. Finish by following the quiet

Alexander Lake reflects gathering storm clouds beyond Ward Creek, its outlet stream.

Baron Lake placidly stretches beyond sunflowers and cinquefoil along the Baron Lake Trail.

water to a small earthen dam that forms 36-foot-deep Baron Lake. An unnamed stream spills over the northern edge of the dam and drops southwest to Kennicott Slough Reservoir. The spillway is the turnaround point for the hike since the creek can run deep. Return back along Baron Lake Trail to the trailhead for a 2.6-mile, round-trip hike. It's possible to cross the dam and follow a trail east along the lake's south shore to the Old Grand Mesa Road, FR 123, passing a church camp and adding another mile to the hike.

Miles and Directions

0.0 Start on the east side of the Ward Way Picnic Area parking lot east of Ward Lake. Walk southeast for 225 feet on a closed dirt road between Ward and Alexander Lakes, passing a gate, to signed Baron Lake Trailhead on the left (GPS: 39 2.2427, -107 58.4376).

0.05 Go left on the trail and hike east through trees along the south shoreline of Alexander Lake.

0.1 Reach a junction with a social trail on the left at the south end of the lake's dam. Continue straight.

0.8 Pass Alexander Lake and reach a junction with an old road on the left from College Drive to the north (GPS: 39 2.3786, -107 57.6641). Cross the road and continue east on Baron Lake Trail.

0.9 Reach a meadow on the western side of Baron Lake. Head southeast on the trail.

1.3 End at the outlet creek's spillway at the north end of Baron Lake's dam (GPS: 39 2.1989, -107 57.3721). Turn around to return to the trailhead. You can also cross the creek and continue another 0.5 mile past a church camp along Baron Lake's south shore to Old Grand Mesa Road/FR 123.

2.6 Arrive back at the start at the Ward Way Picnic Area and parking lot (GPS: 39 2.2685, -107 58.4347).

50 Crag Crest Trail Lakes

This hike climbs to Crag Crest, a narrow, rocky ridge that offers wildflower-splotched meadows, wildlife, and 360-degree views of many lakes.

Start: Crag Crest West Trailhead
Difficulty: Moderate
Trail: Crag Crest Trail #711
Hiking time: 4 to 6 hours
Distance: 7.6 miles out-and-back
Elevation trailhead to lake: 10,430 to 11,189 feet at Crag Crest high point (+759 feet)
Restrictions: Hikers only on crest; mountain bikers and horses to Cottonwood Lakes Trail junction only; leashed dogs only; check at visitor center for conditions; descend off ridge to avoid lightning; bring mosquito repellent; watch children at cliffs; beware of dropoffs
Amenities: Vault toilet at trailhead; services in Grand Junction and Cedaredge
Maps: *DeLorme:* Page 44, E2; Trails Illustrated 136: Grand Mesa; USGS Grand Mesa; trail map available at Grand Mesa Visitor Center
County: Delta
Land status: Grand Mesa National Forest; Grand Valley Ranger District, (970) 242-8211; Grand Mesa Visitor Center, (970) 856-4153

Finding the trailhead: From I-70, take exit 49 and drive east and south on CO 65/Grand Mesa Scenic Byway for 33.5 miles through Mesa to a marked left turn on FR 131 to Crag Crest West Trailhead.

From Cedaredge to the south, drive 17 miles north on CO 65 to right turn to trailhead (GPS: 39 2.5608, -107 59.8606).

The Hike

Crag Crest National Recreation Trail explores the roof of Grand Mesa, the biggest flattop mountain in the world. The described hike, part of a longer 10.3-mile loop, passes glassy lakes, evergreen forests, and meadows splashed with wildflowers before climbing onto Crag Crest, a rocky, 11,000-foot-high ridge that offers hundred-mile views to the San Juan and West Elk Mountains. Below the ridge stretches Grand Mesa and over 300 lakes. While fourteen lakes are visible south of Crag Crest's 11,189-foot summit, over sixty named lakes hide in hollows below. North of the Crest are more lakes including the five Cottonwood Lakes.

Start at Crag Crest West Trailhead off CO 65 and head northeast through meadows and forests to a junction with Crag Crest Loop Trail, the return leg of the loop hike. Continue past a small, unnamed lake below a talus field. The trail continues up the steep south face of Crag Crest, eventually ending on a wooded plateau. Take a breather and look east at narrow Wolverine Lake in the valley below. Continue east, gradually gaining elevation, until the plateau pinches down to a ridgeline.

The next mile is breathtaking with volcanic cliffs and steep slopes falling away to valleys flanked by glacial moraines. The trail weaves along the ridgetop, passing viewpoints above cliffs to the hike's end at Crag Crest's summit, the last high point

Wolverine Lake fills a narrow valley below Crag Crest on Grand Mesa.

Butts Lake, one of over 300 lakes on Grand Mesa, stretches down a valley below the summit of Crag Crest.

Crag Crest Trail Lakes

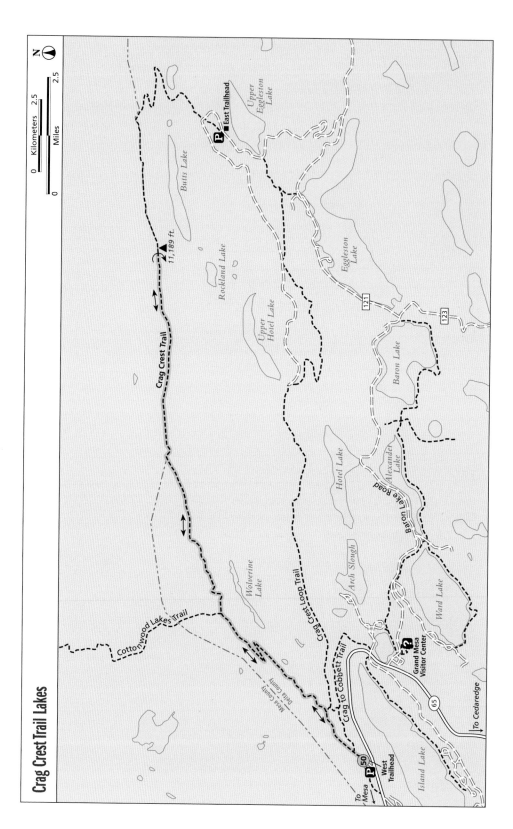

on the ridge before it descends east. Sit on a boulder at the overlook for lunch and views across Grand Mesa to distant mountain ranges. Directly below are Rockland and Butts Lakes. Farther south are more lakes, including Island, Ward, Alexander, and Baron Lakes.

After enjoying the view, reverse your steps back to the trailhead. For a full-value adventure, continue east on Crag Crest Trail to the East Trailhead at Upper Eggleston Lake. Then head west on Crag Crest Loop Trail to the trailhead.

Miles and Directions

0.0 From the parking lot, walk 45 feet on a paved path to the trailhead right of toilets. Keep straight on the trail and hike northwest.

0.05 Reach a junction on the right with Crag to Cobbett Trail #749, a 1-mile trail to Cobbett Lake Campground (GPS: 39 2.5974, –107 59.83). Keep straight.

0.4 Reach a junction with signed Crag Crest Loop Trail #711.1A on right (GPS: 39 2.7661, –107 59.5349). This is the return trail for the 10.3-mile loop hike. Continue straight and hike past a small tarn.

0.8 Stop at the edge of a talus field above an unnamed lake (GPS: 39 2.983, –107 59.2844). Cross the talus and climb the south face of Crag Crest.

0.9 Reach a view east of long, narrow Wolverine Lake at the first switchback.

1.1 Reach the south edge of wide Crag Crest.

1.5 Junction with Cottonwood Lakes Trail #712 (GPS: 39 3.2972, –107 58.9349). Continue northeast on main trail. The next 1.1 miles follows the narrowing ridge through mixed forest. Look for short trails on the right that lead to views.

2.6 Reach the start of the spectacular Crag Crest, a narrow ridge flanked by cliffs (GPS: 39 3.5766, –107 57.8554). Head east along the ridge.

3.8 End the hike at Crag Crest's high point, an overlook on the ridge above two lakes (GPS: 39 3.6397, –107 56.6108). Reach the point by scrambling 20 feet right from trail. Reverse the hike by returning west on the trail to the trailhead.

7.6 Arrive back at the trailhead (GPS: 39 2.5608, –107 59.8606).

EXTRA CREDIT: CRAG CREST LOOP TRAIL

For the 10.3-mile, loop hike, continue 2.7 miles east and south on Crag Crest Trail from the summit to the East Trailhead near Upper Eggleston Lake, then hike 3.4 miles west on Crag Crest Loop Trail to its junction with Crag Crest Trail.

51 Land o' Lakes Trail Lakes

The Land o' Lakes Trail, one of Grand Mesa's best easy hikes, circles out to a dramatic overlook with views of eight lakes tucked onto the wooded mesa.

Start: Land o' Lakes Trailhead
Difficulty: Easy
Trail: Land o' Lakes Trail #713
Hiking time: About 30 minutes
Distance: 0.5 mile loop
Elevation trailhead to lake: 10,745 to 10,825 feet at overlook (+80 feet)
Restrictions: Hikers only; check at visitor center for trail conditions

Amenities: Paved surface; ADA accessible; leashed dogs only; services in Grand Junction and Cedaredge
Maps: *DeLorme*: Page 44, E1; Trails Illustrated 136: Grand Mesa; USGS Mesa Lakes
County: Delta
Land status: Grand Mesa National Forest: Grand Valley Ranger District, (970) 242-8211; Grand Mesa Visitor Center, (970) 856-4153

Finding the trailhead: From I-70, take exit 49 and drive east and south on CO 65/Grand Mesa Scenic Byway for 31.8 miles to a right turn labeled "Land o' Lakes." Follow a short access road to the trailhead (GPS: 39 1.7309, -108 1.2881). From the Grand Mesa Visitor Center, drive northwest on CO 65 for 2.6 miles to the signed trailhead turn.

The Hike

Grand Mesa, the highest flat-topped mountain in the world, is the land of 300 lakes. Glaciers covered the mesa about 20,000 years ago, chiseling rock basins that later became lakes filled with snowmelt. Some were later enlarged with dams for water storage for the thirsty valleys below. The short Land o' Lakes Trail, a loop hike, climbs to an airy overlook that offers views of eight major lakes and distant snowcapped ranges. The trail, paved with asphalt, is wheelchair and stroller accessible, although weather conditions may make it impassable. The best time to hike is between June and October.

Begin at the trailhead on the south side of the parking lot. Walk 20 feet and go left on the trail to a junction. Keep right and follow the easy trail up a slight hill, passing a glassy pond, to the crest of a ridge and a junction with the return trail. Continue along the flat ridge to an overlook on glacier-scraped bedrock. An interpretive sign gives you the names of the jeweled lakes scattered in the forest below. These are, from left to right, Island Lake, Ward Lake, Little Gem Reservoir, Deep Slough Reservoir, Ward Creek Reservoir, January Reservoir, and Scotland Reservoir. Sawtoothed mountain ranges, including the San Juans to the south and the West Elks to the southeast, line the horizon. After enjoying the view, return to the last junction and go right. Follow the path down to the trailhead.

Eight lakes are seen below the Land o' Lakes Overlook on Grand Mesa.

Land o' Lakes Trail ends at a scenic overlook.

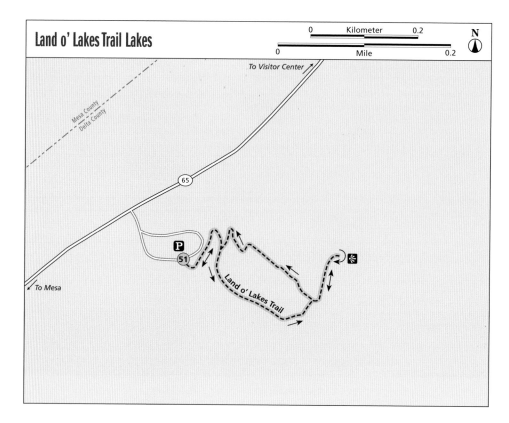

Miles and Directions

0.0 Start at the trailhead on the south side of the parking area and go straight 20 feet on the paved trail. Bend left and follow the trail to a junction past a switchback.

0.05 Keep right at a junction. The left trail is the return loop. Hike southeast past a small tarn.

0.2 Reach a junction. Continue straight and hike northeast along the top of a rocky ridge.

0.25 End at a dramatic overlook with interpretive signs (GPS: 39 1.7434, –108 1.1419).

0.3 Return to the junction. Go right on the return trail and descend northwest.

0.5 Arrive back at the trailhead (GPS: 39 1.7309, –108 1.2881).

52 Mesa Lake Loop

Mesa Lake Shore Trail makes an easy loop hike around Mesa Lake, a horseshoe-shaped lake tucked against rocky slopes at Mesa Lakes Recreation Area on the northwest edge of Grand Mesa.

Start: Glacier Springs Trailhead
Difficulty: Easy
Trail: Mesa Lake Shore Trail #503
Hiking time: About 1 hour
Distance: 1.3 miles loop
Elevations trailhead to lake: 9,858 to 8,850 feet at lake; 9,918 feet at high point above east shore (+60 feet)
Restrictions: Hikers only; leashed dogs only; fee charged at trailhead

Amenities: Vault toilet at trailhead; picnic area; Jumbo Campground; Mesa Lake Lodge (boat rentals); services in Grand Junction
Maps: *DeLorme*: Page 44 E1; Trails Illustrated 136: Grand Mesa; USGS Mesa Lakes
County: Mesa
Land status: Grand Mesa National Forest; Grand Valley Ranger District, (970) 242-8211; Grand Mesa Visitor Center, (970) 856-4153

Finding the trailhead: From I-70, take exit 49 and drive east and south on CO 65/Grand Mesa Scenic Byway for 24.5 miles to a right turn on FR 252 (signed Mesa Lakes Recreation Area) and drive 0.5 mile to Glacier Creek Trailhead (GPS: 39 2.7874, –108 5.4501). From the Grand Mesa Visitor Center, drive northwest on CO 65 for 9.2 miles to the trailhead turnoff.

The Hike

The Mesa Lake Shore Trail offers an easy loop hike around a serene lake surrounded by forest and protected from wind. The trail, one of Grand Mesa's best hikes, is perfect for family treks with a wide surface, gentle grades, and spectacular lake views. Mesa Lake is the largest of the eight Mesa Lakes scattered across a glaciated bench at 9,800 feet. Stop at the historic Mesa Lakes Ranger Station, built in 1941, by Sunset Lake for info about the lakes, trails, and camping.

Begin at Glacier Springs Trailhead and Picnic Ground on the lake's west side and follow the trail north on the west side of a hill above Beaver Lake to Mesa Lakes Picnic Site, a small area with tables and vault toilets on Mesa Lake's northwest arm. Continue hiking along the lake's quiet north and east shorelines, crossing a wide talus field, to moist woods and a boardwalk over the rushing inlet creek. After passing junctions with Lost Lake (see Hike 53) and Glacier Spring Cutoff Trails, finish through tall spruce trees on the lake's south side to the picnic area and trailhead.

The Mesa Lake Shore Trail edges across a talus field on the lake's eastern shore.

A fallen log divides still and choppy water in Mesa Lake.

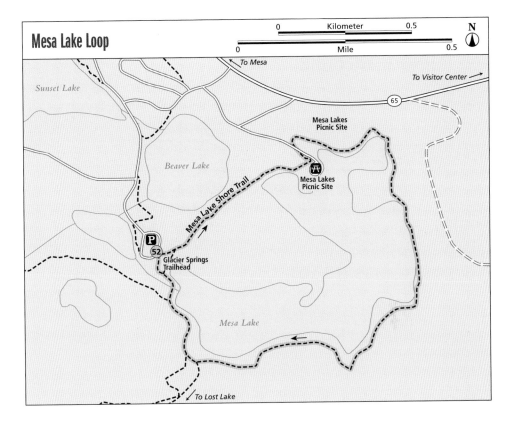

Mesa Lake Loop

Kilometer 0 — 0.5

Mile 0 — 0.5

N

To Mesa

To Visitor Center

Sunset Lake

65

Mesa Lakes
Picnic Site

Beaver Lake

Mesa Lake Shore Trail

Mesa Lakes
Picnic Site

P

52

Glacier Springs
Trailhead

Mesa Lake

To Lost Lake

Miles and Directions

0.0 Start at the signed trailhead right of toilets on the west side of the lake. Go left on a trail below the dam and enter a forest. Pass a sign, "503 Mesa Lake Shore," and hike north across a hillside above Beaver Lake on the left

0.2 Reach a cove on the northwest side of Mesa Lake. Hike northeast to picnic area.

0.25 Arrive at Mesa Lakes Picnic Site and parking lot. Go left and walk west on paved road.

0.3 Go right on marked Mesa Lake Shore Trail (GPS: 39 2.9182, –108 5.2408) and hike east on north shore of lake.

0.4 Reach north end of lake. Follow trail south on east shoreline.

0.5 Cross a large talus field on the good trail on the lake's edge.

0.8 Reach the south end of Mesa Lake and turn west.

1.0 Cross a boardwalk over an inlet creek.

1.1 Reach a junction with Lost Lake Trail #502 on the left (GPS: 39 2.6581, –108 5.3855). Continue straight on the main trail on southwest side of Mesa Lake.

1.3 Arrive back at the trailhead (GPS: 39 2.7874, –108 5.4501).

53 Mesa Lake, South Mesa Lake, and Lost Lake

The Lost Lake Trail climbs past Mesa Lake and South Mesa Lake to Lost Lake, a narrow finger lake hidden between rocky ridges below the North Rim of Grand Mesa.

Start: Glacier Springs Trailhead
Difficulty: Moderate
Trails: Mesa Lake Shore Trail #503, Lost Lake Trail #502
Hiking time: 2 to 3 hours
Distance: 2.4 miles out-and-back
Elevations trailhead to lake: 9,858 to 10,125 feet at trail high point (+267 feet)
Restrictions: Hikers only; leashed dogs only; fee charged at trailhead

Amenities: Vault toilet at trailhead; picnic area; Jumbo Campground; Mesa Lake Lodge (boat rentals); services in Grand Junction
Maps: *DeLorme*: Page 44, E1; Trails Illustrated: 136: Grand Mesa; USGS Mesa Lakes
County: Mesa
Land status: Grand Mesa National Forest; Grand Valley Ranger District, (970) 242-8211; Grand Mesa Visitor Center, (970) 856-4153

Finding the trailhead: From I-70, take exit 49 and drive east and south on CO 65/Grand Mesa Scenic Byway for 24.5 miles to a right turn on FR 252 (signed Mesa Lakes Recreation Area) and drive 0.5 mile to Glacier Creek Trailhead (GPS: 39 2.7874, -108 5.4501). From the Grand Mesa Visitor Center, drive northwest on CO 65 for 9.2 miles to the trailhead turn.

The Hike

The Lost Lake Trail, gaining 425 feet of elevation round-trip, is a fun hike that twists past three lakes—Mesa, South Mesa, and Lost Lakes. The trail is best from June through October since snowdrifts, especially in the spring, block the upper section. Plan on bringing insect repellent since mosquitos are buzzing in summer. The hiker-only trail is easy to follow with a dirt and rock surface, directional signs, and only two steep sections. Despite being in the popular Mesa Lakes Recreation Area, the trail offers solitude and privacy with few other hikers.

Start your adventure at Glacier Springs Trailhead on the west side of Mesa Lake. Hike east along the lake's south shore on Mesa Lake Shore Trail to a junction with Lost Lake Trail. Turn right and follow Lost Lake Trail through damp woods to the stony north shore of South Mesa Lake, a glacial tarn surrounded by spruce trees and talus slopes. Step along the lake's north shore and then make two long switchbacks up a wooded slope to the trail's high point on a rocky ridge. Descend the trail to the northern edge of Lost Lake, a shimmering 0.25-mile-long lake squeezed between steep talus slopes below cliffs on Grand Mesa's North Rim. After enjoying the view, return to Mesa Lake.

Steep talus slopes surround narrow Lost Lake below Grand Mesa's North Rim.

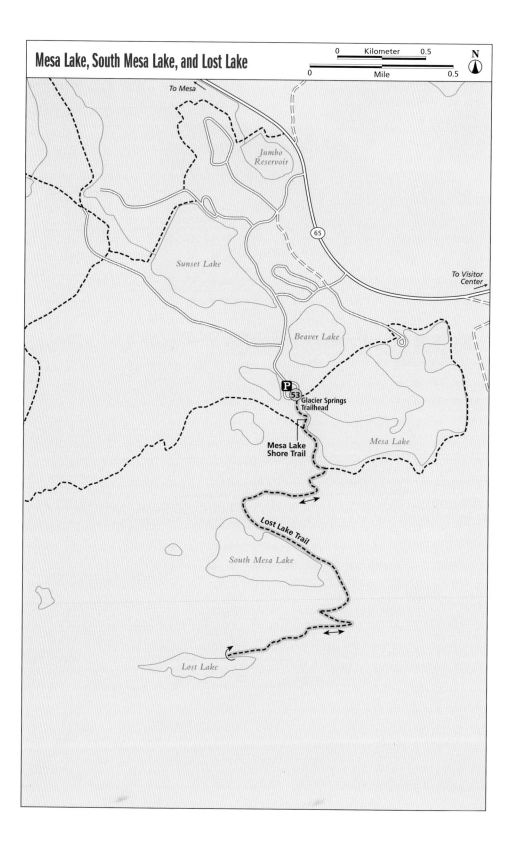

Mesa Lake, South Mesa Lake, and Lost Lake

Kilometer

0   0.5

Mile

0   0.5

N

To Mesa

Jumbo Reservoir

65

To Visitor Center

Sunset Lake

Beaver Lake

P

53

Glacier Springs Trailhead

Mesa Lake Shore Trail

Mesa Lake

Lost Lake Trail

South Mesa Lake

Lost Lake

Rocky slopes drop sharply into Lost Lake, a hidden gem tucked between glacial ridges.

Miles and Directions

0.0 Begin at the signed Glacier Springs Trailhead for Mesa Lake Shore Trail on the west side of Mesa Lake and right of toilets. Go right on the paved trail and hike east through a picnic area past a junction with Deep Creek Cutoff Trail.

0.2 Walk along Mesa Lake's south shore to a wooded junction with Lost Lake Trail on the right (GPS: 39 2.6581, –108 5.3855). Go right and hike southwest past ponds.

0.3 Reach the north shoreline of South Mesa Lake (GPS: 39 2.5483, –108 5.5213). Continue southeast along the lakeshore.

0.7 Begin climbing a rocky, wooded slope east of the lake.

1.0 Reach the trail's high point on a glacial ridge and descend southeast.

1.2 Arrive at the west side of Lost Lake (GPS: 39 2.321, –108 5.6066). Return the way you came.

2.4 Arrive back at the trailhead (GPS: 39 2.7874, –108 5.4501).

EXTRA CREDIT: MESA LAKE SHORE

On the return hike, go right on Mesa Lake Shore Trail to add another 1.1 miles to the hike.

54 Highline Lake

Highline Lake and nearby Mack Mesa Lake lie in the arid Grand Valley west of Grand Junction. Explore the lakes on a long hike over hills and past wetlands.

Start: Highline Lake Trailhead by east boat ramp
Difficulty: Moderate
Trails: Highline Lake Trail, East Bluffs Loop Trail, Eagle Loop Trail
Hiking time: About 2.5 hours
Distance: 4.0 miles loop
Elevation trailhead to lake: 4,714 to 4,695 feet at lake
Restrictions: Fee area; leashed dogs allowed

Amenities: Vault toilets; water at visitor center; park campground; picnic areas; services in Fruita and Grand Junction
Maps: *DeLorme:* Page 42, C2; Trails Illustrated none; USGS Highline Lake; Highline Lake State Park map
County: Mesa
Land status: Highline Lake State Park, (970) 858-7208

Finding the trailhead: Drive west from Grand Junction on I-70 to exit 15. Turn north on CO 139 and drive 4 miles to Q Road, passing through Loma. Turn left on Q Road and drive west for 1.2 miles to 11 8/10 Road. Turn right and drive north 1 mile to Highline Park's east entrance. Pass through the fee station and park at the north end of a parking lot. The trailhead is right of the east boat ramp inspection shack (GPS: 39 16.3016. -108 50.1788).

The Hike

Highline Lake State Park is a verdant oasis with two reservoirs—160-acre Highline Lake and 14-acre Mack Mesa Lake—in the Grand Valley near the Utah border. Highline Lake offers water sports like swimming, standup paddling, and waterskiing as well as mountain biking and hiking on seven trails. The lake's wakeless northern part is renowned as one of the best bird-watching areas in the Grand Valley, boasting over 200 bird species including waterfowl, shorebirds, songbirds, and raptors. The lake's southern part is like a city park with mowed lawns, shady cottonwoods, picnic tables, and campsites. The lake stays full through summer with Colorado River water from the Highline Canal.

This hike, circumnavigating Highline Lake, follows three trails over dry hills dominated by saltbush on the lake's east side and passes wetlands filled with cattails along the north shore. Four short trails on the north head to blinds for bird observation. The Highline Lake Trail is wide and well traveled, while the East Bluffs Loop and Eagle Loop Trails are twisting, singletrack affairs. Shaded tables along the hike make perfect picnic spots.

Begin beside the boat inspection shack by the east boat ramp and hike north on Highline Lake Trail, crossing a bridge over the inlet stream, to a junction. Keep left on winding East Bluffs Loop Trail, a scenic track used by bikers that offers great

Twisting across dry slopes, the East Bluffs Loop Trail offers views across Highline Lake to the Roan Cliffs.

The East Bluffs Loop Trail winds along bluff-tops on the eastern edge of Highline Lake.

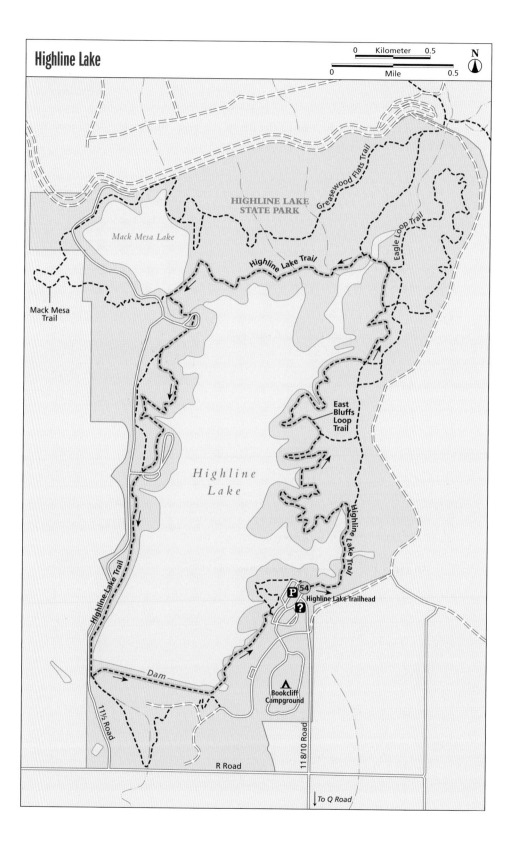

Highline Lake

HIGHLINE LAKE
STATE PARK

GreaseWood Flats Trail

Eagle Loop Trail

Mack Mesa Lake

Highline Lake Trail

Mack Mesa
Trail

East
Bluffs
Loop
Trail

*Highline
Lake*

Highline Lake Trail

Highline Lake Trail

54

P

Highline Lake Trailhead

?

Dam

Bookcliff
Campground

11½ Road

118/10 Road

R Road

To Q Road

0   Kilometer   0.5

0   Mile   0.5

N

views from the bluff tops. Farther north, turn left on Eagle Loop Trail and hike to Highline Lake Trail, which heads west along the north shore to Mack Mesa Lake. The last hike section crosses a couple access roads, passes the west boat ramp, and threads along the shoreline to the dam. Past the dam, jog left across a bridge over the spillway and follow the dam east to the developed area. Finish on a paved path by a swim beach and grassy slopes to the parking lot.

Miles and Directions

0.0 Start at the Highline Lake Trailhead right of the boat inspection shack and north of the visitor center. Hike north on Highline Lake Trail marked with blue posts.

0.3 Cross a bridge over the inlet stream and reach a Y-junction (GPS: 39 16.4461, –108 50.0777). Go left on singletrack East Bluffs Loop Trail (yellow posts) and follow the trail on bluffs east of the lake.

1.0 Reach a junction with a connector trail that goes right to Highline Lake Trail. Go left on East Bluffs Loop.

1.5 Arrive at a junction with Eagle Loop Trail (GPS: 39 16.8256, –108 49.9944). Turn left on Eagle Loop Trail (green posts) and hike north.

1.7 Reach a junction with the connector trail on the right. Keep left on Eagle Loop Trail.

1.8 Reach a junction with Highline Lake Trail (GPS: 39 16.901, –108 49.9822). Go left on Highline Lake Trail and hike west across the north end of the lake.

1.85 Pass a left turn to a wildlife blind and a junction with Greasewood Flats Trail on the right. Continue west past three left turns to wildlife blinds.

2.4 Cross the dam for Mack Mesa Lake to its south end. Turn left on Highline Lake Trail (GPS: 39 16.8457, –108 50.5264) and hike southeast. Don't go straight to parking lot.

2.5 Cross a road, turn right, and recross the road again. Continue southwest above the lake's western shore.

2.9 Reach a restroom and the west boat ramp. Hike south on a slope west of the ramp and cross the ramp road. Continue south along the lake's edge.

3.45 Get to 11½ Road and walk along its east edge past the dam.

3.5 Arrive at a left turn on Highline Lake Trail below the dam (GPS: 39 16.1329, –108 50.7167). Cross a bridge over the spillway and climb onto the dam. Hike east on the dam.

3.8 Reach the dam's east end. Go left on the trail by the lake. Trail becomes concrete and passes a swim beach. Continue northeast on the trail to restrooms.

4.0 Finish at the trailhead on the south end of the parking lot opposite the visitor center (GPS: 39 16.2526, –108 50.2642).

Northwestern Colorado

Meeker, Glenwood Springs, Vail, and Steamboat Springs

An unbroken wall of cliffs and talus rise above a placid cove at Big Fish Lake.

55 Skinny Fish Lake

Skinny Fish Lake spreads a scalloped shoreline lined with spruce trees in a broad, glacier-sculpted cirque below the Chinese Wall, a towering rampart of cliffs and scree fields in the Flat Tops Wilderness Area.

Start: Skinny Fish Trailhead
Difficulty: Moderate
Trail: Skinny Fish Trail #1813
Hiking time: About 3 hours
Distance: 5.2 miles out-and-back
Elevation trailhead to falls viewpoints: 9,240 to 10,192 feet at lake (+952 feet)
Restrictions: Observe wilderness regulations; no camping within 100 feet of lakes, streams, and trails; no motorized vehicles or equipment; dogs must be under control
Amenities: None; services in Meeker and Yampa
Maps: *DeLorme*: Page 25, E8; Trails Illustrated 150: Flat Tops North; USGS Devils Causeway
County: Garfield
Land status: Flat Tops Wilderness Area; White River National Forest, (970) 945-2521; Blanco Ranger District, (970) 878-4039

Finding the trailhead: From Meeker, drive northeast on CO 13 for 1 mile and turn right on Rio Blanco CR 8. Drive east up the North Fork of the White River valley for 39 miles. Turn right on Trappers Lake Road/FR 205 and drive 6.4 miles to the trailhead on the left (GPS: 40 0.9872, -107 14.2874). Alternatively, the trailhead is reached on Flat Tops Trail Scenic Byway from Yampa on CO 131. This 47-mile route follows dirt roads. Allow 2.5 hours to drive from Yampa to the trailhead.

The Hike

Beginning at a trailhead on Trappers Lake Road, a moderate trail climbs to Skinny Fish Lake, a glassy lake below the ragged rim of the Chinese Wall. This abrupt, west-facing escarpment, composed of basalt cliffs, rims the western edge of a high, upland plateau aptly named the Flat Tops. Spacious Skinny Fish Lake and neighboring McGinnis Lake, two of 110 lakes in the Flat Tops, nestle in a broad bowl carved by glaciers.

The Skinny Fish Trail gains over 1,100 feet of cumulative elevation, is easy to follow, has gentle grades, and offers spectacular mountain views. The hike's middle section passes through an area that burned in the Big Fish Fire in 2002, which torched over 17,000 acres around Trappers Lake. However, the Skinny Fish Trail was largely spared destruction by flame and the lakeshore was untouched. The trail now traverses through burned areas that are slowly regenerating with aspen saplings and young spruce among toppled deadfall. Wildflowers, including masses of columbine, blanket the hillsides in summer. After visiting Skinny Fish Lake, hikers can continue to McGinnis Lake, a smaller, spruce-lined tarn that reflects cliffs and sky, and then return on McGinnis Lake Trail to the main path.

Skinny Fish Lake

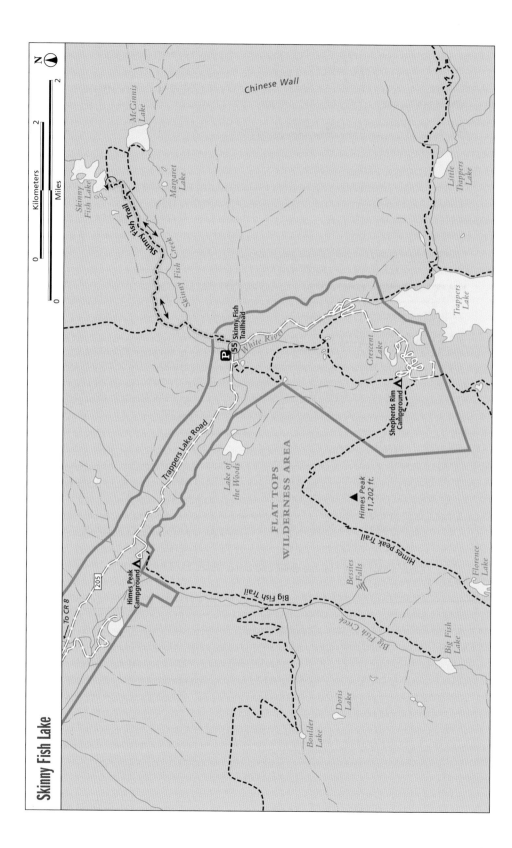

Chinese Wall

McGinnis Lake

Skinny Fish Lake

Margaret Lake

Skinny Fish Trail

Skinny Fish Trail

Skinny Fish Creek

Little Trappers Lake

Skinny Fish Trailhead

55

P

White River

Trappers Lake

Crescent Lake

Trappers Lake Road

Shepherds Rim Campground

FLAT TOPS WILDERNESS AREA

Lake of the Woods

Himes Peak 11,202 ft.

Himes Peak Trail

205

To CR 8

Himes Peak Campground

Bessies Falls

Big Fish Trail

Big Fish Creek

Florence Lake

Doris Lake

Big Fish Lake

Boulder Lake

N

Kilometers
0   2

Miles
0   2

The Chinese Wall rises beyond Skinny Fish Lake in the Flat Tops Wilderness Area.

Miles and Directions

0.0   Start at Skinny Fish Trailhead. Hike steadily up grassy slopes to an aspen and spruce forest.

0.3   Enter the Flat Tops Wilderness Area in an aspen grove. Continue uphill through meadows to Skinny Fish Creek.

0.5   Cross a footbridge over the creek and climb slopes to open meadows.

0.9   Reach a signed junction with Lost Lake Trail (#1812) on the left (GPS: 40 1.5323, -107 14.0611). Continue straight and hike east over rounded ridges covered with deadfall and across side creeks.

2.0   Reach a signed junction with McGinnis Lake Trail (#2213) on the right (GPS: 40 1.7693, -107 12.9151). Continue straight and gradually ascend a long slope to a spruce forest.

2.6   Arrive at the southwest shore of Skinny Fish Lake (GPS: 40 1.93, -107 12.7458). Turn around here and return on Skinny Fish Trail. (***Option:*** From lake, go right on the trail for 0.6 mile to McGinnis Lake, then return to main trail on 0.7-mile McGinnis Lake Trail for a two-lake hike.)

5.2   Arrive back at the trailhead (GPS: 40 0.9872, -107 14.2874).

56 Little Trappers Lake and Coffin Lake

Two gleaming tarns—Little Trappers Lake and Coffin Lake—lie cupped in a wide amphitheater below the Chinese Wall in the heart of the Flat Tops Wilderness Area, one of Colorado's first designated wilderness areas.

Start: Outlet Trailhead
Difficulty: Moderate
Trails: Outlet Trail #1815.1, Carhart Trail #1815, Little Trappers Lake Trail #1814
Hiking time: About 2 hours
Distance: 3.4 miles out-and-back
Elevation trailhead to lake: 9,600 to 9,705 feet at Coffin Lake; 9,926 feet at Little Trappers Lake (+326 feet)
Restrictions: Observe wilderness regulations; no bicycles or motorized vehicles in wilderness area; leashed dogs only; dispose of human waste properly
Amenities: Vault toilets at trailhead; backcountry camping; services in Meeker
Maps: *DeLorme*: Page 35, A8; Trails Illustrated 150: Flat Tops North; USGS Trappers Lake
County: Garfield
Land status: Flat Tops Wilderness Area; White River National Forest, (970) 945-2521; Blanco Ranger District, (970) 878-4039

Finding the trailhead: From Meeker, drive northeast on CO 13 for 1 mile and turn right on Rio Blanco CR 8. Drive east up the North Fork of the White River valley for 39 miles. Turn right on Trappers Lake Road/FR 205 and drive 8 miles to the Outlet Trailhead at the end of the road (GPS: 39 59.932, -107 13.8512). Alternatively, reach the trailhead on Flat Tops Trail Scenic Byway from Yampa on CO 131. This 47-mile route follows dirt roads. Allow 2.5 hours to drive from Yampa to the trailhead.

The Hike

Two glacial lakes, Little Trappers Lake and Coffin Lake, nestle along Cabin Creek in a broad valley west of 180-foot-deep Trappers Lake, the second-largest natural lake in Colorado. A pleasant hike on three trails reaches the lakes, offering gentle grades, minimal elevation gain, and stunning lake and mountain views. A gorgeous old-growth spruce, fir, and lodgepole pine forest covered the area until July 2002, when a lightning strike started the Big Fish Fire. The fire torched 17,056 acres in the Flat Tops Wilderness Area and the surrounding mountains. The hike treks through the burned area, passing deadfall, standing snags, and grassy meadows. Colorful wildflowers splotch the open meadows in midsummer.

The hike begins at the Outlet Trailhead at the end of Trappers Lake Road past the Trappers Lake Lodge and the turnoff to the Trappers Lake Campgrounds. The hike's first section follows Outlet Trail to Carhart Trail, a footpath that follows the perimeter of Trappers Lake, which leads down the east shoreline to Little Trappers Lake Trail. This trail climbs past Coffin Lake and then follows a rounded ridge to Little Trappers Lake. A short trail section traverses an exposed slope that plunges

Coffin Lake, a small, glacial tarn, shines below fire-ravaged trees and deadfall in the Flat Tops Wilderness Area.

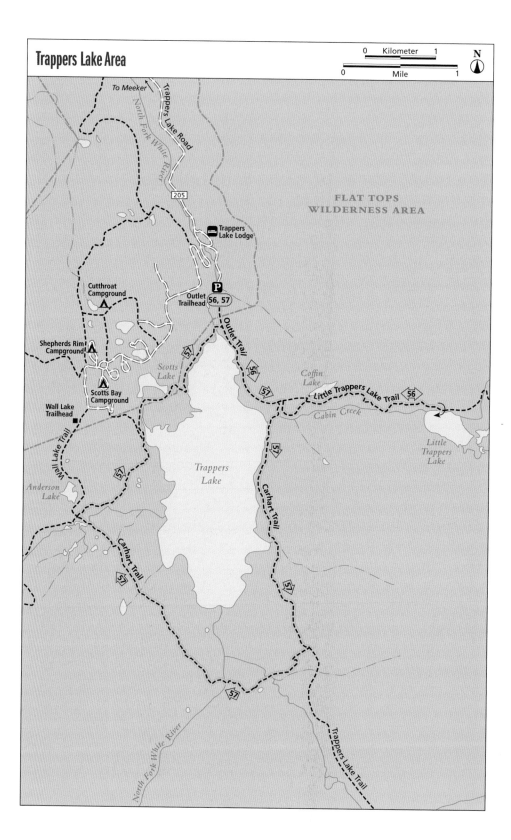

Trappers Lake Area

0 — Kilometer — 1

0 — Mile — 1

N

To Meeker

North Fork White River

Trappers Lake Road

205

**FLAT TOPS
WILDERNESS AREA**

Trappers Lake Lodge

Cutthroat Campground

Outlet Trailhead **P** 56, 57

Shepherds Rim Campground

Scotts Lake

57

56

57

Coffin Lake

Little Trappers Lake Trail 56

Cabin Creek

Little Trappers Lake

Scotts Bay Campground

Wall Lake Trailhead

Wall Lake Trail

Anderson Lake

57

Trappers Lake

57

Carhart Trail

57

Carhart Trail

57

North Fork White River

57

Trappers Lake Trail

Ragged ridges and unnamed peaks on the Chinese Wall rim the sky above Little Trappers Lake.

down to Cabin Creek so watch kids and dogs here. Past the lake, the trail twists up the Chinese Wall for a couple of miles to the Flat Tops, an 11,000-foot upland, and joins the Chinese Wall Trail, which leads north to the mile-long Devils Causeway, a skywalk along an airy ridge above a sheer cliff.

Miles and Directions

0.0 Start at the Outlet Trailhead on the west side of the parking lot. Hike south on the Outlet Trail toward Trappers Lake.

0.1 Enter the Flat Tops Wilderness Area and reach a junction with the Carhart Trail (GPS: 39 59.8131, –107 13.825), which encircles Trappers Lake. Go left on the Carhart Trail and hike along the eastern edge of the lake.

0.4 Pass through a clump of trees and a boulder field. Continue south along the lakeshore.

0.6 Pass an old house by Cabin Creek and reach a signed junction with Little Trappers Lake Trail on the left (GPS: 39 59.482, –107 13.513). Go left on the narrow trail and hike east on the north side of Cabin Creek with gentle ups and downs. Look east for great views of the Chinese Wall, a towering escarpment on the east side of the wide basin.

0.85 Reach a side trail on the left (GPS: 39 59.4875, –107 13.3318) that leads 200 feet down to the western end of Coffin Lake (GPS: 39 59.5107, –107 13.3175). Return to the trail and continue east.

1.1 Stop and enjoy views of Coffin Lake to the left and the Chinese Wall straight ahead.

1.3 The narrow trail edges across a steep slope with a dropoff to the creek. Use caution with children and dogs.

1.4 Continue up gentle slopes littered with deadfall from a 2002 wildfire to a view east of Little Trappers Lake nestled in a wide basin below alpine ridges and cliffs.

1.7 Arrive at the north shoreline of Little Trappers Lake (GPS: 39 59.4562, –107 12.5474). Grab a log seat and enjoy the mountain views, then return back on the trails.

3.4 Arrive back at the trailhead (GPS: 39 59.932, –107 13.8512).

57 Trappers Lake

Carhart Trail explores meadows and low hills covered with deadfall on the shoreline of Trappers Lake, the cradle of American wilderness and Colorado's second-largest natural lake, in the Flat Tops Wilderness Area south of Steamboat Springs.

See map on page 210.
Start: Outlet Trailhead
Difficulty: Moderate
Trails: Outlet Trail #1815.1, Carhart Trail #1815
Hiking time: About 3 hours
Distance: 5.5 miles loop
Elevation trailhead to lake: 9,600 to 9,627 feet at lake (+27 feet)
Restrictions: Observe wilderness regulations; no bicycles or motorized vehicles in wilderness area; leashed dogs only; dispose of human waste properly
Amenities: Vault toilets at trailhead; backcountry camping; services in Meeker and Yampa
Maps: *DeLorme*: Page 35 A8; Trails Illustrated 150: Flat Tops North; USGS Trappers Lake
County: Garfield
Land status: Flat Tops Wilderness Area; White River National Forest, (970) 945-2521; Blanco Ranger District, (970) 878-4039

Finding the trailhead: From Meeker, drive northeast on CO 13 for 1 mile and turn right on Rio Blanco CR 8. Drive east up the North Fork of the White River valley for 39 miles. Turn right on Trappers Lake Road/FR 205 and drive 8 miles to the Outlet Trailhead at the end of the road (GPS: 39 59.932, -107 13.8512). Alternatively, reach the trailhead on Flat Tops Trail Scenic Byway from Yampa on CO 131. This 47-mile route follows dirt roads. Allow 2.5 hours to drive from Yampa to the trailhead.

The Hike

Trappers Lake, the second-largest natural lake in Colorado, sprawls across 302 surface acres in a semicircular amphitheater on the northern edge of the Flat Tops Wilderness Area. One of the state's iconic wonders, the 1.5-mile-long lake offers postcard-worthy scenery with horizontal cliff bands lining flat-topped mountains, clumps of unburned old-growth forest, silvered deadfall torched in a wildfire, wide meadows splotched with wildflowers, and the expansive lake reflecting starlight and storm. The remote lake is a popular destination with five campgrounds on its northwest side, the famed Trappers Lake Lodge, nonmotorized boating, and miles of hiking trails that explore the Flat Tops. The area's old-growth forest was devastated by the Big Fish Fire in July 2002 but now lodgepole pine, fir, and spruce are growing back among the fire-charred trees.

Besides being a beauty spot, Trappers Lake was instrumental in the preservation of pristine public lands as wilderness. After the Flat Tops were protected in 1891 as

A row of unnamed peaks tower beyond the eastern shore of Trappers Lake in the Flat Tops Wilderness Area.

the second national forest in the United States, the US Forest Service wanted to turn Trappers Lake into a playground with a road around the lake, lodges, and dude ranches. A landscape architect, Arthur Carhart, was hired to plan the development in 1919. After hiking the lake area, Carhart recommended that the area should be protected as wilderness, writing that Trappers Lake "should be preserved for all time for the people of the Nation and the world." The plans were dropped and in 1929 the lake became the Flat Tops Primitive Area, which became Colorado's third wilderness area in 1975.

The Carhart Trail, named for its savior, is a fabulous hike that encircles Trappers Lake. Signed at all important junctions, the trail has low grades, minimal elevation gain, and yields spectacular views of lake and peaks. It is best to hike clockwise on the trail, heading down the east side of the lake and passing the turnoff to Little Trappers and Coffin Lakes. Several creek crossings on slippery logs are encountered on the trail so trekking poles are advised for balance. Don't attempt to cross if the creeks are running high, especially early in the summer. The first crossing at Cabin Creek is usually the hardest. Enjoy wildflowers and wildlife, including moose, but bring bug repellent to chase mosquitos away. The west hike section also passes Anderson Lake and Scotts Lake.

Miles and Directions

0.0 Start at the Outlet Trailhead on the west side of the parking lot. Hike south on the Outlet Trail toward Trappers Lake.

0.1 Enter the Flat Tops Wilderness Area and reach a junction with the Carhart Trail (GPS: 39 59.8131, –107 13.825), which encircles Trappers Lake. Go left on the Carhart Trail and hike along the lake's eastern edge.

0.6 Pass an old house by Cabin Creek and reach a signed junction with Little Trappers Lake Trail on the left (GPS: 39 59.482, –107 13.513). Keep right on Carhart Trail.

0.7 Cross Cabin Creek on logs. Use caution when the creek is high. Continue south along the east side of Trappers Lake.

1.5 The trail passes a small pond on the left and swings onto a hill with scenic views of peaks to the south, including unnamed points above the cliff-lined Amphitheatre to the southwest.

2.0 Reach the junction with Trappers Lake Trail (#1816) on the left (GPS: 39 58.4351, –107 13.3037). Go right on Carhart Trail and hike southwest along the edge of a wetland.

2.3 Cross logs to the west bank of Fraser Creek and continue west through deadfall past a small pond.

2.6 Reach the North Fork of the White River at the northern edge of an unburned section of trees (GPS: 39 58.2776, –107 13.7735). Cross the river on logs. Hike west and then northwest on the trail across low hills covered with deadfall and occasional clumps of conifers on the southwest side of Trappers Lake.

3.8 Cross a meandering creek on logs and continue northwest.

3.9 Reach a three-way signed junction with Wall Lake Trail (#1818) on the left (GPS: 39 58.9844, –107 14.6508). Go right on the Carhart Trail and hike northeast across hummocks toward Trappers Lake. The left trail goes north for 350 feet to the south edge of Anderson Lake.

4.5 Reach an unsigned fork on the west side of the lake. Keep right and hike north.

4.6 At another junction, keep right on Carhart Trail and hike north along a creek. The left trail goes to a parking lot at Scotts Bay Picnic Site.

4.8 Reach the south end of Scotts Lake and bend right through forest.

5.0 Reach a junction with a trail on the left. Keep right and hike east to the west shore of Trappers Lake. Go left and hike north across meadows along the shoreline, passing a junction on the left with Scotts Lake Trail (#1815.4).

5.35 Reach the North Fork of the White River, the lake's outlet stream (GPS: 39 59.8025, –107 13.8617). Cross a footbridge and hike east.

5.4 Reach the first junction with the start of the Carhart Trail. Go left on Outlet Trail.

5.5 Arrive back at the trailhead (GPS: 39 59.932, –107 13.8512).

58 Big Fish Lake

Big Fish Lake, fed by creeks originating on the north flank of 12,002-foot Trappers Peak, tucks into a cliff-lined cirque surrounded by subalpine forest, burned snags, and grassy meadows.

Start: Big Fish Trailhead
Difficulty: Moderate
Trail: Big Fish Trail #1819
Hiking time: About 3 hours
Distance: 6.2 miles out-and-back
Elevation trailhead to lake: 8,872 to 9,388 feet at lake (+516 feet)
Restrictions: Observe wilderness regulations; no camping within 100 feet of lakes, streams, and trails; no motorized vehicles or equipment; dogs must be under control

Amenities: None; vault toilets at Himes Peak Campground; services at Meeker and Yampa
Maps: *DeLorme*: Page 25, E8 and page 35, A8; Trails Illustrated 150: Flat Tops North; USGS Ripple Creek, Big Marvine Peak
County: Garfield
Land status: Flat Tops Wilderness Area; White River National Forest, (970) 945-2521; Blanco Ranger District, (970) 878-4039

Finding the trailhead: From Meeker, drive northeast on CO 13 for 1 mile and turn right on Rio Blanco CR 8. Drive east up the North Fork of the White River valley for 39 miles. Turn right on Trappers Lake Road/FR 205 and drive 4.3 miles to Himes Peak Campground turn on the right. Follow campground access road down to the signed Big Fish Trailhead at the campground entrance and a parking lot (GPS: 40 1.6597, –107 16.305). Alternatively, the trailhead is reached on Flat Tops Trail Scenic Byway from Yampa on CO 131. This 47-mile route follows dirt roads. Allow 2.5 hours to drive from Yampa to the trailhead.

The Hike

The Big Fish Trail ascends south up a broad, glaciated valley in the Flat Tops Wilderness Area to a glistening lake encircled by high cliffs. Look for wildlife, including moose, elk, beaver, and mule deer, along the trail and around the lake. Past the lake, the trail continues past a junction with the Himes Peak Trail, which leads to Florence Lake and then climbs to a junction with Oyster Lake Trail near Clinard Lake, Twin Lakes, and Star Lake.

The Big Fish Fire, which began in July 2002, severely burned the valley after a lightning strike near Fish Creek Lake ignited deadfall trees. The fire consumed 17,056 acres in the wilderness area, including the Trappers Lake area and the original Trappers Lake Lodge. The hike to the lake passes through the burned area with standing snags, fallen trunks, aspen groves, and open meadows festooned with wildflowers in June and July.

Begin at the trailhead in Himes Peak Campground and descend to the North Fork of the White River. Cross the river on a footbridge and climb to the wilderness

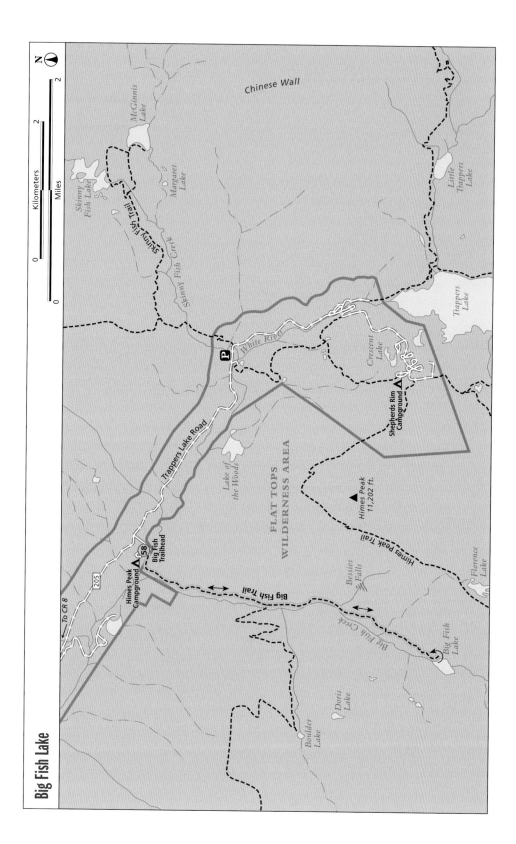

Big Fish Lake

Surrounded by meadows and clumps of unburned spruce trees, Big Fish Lake reflects summer sky and clouds.

boundary. The next section heads up a valley with Big Fish Creek twisting through willows on the right. The trail dips across shallow side creeks. Most are easy to boulder hop or scoot across polished tree trunks. Bring trekking poles for balance and use caution when crossing creeks in high water. As the trail climbs, look for Bessies Falls tumbling down the hillside to the left. After a couple of miles, cross the falls outlet creek and stop in a meadow for a great view of the waterfall. Continue up the trail, gently climbing across meadows and pocket forests to Big Fish Lake, a gorgeous lake tucked in the upper cirque.

Miles and Directions

0.0   Start at Big Fish Trailhead at Himes Peak Campground entrance. Hike downhill to the North Fork of White River.

0.15   Cross the White River on a footbridge and climb a hill.

0.2   Pass the Flat Tops Wilderness Area boundary (GPS: 40 1.6304, –107 16.4903). Go through a gate and hike west on the singletrack trail in meadows south of Big Fish Creek.

1.3   Reach a junction with Boulder Lake Trail on the right. Continue straight.

2.0   Reach a creek crossing below Bessies Falls. **Do not attempt in high water.** Continue west past the falls viewpoint and then climb gradual slopes.

3.1   Arrive at the east side of the lake (GPS: 39 59.3938, –107 17.3188). Retrace your steps back down the trail.

6.2   Arrive back at the trailhead (GPS: 40 1.6597, –107 16.305).

59 Hanging Lake

High above Glenwood Canyon, the East Fork of Dead Horse Creek drops off a cliff into famed Hanging Lake. The hike is steep, but the reward is a mesmerizing emerald pool hidden on a limestone shelf.

Start: Hanging Lake Trailhead
Difficulty: Moderate
Trail: Hanging Lake Trail
Hiking time: About 3 hours
Distance: 2.9 miles out-and-back
Elevation trailhead to lake: 6,120 to 7,500 feet at Hanging Lake (+1,380 feet)
Restrictions: Open year-round, weather dependent; hiking permit required year-round; hikers must carry permit on trail; reserve permits at www.visitglenwood.com/hanginglake; hourly reservation times from 6:30 a.m. to 5:30 p.m.; free shuttles operate from 110 Wulfsohn Road, Glenwood Springs from May 1 to Oct 31, personal vehicles not allowed to park at trailhead during those months; no

toilets at lake or on trail; no cell service; do not stand on log, swim, or fish in the lake; no drones allowed; no dogs, pets, or bicycles allowed; pack out trash; forecasted rain may lead to closure and evacuation of the trail due to terrain damage from the 2020 wildfire
Amenities: Restrooms and water at trailhead; services in Glenwood Springs
Maps: *DeLorme*: Page 35, E8; Trails Illustrated 151: Flat Tops South; USGS Shoshone
County: Garfield
Land status: White River National Forest, (970) 945-2521; Eagle–Holy Cross Ranger District, (970) 827-5715; Hanging Lake Call Center, (970) 384-6309

Finding the trailhead: During peak season (May 1 to Oct 31), personal vehicles are not allowed to drive to the trailhead except by prior reservation. Because of limited parking spots, arrive within 15 minutes either before or after your reservation time, otherwise you will not be allowed to park. Alternatively, park in Glenwood Springs at the Hanging Lake Welcome Center in peak season and ride from 6:45 a.m. to 5 p.m. to the trailhead. Return shuttles operate until 8 p.m. During off-peak season (Nov 1 to Apr 30), vehicles are allowed at the trailhead but hiking permits are required. Be advised that dates, times, and requirements are subject to change.

To reach the trailhead from Glenwood Springs, drive 9 miles east on I-70 East and take exit 125 for Hanging Lake. There is no direct exit to Hanging Lake from westbound I-70. Rather, take exit 121 for Grizzly Creek, go 0.2 mile and turn left to merge onto I-70 East, then drive 3.8 miles to exit 125 for Hanging Lake. There is no re-entry to I-70 East from Hanging Lake; rather, take the interstate west to exit 121 (Grizzly Creek) to get onto I-70 East. Parking is 0.4 mile from the Hanging Lake exit (GPS: 39 35.361, –107 11.406).

The Hike

Hanging Lake, one of Colorado's iconic beauty spots, is filled by 20-foot Bridal Veil Falls and 70-foot "Spouting Rock Falls," a unique waterfall that rushes through a hole in a cliff above the lake. The shallow lake, a designated National Natural Landmark,

Emerald-colored Hanging Lake, reached by a steep hike, is fed by the East Fork of Dead Horse Creek.

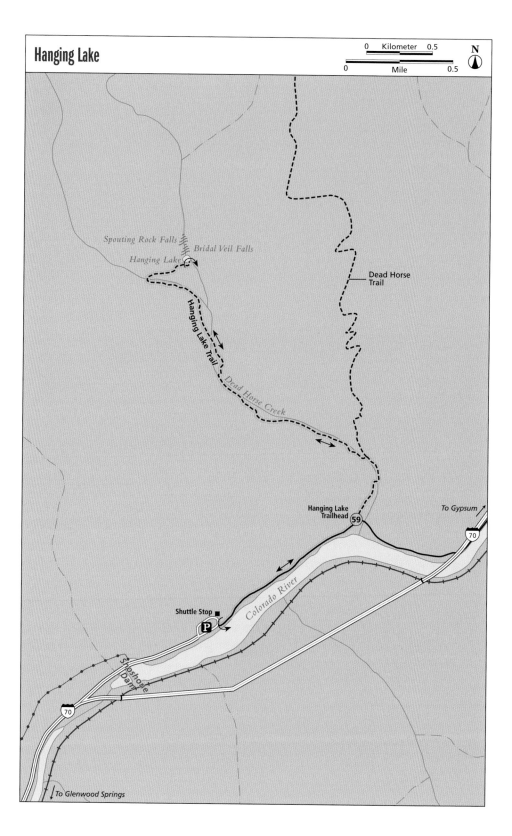

Hanging Lake

Spouting Rock Falls
Bridal Veil Falls
Hanging Lake

Hanging Lake Trail

Dead Horse Creek

Dead Horse Trail

Hanging Lake Trailhead
59

To Gypsum

70

Colorado River

Shuttle Stop
P

Shoshone Dam

70

To Glenwood Springs

0   Kilometer   0.5
0   Mile   0.5

N

Hanging Lake hides on a high shelf in a side canyon above the Colorado River in Glenwood Canyon.

is a rare formation—a small, clear lake formed by a travertine or calcium carbonate dam that perches atop a limestone cliff in a narrow canyon above Glenwood Canyon.

Visitation at popular Hanging Lake jumped from 99,000 in 2014 to almost 200,000 in 2018, causing damage to the lake and surrounding terrain. The US Forest Service then instituted restrictions to keep the lake from being loved to death. The number of daily hikers is limited, and a permit is required for hiking and parking. Be advised that the trail, damaged in 2021 floods, may be rebuilt and rerouted at a future time.

The hike starts on a paved walkway along the north side of the Colorado River in Glenwood Canyon, and heads northeast to Hanging Lake Trail. Leaving the sidewalk, the trail climbs up Dead Horse Creek canyon, gaining almost 1,400 feet of elevation to the lake. Trekking poles are useful, especially on the descent. The trail switchbacks up the canyon, climbs steps, and crosses bridges over the creek. The final section ascends stone steps along an exposed cliff with a safety railing. Finish at a boardwalk along the lake's west side. Plenty of benches let you rest and soak in the stunning scenery at Hanging Lake.

Miles and Directions

0.0 Begin on the paved sidewalk at the parking lot's east end.

0.4 Leave the sidewalk and hike up signed Hanging Lake Trail (#1650) on the left (GPS: 39 35.562, -107 11.053).

0.7 Reach a junction with Dead Horse Trail (#1851) on the right (GPS: 39 35.716, -107 11.049), Go straight on Hanging Lake Trail up the canyon.

1.4 Reach a boardwalk at Hanging Lake and seating areas to view the lake and waterfall (GPS: 39 36.0755, -107 11.4963).

1.45 Reach the end of the boardwalk (GPS: 39 36.08, -107 11.46). Return the way you came.

2.9 Arrive back at the trailhead (GPS: 39 35.361, -107 11.406).

60 Pitkin Lake

Fed by snowmelt and springs on "East" and "West Partner Peaks," Pitkin Lake is one of the prettiest glacier-sculpted tarns in the Gore Range above Vail and I-70.

Start: Pitkin Creek Trailhead
Difficulty: Strenuous
Trail: Pitkin Creek Trail #2012
Hiking time: About 6 hours
Distance: 10.0 miles out-and-back
Elevation trailhead to lake: 8,455 to 11,390 feet at lake (+2,935 feet)
Restrictions: Wilderness rules apply; leashed dogs only; group size limited to 15; parking limited at trailhead; no parking on street by trailhead; no sleeping in cars at trailhead

Amenities: Portapotty at trailhead; services in Vail
Maps: *DeLorme*: Page 37, D8; Trails Illustrated 602: Vail [Local Trails]; USGS Vail East
County: Eagle
Land status: Eagles Nest Wilderness Area; White River National Forest, (970) 945-2521; Eagle-Holy Cross Ranger District, (970) 827-5715

Finding the trailhead: From I-70 in East Vail, take exit 180. On the north side of the interstate, turn right on Fall Line Drive and go 0.3 mile to the trailhead on the left at road's end (GPS: 39 38.5817, -106 18.1841). Limited parking is on both sides of the road.

Alternatively, to alleviate trailhead parking problems, park free at Vail Village or Lionshead and take the free East Vail blue line shuttle from the Vail Transportation Center. Ride to Falls at Vail bus stop and walk east on the road for 0.25 mile to the trailhead.

The Hike

Pitkin Lake glistens on the floor of a steep-walled cirque below 13,041-foot "West Partner Peak" and 13,057-foot "East Partner Peak" on the west side of the Gore Range, a rugged mountain chain that stretches north from Vail Pass to the Colorado River. The popular Pitkin Creek Trail climbs north up a narrow valley east of Vail, passing two waterfalls before switchbacking up to the lake. The trail, gaining almost 3,000 feet of elevation, is strenuous with several long steep sections. It is busy in summer and on weekends. Limited parking is a problem at the trailhead so to ease congestion, park in Vail and take a free shuttle bus to the trailhead area. Also, hike on weekdays to avoid crowds.

Beginning at a trailhead in East Vail, the trail quickly enters Eagles Nest Wilderness Area and climbs north up a steep valley through aspen groves and spruce and fir forest. The trail passes "Lower Pitkin Creek Falls" gushing down a defile that splits a cliff and then heads up through avalanche debris to an overlook below "Upper Pitkin Creek Falls" spilling down broken cliffs. The last section of trail twists up to a final watery reward—picturesque Pitkin Lake nestled below rocky peaks.

Pitkin Lake reflects "East Partner Peak" in the Eagles Nest Wilderness Area near Vail.

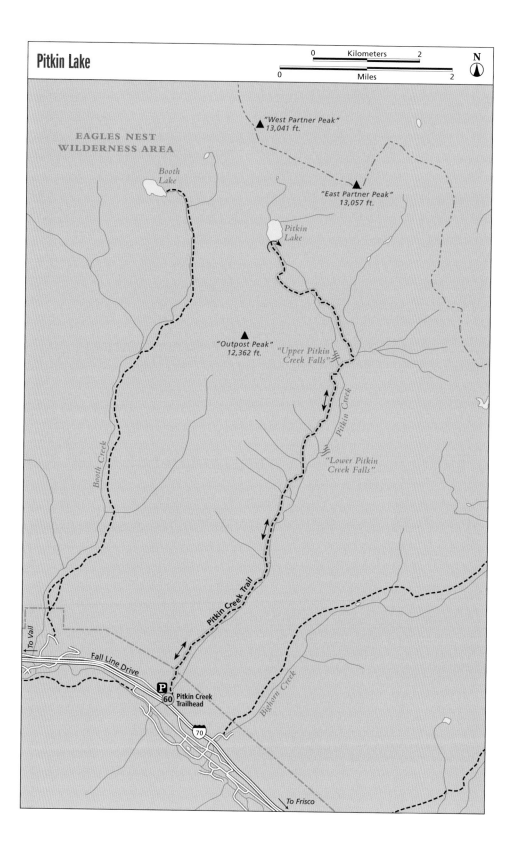

Pitkin Lake

EAGLES NEST
WILDERNESS AREA

Booth
Lake

"West Partner Peak"
13,041 ft.

"East Partner Peak"
13,057 ft.

Pitkin
Lake

"Outpost Peak"
12,362 ft.

"Upper Pitkin
Creek Falls"

Pitkin Creek

"Lower Pitkin
Creek Falls"

Booth Creek

Pitkin Creek Trail

To Vail

Fall Line Drive

P
60   Pitkin Creek
Trailhead

70

Bighorn Creek

To Frisco

Girded by cliffs and talus slopes, "West Partner Peak" looms above glassy Pitkin Lake.

Miles and Directions

0.0 Start at the Pitkin Creek Trailhead on the north side of the parking lot. Hike north on the trail.

0.25 Enter Eagles Nest Wilderness Area and continue north.

2.5 Reach a viewpoint of "Lower Pitkin Creek Falls" (GPS: 39 40.1932, –106 17.0179) in cliffs below. Enjoy the waterfall from a boulder on the trail. Continue up the trail.

3.5 Reach a view of "Upper Pitkin Creek Falls" above the trail (GPS: 39 40.788, –106 16.7116). Continue up the steep trail. Higher, the angle eases and the trail crosses tundra with scattered trees and glacier-smoothed bedrock.

5.0 Arrive at the south end of Pitkin Lake (GPS: 39 41.5932, –106 17.3484). Enjoy views of "East" and "West Partner Peaks" and "Outpost Peak." Return back down the trail.

10.0 Arrive back at the trailhead (GPS: 39 38.5817, –106 18.1841).

61 Steamboat Lake

The Tombstone Nature Trail explores meadows, forests, and wildlife on the scenic northern edge of Steamboat Lake, a huge reservoir filled by five mountain creeks in northern Colorado.

Start: Tombstone Nature Trailhead
Difficulty: Easy
Trail: Tombstone Nature Trail
Hiking time: About 1 hour
Distance: 1.1 miles loop
Elevation trailhead to lake: 8,059 to 8,170 feet at Tombstone Hill summit (+111 feet)
Restrictions: Fee area; vehicles must display valid park pass; dogs must be leashed; no horse, motorcycles, or mountain bikes

Amenities: None at trailhead; restrooms, water, and interpretive displays at visitor center; campgrounds; services in Steamboat Springs
Maps: *DeLorme*: Page 16, C2; Trails Illustrated 116: Hahns Peak, Steamboat Lake; USGS Hahns Peak
County: Routt
Land status: Steamboat Lake State Park, (970) 879-3922

Finding the trailhead: From Steamboat Springs, drive west on US 40 to the west side of town and turn north on CR 129/Elk River Road. Drive north for 24.8 miles to a left turn at the state park visitor center. Drive southwest on a park road for 0.3 mile to a Y-junction. Go left on a dirt road and drive 275 feet to a parking lot on the right. Start at the left trailhead (GPS: 40 48.3655, -106 57.3769). The right trailhead is the hike's endpoint.

The Hike

Steamboat Lake, a 1,101-acre reservoir north of Steamboat Springs, sprawls across a grassy valley south of pointed 10,839-foot Hahns Peak, a mountain named for miner Joseph Hahn. The lake is the centerpiece of Steamboat Lake State Park, one of Colorado's prettiest and most popular state parklands. Unlike other reservoirs, the lake has little fluctuation in its level, making it an ideal destination for watery activities. Besides a visitor center, marina, and two campgrounds, Steamboat Lake has three trails.

The park's best lake hike is the Tombstone Nature Trail, which climbs 8,170-foot Tombstone Hill, a low-browed hillock overlooking Steamboat Lake's ragged shoreline. The trail, with minimal elevation gain, offers marvelous views across the shining lake toward high mountains. Called one of Colorado's best short trails, the park offers an interpretive brochure about the area's natural and cultural history that is keyed to numbered posts along the trail. Look for endangered calypso orchids along the trail in June and moose wading in shallow waters at the trail's north end.

Atop the hill at the trail's high point is a tombstone for two children—Ruth and Sonny Boy—who died in 1928 and 1930, respectively. Both were children of James

The Tombstone Nature Trail twists along the edge of Steamboat Lake below Hahns Peak, a northern Colorado landmark.

The Tombstone Nature Trail offers scenic views across Steamboat Lake to pointed Hahns Peak.

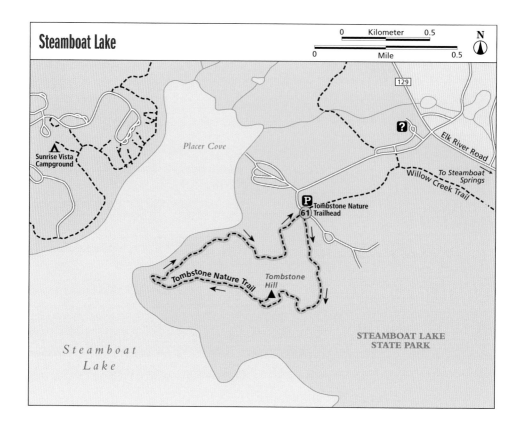

Steamboat Lake

and Rose Wheeler, who homesteaded here on 243 acres in 1921 after driving their Model T car from Sterling in eastern Colorado. Do the hike, enjoy the views and wildlife, and reflect on the hardships and heartaches of those early settlers.

Miles and Directions

0.0 Start at the Tombstone Nature Trailhead on the south side of the parking area. Hike south through a meadow on the singletrack path to an open, mixed forest of spruce, fir, and aspen. As the trail gains elevation, enjoy views of Steamboat Lake below.

0.4 Reach a junction with a side trail labeled "Historic Marker" on the summit of Tombstone Hill. Go right for 85 feet to a tombstone on the graves of two children (GPS: 40 48.2238, -106 57.4651). Return to the trail and hike downhill to the west with views of 10,847-foot Sand Mountain.

0.6 Reach a right turn at the west end of a headland above the lake (GPS: 40 48.2639, -105 57.7316). Hike northeast through meadows and forests on slopes above a cove with views north of Hahns Peak.

0.8 Drop down and reach the edge of Steamboat Lake. Continue northeast above a wetland.

1.1 Arrive back at the trailhead (GPS: 40 48.373, -105 57.3863).

62 Mica Lake

Mica Lake, a placid tarn surrounded by meadows and forest, shines among alpine splendor including rugged Big Agnes Mountain in the Mount Zirkel Wilderness Area.

Start: Slavonia Trailhead
Difficulty: Strenuous
Trails: Gilpin Lake Trail #1161, Mica Basin Trail #1162
Hiking time: About 5 hours
Distance: 8.4 miles out-and-back
Elevation trailhead to lake: 8,428 to 10,248 feet at lake (+1,820 feet)
Restrictions: Observe wilderness regulations; dogs must be under control or on leash; stay on trail; no bicycles or motorized vehicles; no camping within 200 feet of lake

Amenities: Vault toilets at trailhead; nearby campgrounds and dispersed campsites; services in Steamboat Springs
Maps: *DeLorme*: Page 16, C4 and page 17, C5; Trails Illustrated 116: Hahns Peak, Steamboat Lake; USGS Mount Zirkel
County: Routt
Land status: Mount Zirkel Wilderness Area; Routt National Forest, (307) 745-2300; Hahns Peak/Bears Ears Ranger District, (970) 870-2299

Finding the trailhead: From Steamboat Springs, drive west on US 40 to CR 129/Elk River Road on the west edge of Steamboat and turn right. Drive north for 17.6 miles on CR 129 through Clark to Glen Ellen and turn right on Seedhouse Road/CR 60, which turns into FR 400 in Routt National Forest. Continue northeast on the paved and dirt road for 11.8 miles to the Slavonia Trailhead and parking at the road's end (GPS: 40 46.989, -106 43.372).

The Hike

Mica Lake snuggles in Mica Basin, a glaciated cirque below 12,059-foot Big Agnes Mountain and its lower neighbor, 11,497-foot Little Agnes Mountain. The lake and mountains lie in the Sawtooth Range, a minor range jutting west from Mount Zirkel and the Park Range. Located in the Mount Zirkel Wilderness Area, secluded Mica Lake is less visited than nearby lakes, including popular Gilpin, Gold Creek, and Three Island Lakes.

The Mica Lake hike, gaining about 2,000 feet of elevation on two trails, offers rushing cascades and waterfalls, thick conifer forests and open meadows, plentiful summer wildflowers, golden aspen groves in autumn, and sublime campsites near the lake. Also, look for wading moose and bald eagles catching trout in the lake. Mica Lake Trail is well marked and easy to follow. Snow may linger near the lake in June so bring poles and MICROspikes for traction. In summer, don't forget bug spray for mosquitos.

If you are camping near Mica Lake, take a hike up Big Agnes Mountain, the Sawtooth highpoint, up grassy slopes and talus fields to a final exposed ridge and

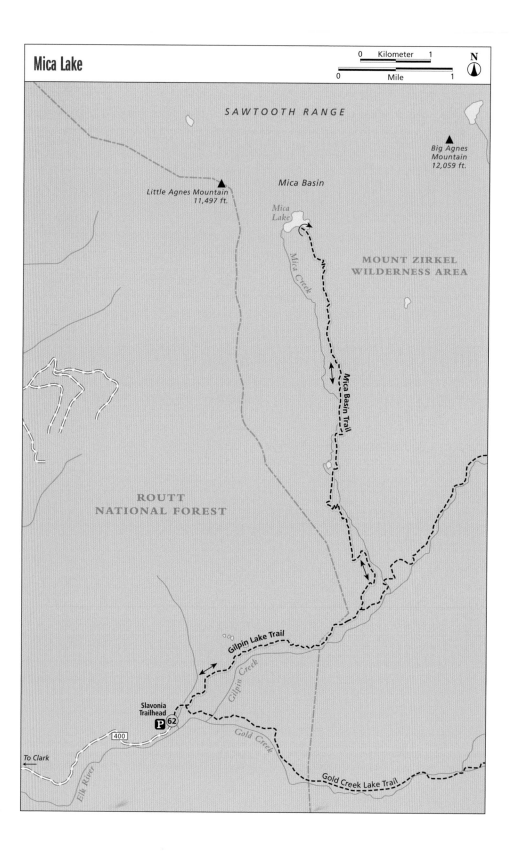

Mica Lake

SAWTOOTH RANGE

Mica Basin

▲ Big Agnes
Mountain
12,059 ft.

▲ Little Agnes Mountain
11,497 ft.

Mica
Lake

MOUNT ZIRKEL
WILDERNESS AREA

Mica Creek

Mica Basin Trail

ROUTT
NATIONAL FOREST

Gilpin Lake Trail

Gilpin Creek

Slavonia
Trailhead

P 62

400

Gold Creek

To Clark

Gold Creek Lake Trail

Elk River

Mirrorlike Mica Lake tucks into a cirque below Little Agnes Mountain in the Mount Zirkel Wilderness Area.

airy summit with forever views across northern Colorado, or romp up the easy south ridge of Little Agnes above the lake.

Miles and Directions

0.0   Start at the Slavonia Trailhead on the northeast side of the parking lot. Hike straight on signed Gilpin Lake Trail.

0.15   Reach a wilderness register and a signed junction with Gold Creek Lake Trail (GPS: 40 47.062, –106 43.288). Sign in the register box and go left on Gilpin Lake Trail. Cross Gilpin Creek a couple of times on rocks and logs and enter the Mount Zirkel Wilderness Area.

1.5   Reach a junction with Mica Basin Trail (GPS: 40 47.538, –106 42.116) at 9,040 feet. Go left on it and climb through spruce, fir, and lodgepole pine forest, meadows, and deadfall along Mica Creek, passing trailside cascades and waterfalls. After the first steep section, the trail crosses to the creek's east bank and the angle eases.

2.7   Cross Mica Creek on rocks or wade across. Continue across a flat area and then switch-back uphill, continuing north with views of Little Agnes Mountain to the northwest and Big Agnes Mountain to the northeast. Continue up easy terrain to a final steep section.

4.2   Reach the south shore of Mica Lake (GPS: 40 49.4077, –106 42.5508). Return back down the trails.

8.4   Arrive back at the trailhead (GPS: 40 46.989, –106 43.372).

Northern Colorado

Walden and Fort Collins

Horsetooth Reservoir, with 25 miles of shoreline, stretches over 6 miles to a dam at its north end.

63 Ruby Jewel Lake

Ruby Jewel Lake reflects sky, clouds, and mountains in an alpine cirque below Clark Peak in the wild heart of the rugged Rawah Range west of Fort Collins.

Start: Ruby Jewel Trailhead
Difficulty: Moderate
Trails: Ruby Jewel four-wheel-drive road, Ruby Jewel Trail
Hiking time: About 3 hours
Distance: 5.4 miles out-and-back
Elevation trailhead to lake: 9,665 to 11,265 feet at lake (+1,600 feet)
Restrictions: Observe wilderness regulations; fee area; trail closed to motorized vehicles; leashed dogs only; no backcountry fires

Amenities: Nearby state park campgrounds and dispersed campsites by reservation; services in Walden
Maps: *DeLorme*: Page 18, E3; Trails Illustrated 112: Poudre River, Cameron Pass; USGS Clark Peak
County: Jackson
Land status: State Forest State Park, (970) 723-8366

Finding the trailhead: From Fort Collins, go north on US 287 for about 10 miles and turn left on CO 14 West at Ted's Place. Drive 69.3 miles, crossing Cameron Pass, and turn right (east) on unpaved CR 41. This turn is 18.7 miles southeast of Walden. Drive 5 miles on CR 41 and bear left at the split for Bockman and Montgomery Pass. Following signs for Ruby Jewel Trailhead, turn right on Ruby Jewel Road and drive 2 miles. Although designated a two-wheel-drive road, a high-clearance, four-wheel-drive vehicle is recommended. Park at the two-wheel-drive parking lot just past the turn for the Clark Peak Yurt (GPS: 35.029, –105 57.690).

The Hike

Living up to its name, Ruby Jewel Lake is a hidden gem tucked in a high cirque below Clark Peak, the highest point in the Rawah Range, a 40-mile extension of Wyoming's Medicine Bow Mountains. The glacial lake—called Jewel Lake on USGS topo maps—sits above timberline, surrounded by meadows, clumps of willows, and talus fields below broken cliffs and tall mountains. Reach the lake by a well-marked trail through a forest of spruce, lodgepole pine, and subalpine fir, flower-strewn meadows, and rocky talus slopes. The lake lies in State Forest State Park, a 70,830-acre parkland that sprawls along the western slope of the Rawahs. Beside hiking, the park offers campgrounds, yurts, cabins, a visitor center, and moose in the wet valleys.

Most hikers park at a lower, two-wheel-drive lot and hike up a rough and rocky, four-wheel-drive road to the official trailhead where the road dead-ends. From there the trail steadily climbs with spacious views of mountains and dark woods for rest-break enjoyment. The trail's upper part may be snow covered in early summer so bring trekking poles and MICROspikes for added traction.

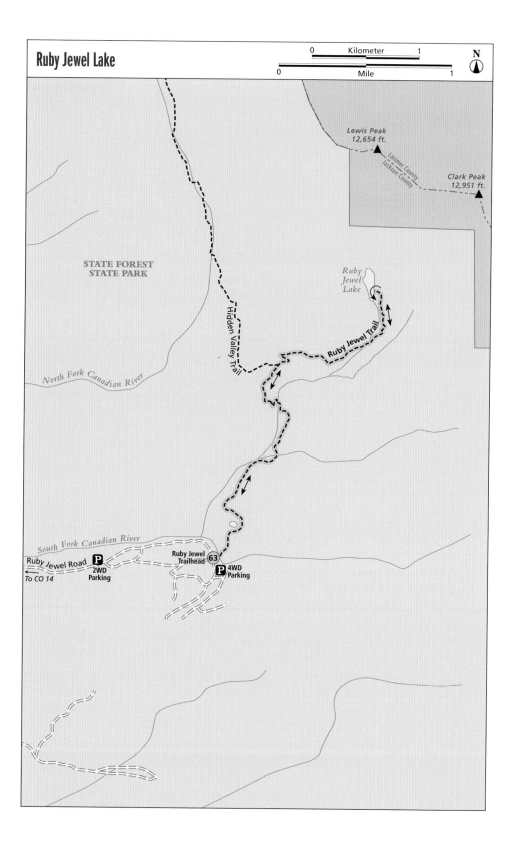

Ruby Jewel Lake

0   Kilometer   1

0   Mile   1

N

Lewis Peak
12,654 ft.

Larimer County
Jackson County

Clark Peak
12,951 ft.

STATE FOREST
STATE PARK

Ruby
Jewel
Lake

Hidden Valley Trail

Ruby Jewel Trail

North Fork Canadian River

South Fork Canadian River

Ruby Jewel Road

To CO 14

P
2WD
Parking

Ruby Jewel
Trailhead

63

P
4WD
Parking

Ruby Jewel Lake gleams in a high basin at the foot of 12,951-foot Clark Peak, the high point of the Rawah Range. Photo by Ben Loftin

Miles and Directions

0.0 Start at the two-wheel-drive parking lot (9,665 feet) and hike east and then north on the road.

1.3 Reach the four-wheel-drive parking area and the Ruby Jewel Trailhead (GPS: 40 35.0511, -105 57.1133). Go north to cross the South Fork of the Canadian River on a split log bridge, then cross the river again on a footbridge over a swampy area on logs and planks.

1.9 Reach the junction with Hidden Valley Trail (GPS: 40 35.7742, -105 56.7957). Continue straight, angling to the right, and hike northeast on the Ruby Jewel Trail.

2.0 Cross a boulderfield on a talus trail and hike east into a meadow. Contour across a slope, cross the river by rock hopping, and climb north into an alpine basin.

2.7 Arrive at the eastern shore of Ruby Jewel Lake (GPS: 40 36.0502, -105 56.3195). Look north to 12,654-foot Lewis Peak and northeast to 12,951-foot Clark Peak, the high point of the Rawah Range. Return down the trail.

5.4 Arrive back at the trailhead (GPS: 35.029, -105 57.690).

64 Lake Agnes

Lake Agnes, a classic glaciated tarn, floors an unspoiled alpine cirque amid skyscraping peaks and clear horizons in State Forest State Park.

Start: Lake Agnes Trailhead
Difficulty: Moderate
Trail: Lake Agnes Trail
Hiking time: 1 to 2 hours
Distance: 1.6 miles out-and-back
Elevation trailhead to lake: 10,265 to 10,663 feet at lake (+398 feet)
Restrictions: Fee area; no camping or fires (stoves only); stay on designated trails; boats, bikes, and horses prohibited; dogs must be leashed; pack out trash
Amenities: Toilets at trailhead; Moose Visitor Center in state park; services in Walden
Maps: *DeLorme:* Page 28, A3; Trails Illustrated 200: Rocky Mountain National Park; USGS Mount Richthofen
County: Jackson
Land status: State Forest State Park, (970) 723-8366

Finding the trailhead: From Fort Collins, go north on US 287 for about 10 miles and turn left on CO 14 West at Ted's Place. Drive 60.3 miles, crossing Cameron Pass, and make a hard left on CR 62 toward Lake Agnes. The turn is 27.7 miles southeast of Walden and 2.3 miles west of Cameron Pass. Drive 0.7 mile up CR 62 and turn right on FR 170. Cross a bridge over the Michigan River and the left turn for Crags Campground and drive up the rough road for 1.2 miles to the trailhead (GPS: 40 29.3945, -105 54.1979).

The Hike

Lake Agnes, anchoring the northern end of the Never Summer Mountains, is a glassy tarn nestled below towering peaks, including 12,951-foot Mount Richthofen and the rugged Nokhu Crags, named with the Arapaho word for "eagle's nest." The alpine lake, reached by a short, steep trail in State Forest State Park, was named for Agnes, the youngest daughter of miner John Zimmerman, who built a historic cabin at the trailhead for a boy's summer camp. The Lake Agnes area and nearby North Park is Colorado's moose capital, so watch for these massive mammals along the trail as well as elk, mule deer, and bighorn sheep.

The popular trail, gaining 480 feet, is well marked and easy to follow. Starting at the old cabin, the trail switchbacks past Upper Michigan Ditch with views of Nokhu Crags and then levels out and drops to the lake. At a rocky beach on the lake's northern shore are breathtaking vistas of the sparkling lake, a unique rock island, and surrounding mountains. It's possible to circumnavigate the lake, but the western shore is impassable in places with cliffs dropping into the water. Instead, hike along a rough trail on the east shore below a talus field to the south shore and then turn around. Lake Agnes is a good snowshoe hike in winter. Park where the road closes in winter and hike the road for 1.5 miles to the summer trailhead.

Mount Richthofen and Mount Mahler scrape the sky above the azure water of Lake Agnes in State Forest State Park. Photo by Ben Loftin

Lake Agnes and its iconic island nestle in a cirque below Mount Richthofen and Mount Mahler in the Never Summer Mountains. Photo by Ben Loftin

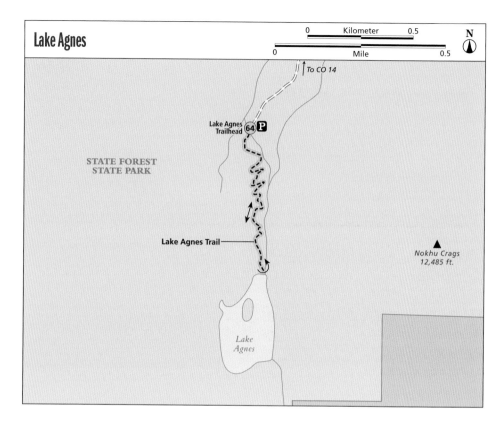

Lake Agnes

Miles and Directions

0.0 Begin at the Lake Agnes Trailhead. Hike south on Lake Agnes Trail.

0.8 Reach the north shore of Lake Agnes (GPS: 40 29.0425, –105 54.1493). Return back on the trail.

1.6 Arrive back at the trailhead (GPS: 40 29.3945, –105 54.1979).

65 Horsetooth Reservoir

The Foothills Trail follows the eastern shoreline of 6-mile-long Horsetooth Reservoir past rock outcrops and rocky beaches to a designated swim area on the west side of Fort Collins.

Start: Foothills Trailhead at Rotary Park
Difficulty: Easy
Trail: Foothills Trail
Hiking time: 1 to 2 hours
Distance: 2.8 miles out-and-back
Elevation trailhead to lake: 5,657 to 5,400 feet at lake (depending on water level); 5,438 feet at Sunrise Day Use Area (–219 feet)
Restrictions: Fee area; open daily 5 a.m. to 11 p.m.; park only in designated spots;

leashed dogs allowed; stay on trail; mountain bikers and equestrians share trail; no fires, fireworks, or glass containers
Amenities: Vault toilet at trailhead; swim beach; services in Fort Collins
Maps: *DeLorme*: Page 20, E2; Trails Illustrated None: USGS Horsetooth Reservoir
County: Larimer
Land status: Fort Collins Natural Areas Program, (970) 416-2815

Finding the trailhead: From Fort Collins, reach the trailhead on Centennial Drive/N. CR 23 on the east side of Horsetooth Reservoir by either CR 42C/Dixon Canyon Road or W. CR 38E. Drive north on CR 23 to Rotary Park and a long parking area on the west side of the road. Enter the lot on its south side, park in a designated spot, and buy an entrance permit at a kiosk. Start at the Foothills Trailhead at the north end of the lot (GPS: 40 34.0414, –105 9.3167).

The Hike

Horsetooth Reservoir, named for a distinctive rock formation on Horsetooth Mountain above the lake, is a long, narrow reservoir hidden between a hogback and the Front Range foothills. Supplying water to Fort Collins, the lake lies in Horsetooth Reservoir County Park and offers campgrounds, boating, world-class bouldering, and many hiking trails. This hike follows the excellent middle section of 6.8-mile Foothills Trail, which twists along the lake's eastern shoreline from Rotary Park to the Sunrise Day Use Area. The trail is easy to follow with gentle grades and marvelous views across the shimmering lake.

Begin at the Foothills Trailhead at the northern end of the Rotary Park parking area. Keep left at a brown post labeled "Foothills Trail." The wide path heads north above low cliffs and makes a couple switchbacks down brushy slopes before gently descending north. After about a half-mile, the trail reaches the edge of eroded bluffs above the lake. Depending on the lake level, the water may be near the trail or 60 feet below on stony beaches. Hike north on the easy trail, passing beneath The Scoop, a cliff band used by toprope climbers, and end at the Sunrise Day Use Area, a popular summer swimming hole with parking and restrooms.

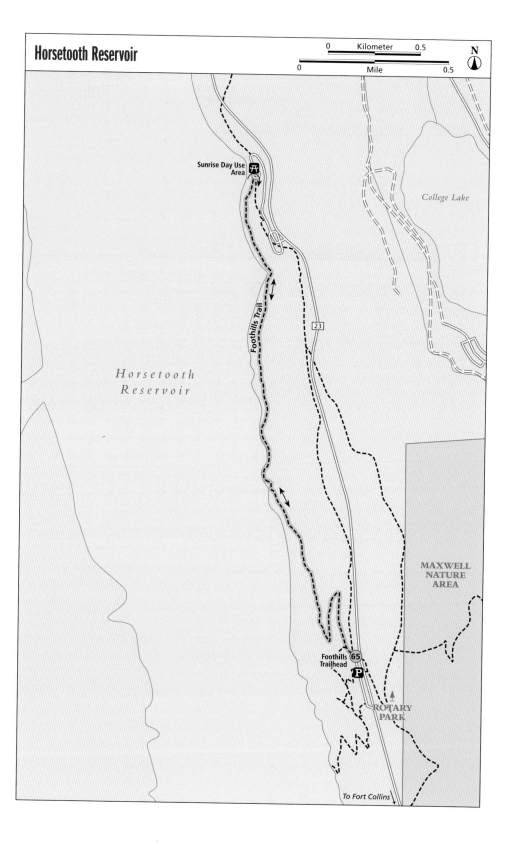

Horsetooth Reservoir

0 Kilometer 0.5
0 Mile 0.5

N

Sunrise Day Use
Area

College Lake

Foothills Trail

23

*Horsetooth
Reservoir*

MAXWELL
NATURE
AREA

Foothills 65
Trailhead
P

ROTARY
PARK

To Fort Collins

Hikers walk leashed dogs on the Foothills Trail above Horsetooth Reservoir.

Miles and Directions

0.0 Start at the Foothills Trailhead at the north end of the Rotary Park parking lot. Keep left at a signpost on Foothills Trail. The right trail climbs to the top of the hogback. Hike north on the west side of the ridge.

0.6 Reach a terrace above the lake's east shore (GPS: 40 34.2787, –105 9.4823). Continue north near the shoreline.

1.1 A cliff band, called The Scoop climbing area, rims the ridge above the trail. Access the cliff from its lower north end by a social trail along the cliff base.

1.4 Reach the hike's northern end at the Sunrise Day Use Area, swim beach, parking lot, and restrooms (GPS: 40 34.9116, –105 9.5821). Turn around here and return on the trail to Rotary Park.

2.8 Arrive back at the trailhead (GPS: 40 34.0414, –105 9.3167).

66 Fossil Creek Reservoir

Three short trails explore the southern edge of Fossil Creek Reservoir, an outstanding bird-watching and wildlife area with prairie, wetlands, and a lakeshore lined with cottonwood trees on the southeastern edge of Fort Collins.

Start: Trailhead by visitor center at west side of parking lot
Difficulty: Easy
Trails: Heron Loop Trail (ADA accessible), Sandpiper Trail, Cattail Flats Trail
Hiking time: About 1 hour
Distance: 3.2 miles loop and out-and-back
Elevation trailhead to lake: 4,895 to 4,865 feet at lake; 4,872 feet at Heron Loop Trail lake blind (-23 feet)
Restrictions: Open daily sunrise to sunset; stay on trails; do not disturb wildlife; bikes,
horses, and dogs not allowed; no water recreation including fishing, boating, swimming, and wading; watch for rattlesnakes; seasonal trail closures for nesting birds; Cattail Flats Trail closed Nov 15 to Mar 1
Amenities: Restrooms; educational programs and activities available; services in Fort Collins
Maps: *DeLorme:* Page 30, A3; Trails Illustrated None; USGS Loveland
County: Larimer
Land status: City of Fort Collins, Natural Areas Department, (970) 416-2480

Finding the trailhead: From Denver, drive north on I-25 and take exit 262. Go west on East CR 32/CO 392 for 0.8 mile to a marked right turn for Fossil Creek Reservoir. Drive northwest for 0.5 mile to a parking lot and the trailhead (GPS: 40 29.0161, -105 0.9539).

The Hike

Fossil Creek Reservoir, protected in 1,398-acre Fossil Creek Reservoir Natural Area, is a 754-acre lake that was designated as an Important Bird Area by the National Audubon Society for its critical habitat for nesting and roosting migratory and resident birds. The southern side of the lake, easily accessed from I-25, offers three trails—Heron Loop, Sandpiper, and Cattail Flats. Combine them for longer hikes.

The paved, ADA-accessible Heron Loop Trail makes an 0.5-mile circle with stops at picnic tables and a bird blind that hangs over the lake's edge. The Sandpiper Trail, an out-and-back, 1-mile hike from the trailhead, ends at a quiet blind to the west. Cattail Flats Trail, a 1.7-mile, round-trip hike from the trailhead, makes a lollipop loop.

Hiking is the only activity allowed at the lake to minimize human impact on wildlife, including over 145 species of birds. Hike in the early morning or evening to see shorebirds, waterfowl, gulls, terns, wading birds, and raptors. Viewing blinds and observation decks are found along the trails with information about the birdlife. The lake, one of northern Colorado's best birding areas, boasts as many as 20,000 geese and ducks wintering here as well as bald eagles. January and February are the best months to spot the eagles. Bring a camera, spotting scope, and binoculars to get up close.

Fossil Creek Reservoir, one of the Front Range's best bird-watching areas, reflects clouds and sky on an autumn afternoon.

Hikers follow Heron Loop Trail, an ADA-accessible hike at Fossil Creek Reservoir Natural Area.

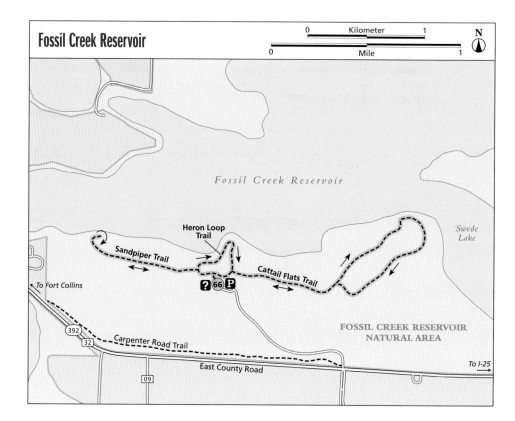

Miles and Directions

Heron Loop Trail

0.0 Start at trailhead right of visitor center. Walk north on the paved trail.

0.05 Reach T-junction with paved trail. Go left.

0.1 Reach a junction with Sandpiper Trail on the left (GPS: 40 29.0515, –105 1.0265). Continue northeast parallel to the lakeshore on the paved trail.

0.25 Junction with a short, paved trail on the left that leads 75 feet to a bird blind and lake views (GPS: 40 29.1264, –105 0.915).

0.35 Reach a junction with the start of the Cattail Flats Trail (GPS: 40 29.0476, –105 0.9023). Continue southwest on paved trail.

0.4 Return to the first trail junction. Go left to parking lot.

0.5 Arrive back at the trailhead (GPS: 40 29.0161, –105 0.9539).

A raised overlook on the Heron Loop Trail lets hikers spot ducks, geese, and bald eagles at Fossil Creek Reservoir Natural Area.

Sandpiper Trail

0.0 Start at the trailhead right of the visitor center. Walk north on the paved trail.

0.05 Reach T-junction with paved Heron Loop Trail. Go left.

0.1 Reach junction with Sandpiper Trail on the left (GPS: 40 29.0515, –105 1.0265). Go left on dirt trail.

0.5 End of the trail at a bird blind on the lake's edge (GPS: 40 29.1424, –105 1.3889).

1.0 Arrive back at the trailhead.

Cattail Flats Trail

0.0 Start at the trailhead right of the visitor center. Walk north on the paved trail.

0.05 Reach T-junction with paved Heron Loop Trail. Go right.

0.1 Junction with Cattail Flats Trail (GPS: 40 29.0476, –105 0.9023). Go right on dirt trail.

0.5 Reach a Y-junction and start of loop (GPS: 40 29.0167, –105 0.519). Keep on left trail.

0.7 Reach a bird blind by the lakeshore.

1.2 Return to the start of the loop. Go left and hike west to Heron Loop Trail, then return back to the parking lot.

1.7 Arrive back at the trailhead.

Rocky Mountain National Park

Estes Park, Allenspark, and Grand Lake

An easy trail makes Sprague Lake a family favorite hike in Rocky Mountain National Park.

67 Gem Lake

Gem Lake, tucked into a hidden basin, is a shallow, jewel-like tarn surrounded by towering granite cliffs and domes in Rocky Mountain National Park's northeastern sector.

Start: Lumpy Ridge Trailhead
Difficulty: Moderate
Trails: Lumpy Ridge Trail, Gem Lake Trail
Hiking time: 2 to 3 hours
Distance: 3.2 miles out-and-back
Elevation trailhead to lake: 7,854 to 8,835 feet at lake (+981 feet)
Restrictions: Limited parking; no dogs or mountain bikes; no wading or swimming in lake

Amenities: Trailhead vault toilets; interpretive signs; services in Estes Park
Maps: *DeLorme*: Page 29, B7; Trails Illustrated 200: Rocky Mountain National Park; USGS Estes Park
County: Larimer
Land status: Rocky Mountain National Park, (970) 586-1206

Finding the trailhead: From Estes Park, drive north on Wonderview Avenue past the historic Stanley Hotel and turn right on MacGregor Avenue, which becomes Devils Gulch Road. Drive 1.3 miles and turn left on Lumpy Ridge Road, then continue 0.3 mile to a parking lot and the Lumpy Ridge Trailhead (GPS: 40 23.7907, -105 30.7832).

The Hike

Gem Lake, cradled in a cliff-lined bowl, is a glistening tarn on the eastern end of Lumpy Ridge, a rocky escarpment stretched across Estes Park's northern skyline. The Arapahos named the ridge *That-aa-ai-atah* or "Mountain with Little Lumps." Later settlers simplified the native name to Lumpy Ridge. The popular Gem Lake Trail climbs steeply to the lake, offering postcard-worthy views south to 14,259-foot Longs Peak and a line of snowy peaks on the Continental Divide. Besides gorgeous scenery, the lake and hike boast summer wildflower displays, including the rare *Telesonix jamesii*, a pink flower brightening cliffs above Gem Lake, and golden groves of quaking aspen in autumn.

The trail is easy to follow but steep and rocky in places. A self-composting toilet with a mountain view is on the trail below the lake. Avoid polluting the lake by not swimming or wading. Gem Lake is unique because it has no inlet or outlet stream. Instead, trapped snowmelt and rainwater collects in a granite basin, forming the pond. The trailhead parking lot fills on summer weekends and holidays. Arrive early to snag a spot.

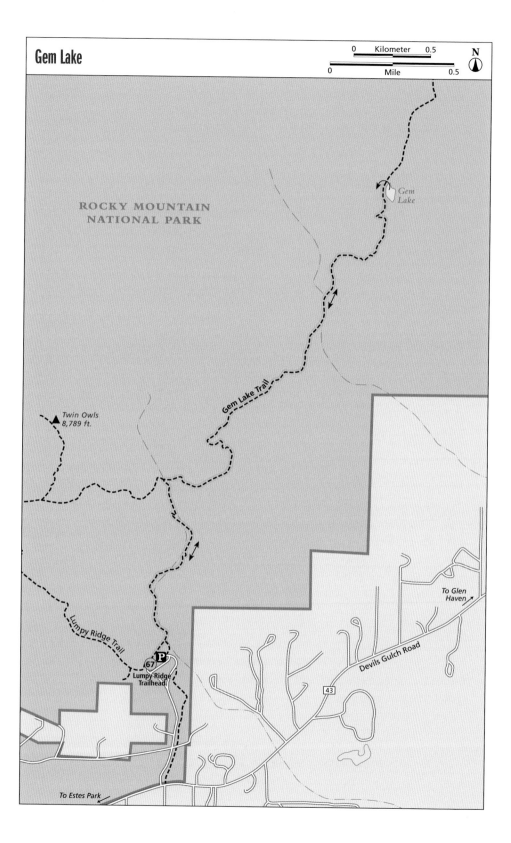

Gem Lake

ROCKY MOUNTAIN
NATIONAL PARK

Gem
Lake

▲ Twin Owls
8,789 ft.

Gem Lake Trail

Lumpy Ridge Trail

To Glen
Haven

P
67
Lumpy Ridge
Trailhead

Devils Gulch Road

43

To Estes Park

Rimmed by ancient granite, Gem Lake yields stunning views south from Lumpy Ridge to Longs Peak, the highest point in Rocky Mountain National Park.

Miles and Directions

0.0   Start on the right side of the toilets at the Lumpy Ridge Trailhead. Following signs for "Gem Lake," go right on Lumpy Ridge Trail and hike north up a cliff-lined canyon.

0.5   Reach a junction with Black Canyon Trail. Go right on Gem Lake Trail (GPS: 40 24.1261, –105 30.7574) and hike up the steep trail below cliffs with views south of Longs Peak and the Continental Divide peaks.

1.6   Reach the sandy west side of Gem Lake in a cliff-rimmed bowl (GPS: 40 24.6673, –105 30.2226). Return down the trail.

3.2   Arrive back at the trailhead (GPS: 40 23.7907, –105 30.7832).

68 Ypsilon Lake and Chipmunk Lake

Ypsilon Lake, a remote tarn in the Mummy Range, hides in a rugged cirque below Ypsilon Mountain and the twin Spectacle Lakes above the Old Fall River Road in Rocky Mountain National Park. The hike also passes small Chipmunk Lake.

Start: Lawn Lake Trailhead
Trails: Lawn Lake Trail, Ypsilon Lake Trail
Difficulty: Strenuous
Hiking time: About 6 hours
Distance: 8.8 miles out-and-back
Elevation trailhead to lake: 8,540 to 10,550 feet (+2,010 feet)
Restrictions: Fee area; follow wilderness regulations; no dogs

Amenities: Vault toilets at trailhead; nearby Fall River Visitor Center
Maps: *DeLorme*: Page 29, A5 and B6; Trails Illustrated 200: Rocky Mountain National Park; USGS Trail Ridge
County: Larimer
Land status: Rocky Mountain National Park, (970) 586-1206

Finding the trailhead: From Estes Park, drive on US 34 West/Fall River Road for 4.7 miles to the Fall River Entrance to Rocky Mountain National Park. Continue 2.1 miles past the entrance on US 34 and turn right on Old Fall River Road. Drive 0.1 mile to the signed Lawn Lake Trailhead parking area on the right (GPS: 40 24.4327, –105 37.5704).

The Hike

Granite cliffs, talus slopes, and pockets of spruce surround clear Ypsilon Lake, a glacial tarn tucked into a cirque on the south flank of the Mummy Range. The lake lies below the abrupt, southeastern face of 13,514-foot Ypsilon Mountain, the fifth-highest peak in Rocky Mountain National Park, although the mountain with its distinctive Y-shaped gullies is unseen from the lake. In a higher cirque below the rocky peak are the Spectacle Lakes, two dramatic lakes reached by a steep, unofficial path that scrambles up bedrock and talus.

The Ypsilon Lake Trail, listed on the National Register of Historic Places, climbs steadily up a blunt ridge from its junction with the Lawn Lake Trail. Besides the lovely lake at trail's end, the path swings past spruce-fringed Chipmunk Lake and wilderness campsites. Just beyond the lake is noisy "Ypsilon Falls," a two-tiered waterfall that fills a plunge pool, then squeezes through a granite gap to Ypsilon Lake.

The Ypsilon Lake Trail, built between 1907 and 1912, predates the establishment of the national park and was included on tourist maps as early as 1915. Early mountaineer Frederick Chapin and his wife, Alice, named the mountain in 1887. Chapin recalled that the pair, lounging in a meadow, saw a "great peak with a steep wall facing the east. . . . A large snowfield lay on the eastern face, two flittering bands of ice extended skyward to the ridge of the mountain, forming a perfect Y. My wife said to me, 'Its name shall be Ypsilon Peak.'"

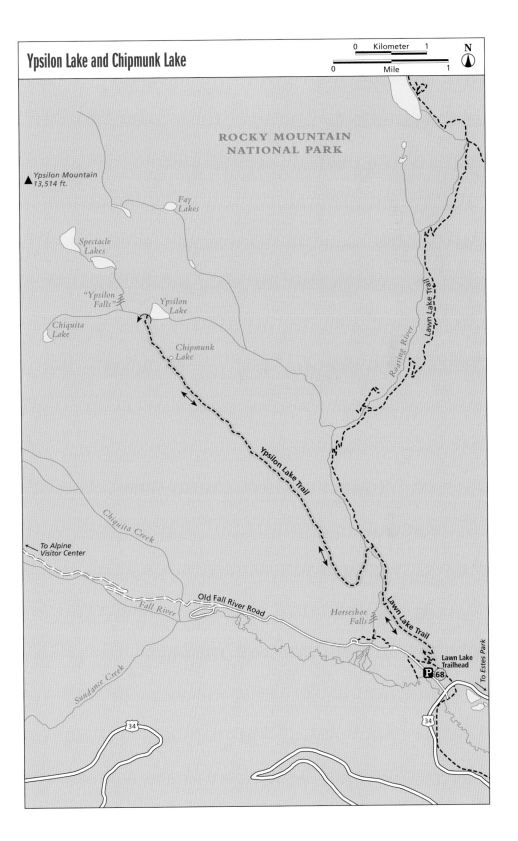

ROCKY MOUNTAIN
NATIONAL PARK

▲ Ypsilon Mountain
13,514 ft.

Fay
Lakes

Spectacle
Lakes

"Ypsilon
Falls"

Ypsilon
Lake

Chiquita
Lake

Chipmunk
Lake

Roaring River

Lawn Lake Trail

Ypsilon Lake Trail

Chiquita Creek

To Alpine
Visitor Center

Fall River

Old Fall River Road

Horseshoe
Falls

Lawn Lake Trail

Sundance Creek

Lawn Lake
Trailhead

P 68

To Estes Park

34

34

0   Kilometer   1

0   Mile   1

N

An afternoon rainstorm envelops Ypsilon Lake on the south flank of the Mummy Range.

Miles and Directions

0.0 Begin at the Lawn Lake Trailhead. Hike north on the Lawn Lake Trail, and after 0.1 mile, bear left at a trail junction and stay on the trail. Follow the trail north above a gorge carved by the Lawn Lake flood.

1.5 Reach a junction with Ypsilon Lake Trail (GPS: 40 25.2032, -105 38.0875). Go left on it, cross a footbridge over Roaring River, and then ascend timber steps. The trail climbs steadily northwest through forest on a blunt ridge with limited views.

4.0 Reach Chipmunk Lake on the right (GPS: 40 26.3447, -105 39.7519). Continue past backcountry campsites.

4.4 Arrive at Ypsilon Lake's wooded southern shore (GPS: 40 26.6074, -105 39.9005). To see Ypsilon Falls, continue around the west side of the lake for 0.1 mile to the waterfall. From the lake, descend down the trail.

8.8 Arrive back at the trailhead (GPS: 40 24.4327, -105 37.5704).

69 Fern Lake and Odessa Lake

This excellent hike explores the heart of Rocky Mountain National Park, passing waterfalls, wildlife, and two elegant lakes. Extra credit hike options visit three other alpine lakes.

Start: Fern Lake Trailhead
Difficulty: Moderate
Trail: Fern Lake Trail
Hiking time: About 6 hours
Distance: 9.4 miles out-and-back
Elevation trailhead to lakes: 8,165 to 9,503 feet at Fern Lake (+1,338 feet); 10,055 feet at Odessa Lake (+1,890 feet)
Restrictions: Fee area; day-use only; back-country camping by permit; no dogs allowed;

arrive early for parking; stay on trails; trail from Odessa to Helene has snowdrifts in June
Amenities: Trailhead vault toilets; picnic areas; full services in Estes Park
Maps: *DeLorme*: Page 29, B5 and B6; Trails Illustrated 200: Rocky Mountain National Park; USGS McHenrys Peak
County: Larimer
Land status: Rocky Mountain National Park, (970) 586-1206

Finding the trailhead: From Estes Park, take US 36 west for 3.8 miles to the Beaver Meadows Entrance Station at Rocky Mountain National Park. Drive 0.2 mile and turn left (south) on Bear Lake Road. Drive 1.2 miles and turn right toward Moraine Park Campground. Drive 0.5 mile and turn left on Fern Lake Road. Continue 1.5 miles to the Cub Lake Trailhead where the road becomes unpaved. Continue 0.7 mile to a parking lot and the trailhead (GPS: 40 21.2897, –105 37.8688). Lot fills in summer and on weekends. Avoid parking problems by boarding the Moraine Park shuttle at the Park and Ride opposite Glacier Basin Campground and ride to the Fern Lake bus stop. Hike 0.8 mile to the trailhead from there (adds 1.6 miles to total hike mileage).

The Hike

The Fern Lake Trail offers dramatic alpine scenery, two waterfalls, golden aspens in autumn, plentiful wildlife, and Fern Lake and Odessa Lake—two of Rocky Mountain National Park's most beautiful lakes. The lakes shimmer in a deep, glacier-carved gorge below 12,129-foot Notchtop Mountain, Little Matterhorn, and Gabletop Mountain.

The trail, gaining over 1,800 feet from trailhead to Odessa Lake, has plenty of uphill sections. Hike at a slow pace and take rest breaks, especially if you're coming from a lower elevation. Be prepared for inclement weather by bringing rain jackets and extra clothes, even in summer.

Start the hike at the Fern Lake Trailhead and hike west along the Big Thompson River to The Pool, gaining little elevation, which makes it an easy kid hike. The trail switchbacks up wooded slopes past Fern Falls to a junction with Spruce Lake Trail on the right before Fern Lake. At Fern Lake, look for moose wading in the shallows. The best mountain views are from the lake's north end. Continue another mile to a side

Notchtop Mountain, Little Matterhorn, and Gabletop Mountain rise above the outlet stream at Fern Lake.

A cow moose wades through the shallows on the edge of Fern Lake.

Notchtop Mountain towers above Odessa Lake in the heart of Rocky Mountain National Park.

Fern Lake and Odessa Lake; Cub Lake

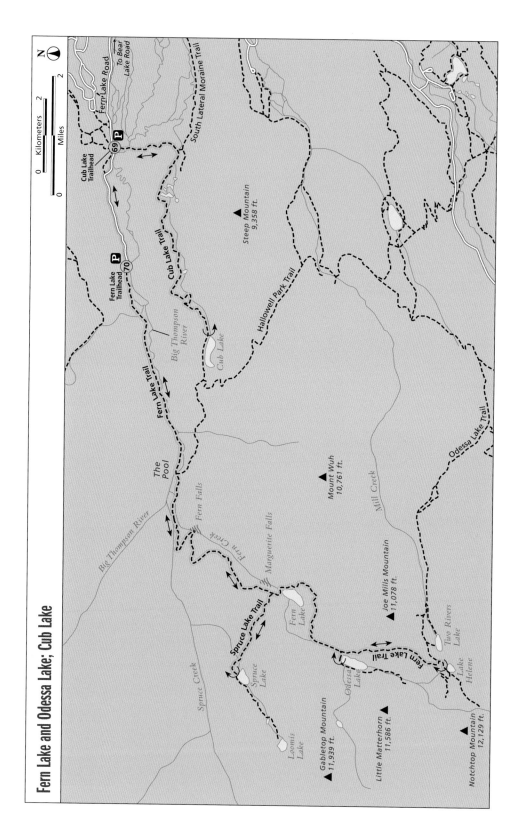

N

0   Kilometers   2

0   Miles   2

Fern Lake Road

To Bear Lake Road

Cub Lake Trailhead   69   P

Fern Lake Trailhead   70   P

Big Thompson River

Fern Lake Trail

The Pool

Big Thompson River

Cub Lake Trail

Cub Lake

South Lateral Moraine Trail

Steep Mountain
9,358 ft.

Hallowell Park Trail

Fern Falls

Fern Creek

Marguerite Falls

Mount Wuh
10,761 ft.

Mill Creek

Spruce Creek

Spruce Lake Trail

Spruce Lake

Loomis Lake

Gabletop Mountain
11,939 ft.

Fern Lake

Odessa Lake

Little Matterhorn
11,586 ft.

Joe Mills Mountain
11,078 ft.

Fern Lake Trail

Odessa Lake Trail

Two Rivers Lake

Lake Helene

Notchtop Mountain
12,129 ft.

trail that leads to a rocky beach at Odessa Lake's north side and more breathtaking views. Turn around here to return to the trailhead.

For extra credit, continue up the Fern Lake Trail from Odessa Lake for a mile to lovely 10,610-foot Lake Helene and Two Rivers Lake below Notchtop's sheer north face. Another extra credit hike follows Spruce Lake Trail to a spruce-ringed tarn that reflects pointed Castle Rock.

Miles and Directions

0.0 Start at the Fern Lake Trailhead and hike west on the north bank of the Big Thompson River.

1.7 Cross the river on a footbridge and reach a junction on the left with Cub Lake Trail. Continue straight past The Pool on the right.

1.9 Cross a bridge over Fern Creek.

2.6 Reach Fern Falls (GPS: 40 20.841, –105 40.062). Continue south up the trail.

3.7 Reach a junction on the right with Spruce Lake Trail (GPS: 40 20.3263. –105 40.5706). An extra credit hike follows this trail. Continue straight to Fern Lake.

3.8 Reach the north shore of Fern Lake (GPS: 40 20.2841, –105 40.5728) and admire the view. To hike to Odessa Lake, go east and cross a bridge over Fern Creek and turn right on Fern Lake Trail.

4.0 Reach a fine overlook above Fern Lake. Continue south on the trail.

4.6 Reach a junction on the right with a side trail to Odessa Lake. Go right and descend to a bridge over Fern Creek and hike south along the creek's west bank.

4.7 Arrive at Odessa Lake (GPS: 40 19.9013, –105 41.0677). To return, descend Fern Lake Trail. For extra credit, continue up Fern Lake Trail to Lake Helene.

9.4 Arrive back at the trailhead (GPS: 40 21.2897, –105 37.8688).

EXTRA CREDIT: SPRUCE LAKE AND LAKE HELENE

SPRUCE LAKE: Below Fern Lake at 3.7 miles, go right on Spruce Lake Trail. Hike 0.8 mile west to the remote lake and a backcountry campsite (GPS: 40 20.5624, –105 41.2227). Return to the main trail for a 1.6-mile side trip.

LAKE HELENE: From Odessa Lake, continue south on Fern Lake Trail for 1 mile, climbing talus slopes on Joe Mills Mountain's west side. This trail section often holds snow until late June. Check with a ranger before hiking and bring MICROspikes and trekking poles. After crossing a pass, reach an unmarked junction. Descend south on a trail for 0.1 mile to gorgeous Lake Helene (GPS: 40 19.25, –105 41.1528). Two Rivers Lake is to the east. Return to Odessa Lake for an extra 2.2-mile, round-trip hike.

70 Cub Lake

Cub Lake, reached by Cub Lake Trail, is a picturesque pond covered with water lilies and nestled in a high valley west of Moraine Park.

See map on page 256.
Start: Cub Lake Trailhead
Difficulty: Easy
Trail: Cub Lake Trail
Hiking time: 2 to 3 hours
Distance: 4.6 miles out-and-back
Elevation trailhead to lake: 8,080 to 8,620 feet at Cub Lake (+540 feet)
Restrictions: Fee area; open 24 hours year-round, weather permitting; vault toilets at Cub Lake shuttle stop; no dogs, no bikes, and no motorized vehicles allowed; wilderness rules apply
Amenities: Toilets at shuttle stop; campgrounds; services in Estes Park
Maps: *DeLorme*: Page 29, B5 and B6; Trails Illustrated 200: Rocky Mountain National Park; USGS McHenrys Peak
County: Larimer
Land status: Rocky Mountain National Park, (970) 586-1206

Finding the trailhead: From Estes Park, take US 36 west for 3.8 miles to the Beaver Meadows Entrance Station at Rocky Mountain National Park. Drive 0.2 mile and turn left (south) on Bear Lake Road. Drive 1.2 miles and turn right toward Moraine Park Campground. Drive 0.5 mile and turn left on Fern Lake Road. Continue 1.5 miles to Cub Lake Trailhead (GPS: 40 21.37, -105 36.9503). Additional lots exist east of the trailhead and at the bus stop west of the trailhead. Lots fill quickly in summer and on weekends. Avoid parking problems by boarding the Moraine Park shuttle at the Park and Ride opposite Glacier Basin Campground on Bear Lake Road and ride to the Cub Lake bus stop.

The Hike

The Cub Lake Trail begins at the western edge of Moraine Park, crosses a flat valley, and climbs to hidden Cub Lake tucked in a shallow basin above the Big Thompson River canyon. Cub Lake Trail is a fun hike for families with gentle grades, wildlife, and spectacular scenery.

Over eighty wildflower species bloom along the trail in summer, and the lake is famed for a profusion of water lily pads adorned with yellow flowers. The first trail section passes willow-covered marshlands and beaver ponds. Watch for moose foraging in the willow thickets. The Cub Lake area was burned in the 2012 Fern Lake Fire, which lasted three months before snow extinguished it in early January.

Start the hike at the Cub Lake Trailhead. Hike south through meadows and wetlands before steadily climbing through pine forest to the lily pad–covered lake and the burned area. Stop at the east end of the lake for the best views of the Continental Divide peaks. Return back to the trailhead on the same trail.

Cub Lake nestles in a shallow basin below mountain slopes burned in the Fern Lake Fire in 2012.

The Cub Lake Trail heads up a marshy valley on the western edge of Moraine Park.

Cub Lake reflects blue sky, clouds, and snowcapped Stones Peak.

Miles and Directions

0.0 Start at the Cub Lake Trailhead. Hike south for 260 feet, cross a footbridge over the Big Thompson River, and continue south on the west side of Moraine Park through meadows and wetlands.

0.5 Reach a junction on the left with South Lateral Moraine Trail at the southwest corner of Moraine Park (GPS: 40 20.9831, –105 36.9659). Keep on the main trail and hike west up a glaciated valley.

0.8 Cross a rock outcrop and pass beaver ponds to the left (GPS: 40 21.0667, –105 37.2381). Look for moose in the ponds.

1.4 Reach the valley's end below a cliff and hike west up pine-covered slopes.

1.5 Pass more beaver ponds in an upper valley and continue uphill.

2.3 Arrive at the northeast side of Cub Lake (GPS: 40 20.7742, –105 38.4829) and the best mountain views. After admiring the vista, turn around and return the way you came.

4.6 Arrive back at the trailhead (GPS: 40 21.37, –105 36.9503).

EXTRA CREDIT: LOOP HIKE PAST THE POOL AND BIG THOMPSON RIVER

For a 6-mile loop hike, continue past Cub Lake to the junction with Hallowell Park Trail. Stay right on Cub Lake Trail. The trail climbs a saddle, descends, and crosses rugged terrain on north-facing slopes. At 3.5 miles, go right onto Fern Lake Trail (GPS: 40 20.9616, –105 39.5839). Cross a footbridge over the Big Thompson River and hike east to the Fern Lake Trailhead at 5.0 miles (GPS: 40 21.2897, –105 37.8688). Walk east on the edge of dirt Fern Lake Road to the Fern Lake bus stop. Take a trail from the stop's north side back to the Cub Lake Trailhead at 6.0 miles.

71 Sprague Lake

The popular Sprague Lake Loop Trail, one of Rocky Mountain National Park's iconic lake hikes, encircles the lake's edge, offering majestic mountain views, glimpses of wildlife, and educational signs.

Start: Sprague Lake Trailhead
Difficulty: Easy
Trail: Sprague Lake Loop Trail
Hiking time: 30 minutes to 1 hour
Distance: 0.8 mile lollipop
Elevation trailhead to lake: 8,690 to 8,688 feet at lake (–2 feet)
Restrictions: Entrance fee; parking lot fills in summer; free shuttle bus to trailhead from Park & Ride lot on Bear Lake Road across

from Glacier Basin Campground; no dogs allowed
Amenities: Toilets at trailhead; services in Estes Park
Maps: *DeLorme*: Page 29, C6; Trails Illustrated 200: Rocky Mountain National Park; USGS Longs Peak
County: Larimer
Land status: Rocky Mountain National Park, (970) 586-1206

Finding the trailhead: From Estes Park, take US 36 west for 3.8 miles to the Beaver Meadows Entrance Station at Rocky Mountain National Park. Continue west on US 36 for 0.2 mile and turn left on Bear Lake Road. Drive 5.7 miles to a left turn on Sprague Lake Road. Drive 0.3 mile to the parking lot and trailhead (GPS: 40 19.2268, –105 36.4716).

The Hike

The Sprague Lake Loop Trail, one of Rocky Mountain National Park's most popular easy hikes, loops around the perimeter of the 13-acre lake, offering marvelous views of the snowcapped Continental Divide mountains to the west, including Hallett Peak, Otis Peak, Flattop Mountain, and Notchtop Mountain. The hike is a favorite for families and seniors with an elevation gain of only 20 feet. The trail's packed gravel surface and gentle grades make it wheelchair- and stroller-accessible in dry conditions. The scenic lake was built in the early 1900s by Abner and Alberta Sprague for guests at their Sprague Hotel, located at today's lake parking lot. They dammed nearby Boulder Brook to create the lake.

Start at the Sprague Lake Trailhead and cross a wooden footbridge over Boulder Brook. The trail heads to a Y-junction. While you can go either right or left, this description turns left and makes a clockwise circuit. Follow the wide trail around the perimeter of Sprague Lake, passing rest benches and interpretive signs that detail the area's geology history, and natural history. Keep alert for wildlife along the trail, including beaver, moose, and ducks. Early morning is the best time to see animals. Find the best mountain views on the east side of the lake. Get there at sunrise to snap photos of alpenglow painting the peaks red and reflecting them in Sprague Lake's glassy surface.

A moose feeds in shallow water on the northern edge of Sprague Lake.

Marsh grass and wildflowers edge the southern shoreline of Sprague Lake.

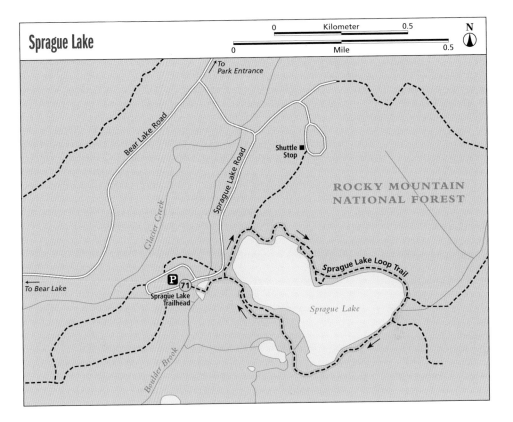

Sprague Lake

Miles and Directions

0.0 Start at the Sprague Lake Trailhead at the southeast corner of the parking lot. Hike east across a bridge and follow the trail paralleling the road.

0.05 Reach a junction at the start of the lake loop (GPS: 40 19.2359, –105 36.4213). Go left.

0.2 Reach a junction. Keep left on the main trail or go right and walk a short path along the northern lakeshore.

0.25 Reach a junction with the lakeshore spur. Continue straight on the main trail around the lake.

0.75 Return to the first Y-junction and turn left.

0.8 Arrive back at the trailhead (GPS: 40 19.2268, –105 36.4716).

72 Glacier Gorge Lakes: Mills Lake, Jewel Lake, and Black Lake

A string of shiny lakes, reached by Glacier Gorge Trail, scatter along the wooded floor of spectacular Glacier Gorge, a deep, alpine valley lined with sharp mountains including 14,259-foot Longs Peak, the high point of Rocky Mountain National Park.

Start: Glacier Gorge Trailhead
Difficulty: Moderate
Trail: Glacier Gorge Trail
Hiking time: About 7 hours for Black Lake
Distance: 9.6 miles out-and-back for Black Lake
Elevation trailhead to lakes: 9,180 to 10,630 feet at Black Lake (+1,450 feet)
Restrictions: Fee area; day-use only; no dogs; wilderness rules apply

Amenities: Trailhead vault toilets; free shuttle service; services in Estes Park
Maps: *DeLorme*: Page 29, C5 and C6; Trails Illustrated 200: Rocky Mountain National Park; USGS McHenrys Peak
County: Larimer
Land status: Rocky Mountain National Park, (970) 586-1206

Finding the trailhead: From Estes Park, take US 36 West for 3.8 miles to the Beaver Meadows Entrance Station at Rocky Mountain National Park. Drive 0.2 mile and turn left (south) onto Bear Lake Road, then go 8.1 miles to a paved parking area on the road's left side at the trailhead. The lot quickly fills in summer and on weekends. Avoid parking problems by boarding the Bear Lake shuttle at the Park and Ride opposite Glacier Basin Campground and ride to the Glacier Basin bus stop and trailhead (GPS: 40 18.621, -105 38.421).

The Hike

Glacier Gorge, one of Rocky Mountain National Park's beauty spots, plunges north from Longs Peak, Pagoda Peak, and Chiefs Head Peak to Loch Vale. The glacier-scoured valley, lined with granite cliffs and skyscraping mountains, offers three majestic lakes along Glacier Gorge Trail. Mills Lake, named for the park's founding father, Enos Mills, lies at the gorge's north end, a crystal lake reflecting sky, clouds, and peaks. Jewel Lake is a shiny gem muffled by thick forest along its shoreline. Follow a side trail on its eastern side for views across this quiet lake. The hike ends at Black Lake, a dark tarn surrounded by cliffs below McHenrys Peak. Farther up the gorge are more lakes, including Blue Lake, Frozen Lake, Green Lake below The Spearhead, and "Italy Lake," the highest in the basin at 11,620 feet. These are reached by continuing up the rough trail to the upper cirque.

The popular Glacier Gorge Trail, beginning at Glacier Gorge Trailhead, twists south past Alberta Falls and then bends up Glacier Creek in lower Loch Vale before busting south up bedrock past Glacier Falls to Mills Lake. Sit on shoreline granite to enjoy the spacious lake and wide views. The trail hugs the lake's east shore to Jewel

Black Lake lies in a cliff-lined cirque below McHenrys Peak in Glacier Gorge.

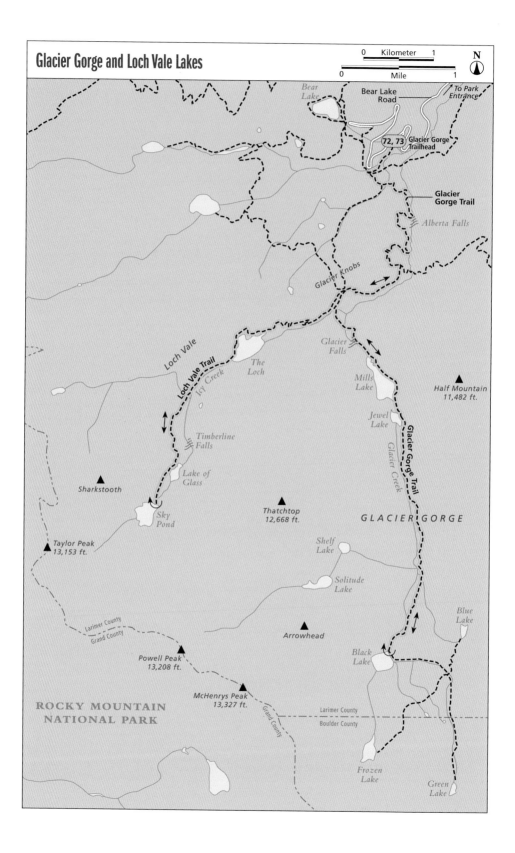

Glacier Gorge and Loch Vale Lakes

0 **Kilometer** 1

0 **Mile** 1

N

Bear Lake

Bear Lake Road

To Park Entrance

72, 73   Glacier Gorge Trailhead

Glacier Gorge Trail

Alberta Falls

Glacier Knobs

Loch Vale

Loch Vale Trail

Icy Creek

The Loch

Glacier Falls

Mills Lake

▲ Half Mountain
11,482 ft.

Jewel Lake

Timberline Falls

Glacier Creek

Glacier Gorge Trail

▲ Sharkstooth

Lake of Glass

Sky Pond

▲ Thatchtop
12,668 ft.

GLACIER GORGE

▲ Taylor Peak
13,153 ft.

Shelf Lake

Solitude Lake

Blue Lake

Larimer County

Grand County

▲ Arrowhead

Black Lake

▲ Powell Peak
13,208 ft.

▲ McHenrys Peak
13,327 ft.

Grand County

Larimer County

Boulder County

**ROCKY MOUNTAIN
NATIONAL PARK**

Frozen Lake

Green Lake

Mills Lake, named for Enos Mills, father of Rocky Mountain National Park, reflects sky and clouds in Glacier Gorge.

Lake and continues across wetlands on a boardwalk to dense forest along Glacier Creek. After passing "Slide Falls" and pretty Ribbon Falls, the trail climbs to Black Lake and the turnaround point. Plan on a full-day adventure to see all of the lakes. Bring extra clothes, rain gear, water, snacks, and trekking poles.

Miles and Directions

0.0 Begin at the Glacier Gorge Trailhead. Hike south on the Glacier Gorge Trail.

0.3 Reach Glacier Gorge Junction and turn left (GPS: 40 18.4589, –105 38.6083). Hike uphill past Alberta Falls to a ridgetop east of the twin Glacier Knobs.

1.6 Reach a junction with North Longs Peak Trail on the left (GPS: 40 17.9826, –105 38.3886). Bend right on Glacier Gorge Trail and hike west across a slope above Glacier Creek.

2.1 Reach a junction with signed Loch Vale Trail. Go left on Glacier Gorge Trail toward Mills Lake and cross a bridge over the creek. Climb south, passing Glacier Falls on the left.

2.5 Reach the north edge of Mills Lake (GPS: 40 17.503, –105 38.5828). Follow the trail around the lake's left (east) side to its south shore and inlet stream.

3.0 Arrive at the east shore of Jewel Lake (GPS: 40 17.1952, –105 38.3601). Continue south through trees past the lake and follow Glacier Creek south.

4.4 Reach "Slide Falls" to the right. Follow a short side trail to the waterfall.

4.6 Reach Ribbon Falls (GPS: 40 16.045, –105 38.399) on the right. Climb steps up the trail right of the waterfall and continue south. Follow the trail if it's dry or rock-hop alongside the creek.

4.8 Arrive at Black Lake below McHenrys Peak (GPS: 40 15.984, –105 38.431). Look across the lake to dramatic "Black Lake Falls." Return north, following the trails back to the trailhead.

9.6 Arrive back at the trailhead (GPS: 40 18.621, –105 38.421).

73 Loch Vale Lakes: The Loch, Lake of Glass, and Sky Pond

Icy Brook fills three lakes—The Loch, Lake of Glass, and Sky Pond, a shining lake below a tableau of sawtoothed peaks—in cliff-lined Loch Vale, a glaciated gorge east of the Continental Divide.

See map on page 266.
Start: Glacier Gorge Trailhead
Difficulty: Strenuous
Trails: Glacier Gorge Trail, Loch Vale Trail
Hiking time: About 6 hours for Sky Pond
Distance: 8.8 miles out-and-back for Sky Pond
Elevation trailhead to lakes: 9,180 to 10,865 feet at Sky Pond (+1,685 feet)

Restrictions: Fee area; day-use only; no dogs; wilderness rules apply
Amenities: Trailhead vault toilets; free shuttle service; services in Estes Park
Maps: *DeLorme:* Page 29, C5 and C6; Trails Illustrated 200: Rocky Mountain National Park; USGS McHenrys Peak
County: Larimer
Land status: Rocky Mountain National Park, (970) 586-1206

Finding the trailhead: From Estes Park, take US 36 West for 3.8 miles to the Beaver Meadows Entrance Station at Rocky Mountain National Park. Drive 0.2 mile and turn left (south) on Bear Lake Road, then go 8.1 miles to a paved parking area at Glacier Gorge Trailhead on the road's left side. The lot quickly fills in summer and on weekends. Avoid parking problems by boarding the Bear Lake shuttle at the Park and Ride opposite Glacier Basin Campground and ride to the Glacier Basin bus stop and trailhead (GPS: 40 18.621, -105 38.421).

The Hike

Rising from Taylor Glacier on the Continental Divide, Icy Brook flows east down Loch Vale, a 2-mile, glaciated valley, pooling in three magnificent lakes—Sky Pond, Lake of Glass, and The Loch—and plunging over Timberline Falls. Loch Vale, one of Rocky Mountain National Park's splendid spots, is lined with jagged peaks including Sharkstooth, The Petit Grepon, the Saber, and Cathedral Wall, while 13,153-foot Taylor Peak lords over the upper cirque. The Loch, a popular destination by itself, fills the lower valley floor. Admire the lake and the mountains beyond from rocky outcrops along the wooded shore. Timberline Falls, the next natural wonder, splatters 75 feet off a cliff, shattering to foam at the base. The striking upper basin is floored by Lake of Glass, a shelf lake above the waterfall, and aquamarine-colored Sky Pond, perhaps Colorado's most beautiful lake. Sky Pond sprawls across the magical valley, its northern skyline etched by soaring granite spires.

Beginning at Glacier Gorge Trailhead, the hike follows Glacier Gorge Trail past Alberta Falls to a junction with Loch Vale Trail, which is followed west up the

The Sharkstooth and Petit Grepon tower above Sky Pond, one of Rocky Mountain National Park's beauty spots.

valley. The busy trail traverses slopes above Icy Brook, which tumbles down cascades below, and climbs to Loch Vale. The hike's steepest section climbs stone steps up a talus slope to Timberline Falls. The next segment scrambles up a broken cliff right of the waterfall. This is the crux of the hike with exposed rock scrambling up narrow ledges. The first 100 feet is dangerous and exposed, especially if the rock is wet or icy. Use extreme caution when climbing up and down this section. Serious accidents have occurred here when ill-equipped hikers have slipped on steep snow. The Park Service advises bringing crampons and an ice axe in early summer when snow still covers the cliff. It's a long day to hike to Sky Pond so plan on an early start to avoid afternoon thunderstorms. Also, bring extra clothes, rain gear, water, food, MICROspikes, and trekking poles.

Miles and Directions

0.0 Begin at the Glacier Gorge Trailhead. Hike south on Glacier Gorge Trail.

0.3 Reach Glacier Gorge Junction and turn left (GPS: 40 18.4589, –105 38.6083). Hike uphill past Alberta Falls at 0.8 mile to a ridgetop east of the twin Glacier Knobs.

1.6 Arrive at a junction with North Longs Peak Trail (GPS: 40 17.9826, –105 38.3886). Bend right on Glacier Gorge Trail and hike west across a slope above Glacier Creek.

2.1 Reach a junction with signed Loch Vale Trail (GPS: 40 17.845, –105 38.76). Go right on Loch Vale Trail.

2.8 Arrive at the east end of The Loch (GPS: 40 17.638, –105 39.272). Enjoy spectacular views west across the lake. Continue on the trail along the right side of the lake.

3.2 Reach the west end of The Loch. Continue west and follow Icy Brook.

3.6 Reach the junction with Andrews Glacier Trail on the right at Andrews Creek. Stay straight on Loch Vale Trail toward Sky Pond.

3.9 Timberline Falls comes into view in the cliffs ahead. Climb stone steps up a steep talus slope to the base of the waterfall.

4.0 Arrive at Timberline Falls (GPS: 40 16.993, -105 39.887). Scramble up steep rock (Class 3) using hands and feet right of the waterfall. Use caution on wet and icy rock. Above the steep section, continue scrambling up lower-angle rock.

4.1 Reach the Lake of Glass (GPS: 40 16.9305, -105 39.9269). Continue on the trail across rocky terrain on its north side.

4.4 Arrive at the east end of Sky Pond (GPS: 40 16.7257, -105 40.068). After a snack, reverse the trail and hike back down Loch Vale. Again, use caution descending the cliff at Timberline Falls.

8.8 Arrive back at the trailhead (GPS: 40 18.621, -105 38.421).

74 Bear Lake

Bear Lake, a glacial lake explored by a wheelchair-accessible shoreline trail, offers breathtaking views, reflections of clouds and peaks, and tranquil beauty in the heart of Rocky Mountain National Park.

Start: Bear Lake Trailhead
Difficulty: Easy; handicapped accessible for segments
Trail: Bear Lake Trail
Hiking time: About 30 minutes
Distance: 0.7 mile loop
Elevation trailhead to lakes: 9,457 to 9,475 feet at Bear Lake (+18 feet)
Restrictions: Fee area; no dogs, swimming, or fishing; no motorized vehicles or equipment; parking lot fills early; take shuttle to avoid parking problems
Amenities: Vault toilets and ranger station at trailhead; free shuttle from Bear Lake Park and Ride; services in Estes Park
Maps: *DeLorme*: Page 29, C5; Trails Illustrated 200: Rocky Mountain National Park; USGS McHenrys Peak
County: Larimer
Land status: Rocky Mountain National Park, (970) 586-1206

Finding the trailhead: From Estes Park, take US 36 west for 3.8 miles to the Beaver Meadows Entrance Station at Rocky Mountain National Park. Drive 0.2 mile past the entrance and turn left (south) on Bear Lake Road. Drive 9.4 miles up Bear Lake Road from the turnoff to a parking lot and trailhead at the road's end (GPS: 40 18.7177, -105 38.7584). The parking lot quickly fills in summer and on weekends. Avoid parking problems by boarding the Bear Lake shuttle at the Park and Ride station opposite Glacier Basin Campground and ride to the Bear Lake stop. The shuttle runs from late May to mid-October, with shuttles departing about every 15 minutes from 6:30 a.m. to 7:30 p.m.

The Hike

Bear Lake, a gorgeous lake below Tyndall Gorge and the Continental Divide, is one of Rocky Mountain National Park's most beloved wonders. The lake is ideal for casual hikers, with easy accessibility, a handicap-accessible trail encircling the lake, less than 30 feet of elevation gain, spectacular views of 12,713-foot Hallett Peak and 14,259-foot Longs Peak, and plenty of rest benches. It's also the gateway to a ladder of lakes—Nymph, Dream, and Emerald Lakes—in the gorge above. Before hiking, pick up an interpretive guide, keyed to bear paw markers, that explains the area's natural history, geology, and human history along the route. Ask at the trailhead ranger station for the booklet.

The Bear Lake Trail, one of four handicapped-accessible trails in Rocky Mountain National Park, is wheelchair friendly with assistance on several sections with grades up to 14 percent. Trail sections at the loop's start and end are fully accessible without assistance. The packed dirt trail averages 60 inches wide with a firm, packed-dirt surface.

Reflections of sky, clouds, and Longs Peak, high point of Rocky Mountain National Park, in Bear Lake.

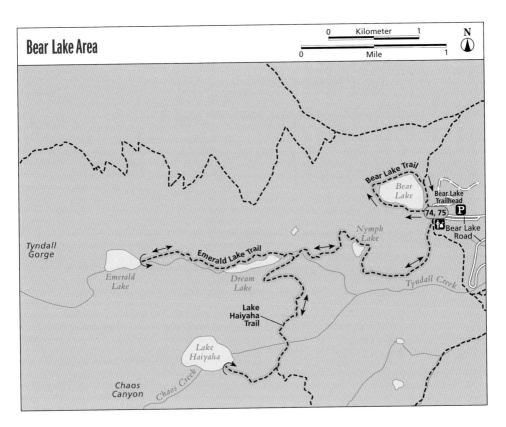

Bear Lake, the park's most visited lake, is a busy place, especially during the summer. The parking lot at the trailhead quickly fills in the morning so if you arrive later, plan to be turned around by a ranger. It's best to park at the Bear Lake Park and Ride opposite Glacier Basin Campground and ride a free shuttle to the trailhead.

Miles and Directions

0.0 Start at the Bear Lake Trailhead by the ranger station at the west side of the parking lot. Cross a bridge and pass a junction on the left for the Emerald Lake Trail. Hike northwest on paved Bear Lake Trail.

0.03 Reach a trail junction and the start of the loop hike (GPS: 40 18.7308, –105 38.7926). Go left on the trail.

0.15 Pass a photo viewpoint. The fully accessible trail section ends just past here with a short 16 percent hill.

0.3 Reach the lake's northwest corner and bend right on the trail along the lake's north shoreline. Stop for views south to Longs Peak.

0.5 Reach the northeast corner of the lake and continue south along the east shoreline. Below a short 14 percent grade, the trail becomes fully accessible again.

0.6 Stop at a lakeside viewpoint that looks west to Hallett Peak. Continue south to the first junction and go left on the wide trail.

0.7 Arrive back at the trailhead (GPS: 40 18.7177, –105 38.7584).

75 Nymph Lake, Dream Lake, and Emerald Lake

Tyndall Creek plunges east between Hallett Peak and Flattop Mountain and pools in four exquisite glacial lakes—Bear, Nymph, Dream, and Emerald Lakes—while Lake Haiyaha, reached by an extra credit hike, nestles to the south in Chaos Canyon. This hike explores the lakes, offering an unforgettable adventure in Rocky Mountain National Park.

See map on page 273.
Start: Bear Lake Trailhead
Difficulty: Moderate
Trail: Emerald Lake Trail, Lake Haiyaha Trail
Hiking time: 3 to 5 hours
Distance: 3.6 miles out-and-back to Emerald Lake; 5.6 miles out-and-back with Lake Haiyaha; 6.3 miles for a five-lake hike
Elevation trailhead to lake: 9,475 to 10,090 feet at Emerald Lake (+615 feet)

Restrictions: Fee area; no dogs; no motorized vehicles or equipment; parking lot fills early
Amenities: Vault toilets; ranger station at trailhead; services in Estes Park
Maps: *DeLorme*: Page 29, C5; Trails Illustrated 200: Rocky Mountain National Park; USGS McHenrys Peak
County: Larimer
Land status: Rocky Mountain National Park, (970) 586-1206

Finding the trailhead: From Estes Park, take US 36 west for 3.8 miles to the Beaver Meadows Entrance Station at Rocky Mountain National Park. Drive 0.2 mile and turn left (south) on Bear Lake Road. Drive 9.4 miles up Bear Lake Road from the turnoff to a parking lot and trailhead at road's end (GPS: 40 18.7177, –105 38.7584). The parking lot fills in summer and on weekends. Avoid parking problems by boarding the Bear Lake shuttle at the Park and Ride station opposite Glacier Basin Campground and ride to the Bear Lake stop. The shuttle runs from late May to mid-October, with shuttles departing about every 15 minutes from 6:30 a.m. to 7:30 p.m.

The Hike

The Emerald Lake Trail is deservedly one of Rocky Mountain National Park's most popular hikes. The trail offers gorgeous mountain scenery and passes four glacial lakes—Bear, Nymph, Dream, and Emerald Lakes—and accesses a fifth one, Lake Haiyaha. The five-lake hike is easy to follow, has few steep grades, and offers bucket-list photo ops. The hike starts at Bear Lake, the park's most visited lake, so plan on arriving early or taking a free shuttle to avoid parking problems. An early start also guarantees reflections of high peaks in still lake water.

From the trailhead, have a quick peek at Bear Lake and then head up marked Emerald Lake Trail to Nymph Lake, a placid tarn filled with lily pads. Continue another half-mile to Dream Lake, a forest-fringed lake often called the park's most beautiful lake. Hallett Peak's rugged cliffs lord above the lake and Tyndall Gorge. The trail edges

Summer storm clouds swirl over Hallett Peak and Nymph Lake in the heart of Rocky Mountain National Park.

past Dream Lake and climbs the glaciated valley to Emerald Lake, a green jewel set in scenic splendor below Hallett Peak's northeast face and skyscraping spires on Flattop Mountain. On the descent, take a right turn below Dream Lake and hike a mile to Lake Haiyaha, another shiny gem surrounded by rugged peaks. Finish the five-lake challenge by returning to the trailhead and walking the easy trail around Bear Lake.

Miles and Directions

0.0   Start at the Bear Lake Trailhead by the ranger station at the west side of the parking lot. Cross a bridge to a junction for the Emerald Lake Trail. Go left on it and hike uphill through a spruce and lodgepole pine forest.

0.5   After gaining 255 feet, reach the south edge of Nymph Lake (GPS: 40 18.575, –105 39.0805). Continue along its east shore with views west to Hallett Peak, then turn left along the north shore and climb below cliffs.

1.0   Reach a junction with the Lake Haiyaha Trail on the left (GPS: 40 18.5821, –105 39.3635). Continue straight and hike west. For extra credit, return to this junction on the descent and hike to Lake Haiyaha.

1.1   Reach the eastern end of narrow Dream Lake and great mountain views to the west. Hike along the rocky north shore and climb west above Tyndall Creek.

1.8   Arrive at a rocky overlook on the east side of Emerald Lake (GPS: 40 18.5798, –105 40.0065). After enjoying the view, return back down the trail.

3.6   Arrive back at the trailhead (GPS: 40 18.7177, –105 38.7584).

EXTRA CREDIT: LAKE HAIYAHA

To hike to Lake Haiyaha, return to the junction east of Dream Lake and go right (south) on the signed trail. Hike 1 mile up to Lake Haiyaha (GPS: 40 18.2479, –105 39.6625) and then return to the junction for 2 extra miles. Elevation is 10,223 feet at Lake Haiyaha (+748 feet). For the full-value, five-lake hike, continue down to the trailhead from Lake Haiyaha and hike 0.7 mile on the perimeter path around Bear Lake for a 6.3-mile trek.

76 Lily Lake

A gentle, ADA-accessible trail follows the shoreline of scenic Lily Lake in a wide valley on the east side of Rocky Mountain National Park.

Start: Lily Lake Trailhead
Difficulty: Easy; handicapped accessible
Trail: Lily Lake Trail
Hiking time: About 1 hour
Distance: 0.8 mile loop
Elevation trailhead to lake: 8,930 feet at trailhead and lake
Restrictions: Limited parking; no dogs or mountain bikes; no wading or swimming in lake

Amenities: Trailhead vault toilets; picnic tables; interpretive signs; services in Estes Park
Maps: *DeLorme*: Page 29, C6; Trails Illustrated 200: Rocky Mountain National Park; USGS Longs Peak
County: Boulder
Land status: Rocky Mountain National Park, (970) 586-1206

Finding the trailhead: From the junction of US 36 and CO 7 in Estes Park, drive south for 6.3 miles on CO 7 to a right (west) turn to a parking lot, restrooms, and the Lily Lake Trailhead (GPS: 40 18.4003, -105 32.275). Overflow parking is on the east side of CO 7.

The Hike

Lily Lake, lying on the eastern edge of Rocky Mountain National Park, is a lovely, 18-acre lake nestled in a valley against 9,786-foot Lily Mountain's south flank. The lake, dammed and enlarged in 1915, was originally private property. The water and recreation rights were bought by Larimer County Parks & Open Lands and the Estes Valley Land Trust to protect the scenic lake from development.

The Lily Lake Trail explores the shoreline of the popular lake, offering stunning views of 14,259-foot Longs Peak, Estes Cone, and Twin Sisters. The wide trail, one of four handicapped-accessible trails in the park, is easily traversed by wheelchairs and strollers. The restrooms, picnic tables, and pier are also ADA accessible. The hike around the lake, one of the national park's no-fee areas, is kid-friendly with minimal elevation gain and wildlife watching, including moose wading in the shallows. A couple of side trails, including Lily Ridge Trail, allow hikers to extend their adventure. Rock climbers also use the trail to reach a steep path to cliffs at Jurassic Park high on Lily Mountain.

The Twin Sisters fill the eastern skyline above Lily Lake in Rocky Mountain National Park.

EXTRA CREDIT: NEW STORM PASS TRAIL AND LILY RIDGE TRAIL

Go left at 0.2 mile on New Storm Pass Trail and hike 0.25 mile to a junction where the trail goes right. Keep left and hike 0.15 mile on a spur back to the trail. This short loop makes a 0.5-mile hike. For a longer hike with views of Longs Peak, follow Lily Lake Trail to the junction with Lily Ridge Trail at 0.4 mile. Go left on the Lily Ridge Trail for 0.7 mile, gaining 100 feet, before dropping down to Lily Lake Trail. This option makes a 1.1-mile hike.

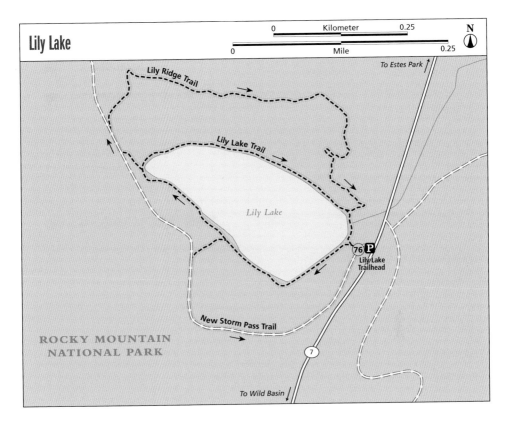

Lily Lake

Miles and Directions

0.0 Start at the Lily Lake Trailhead and go left on the trail. Hike along the lake's edge to a boardwalk over a marsh.

0.2 Reach a junction on the left with New Storm Pass Trail (GPS: 40 18.409, –105 32.4797), which heads southwest to Estes Cone. Continue northwest along the lake's south shoreline.

0.4 Reach the junction with the Lily Ridge Trail on the left (GPS: 40 18.4962, –105 32.6156). Continue on the main trail, which bends right and follows the north shore of Lily Lake.

0.7 Reach a junction with the eastern end of Lily Ridge Trail. Keep right on the trail and cross a levee at the lake's eastern end.

0.8 Arrive back at the trailhead (GPS: 40 18.4003, –105 32.275).

77 Peacock Pool and Chasm Lake

This excellent hike, gaining 2,500 feet of elevation, climbs to Chasm Lake, a dramatic high-elevation lake hidden in a glacier-chiseled cirque below the looming east face of Longs Peak.

Start: Longs Peak Trailhead
Difficulty: Strenuous
Trails: East Longs Peak Trail, Chasm Lake Trail
Hiking time: 4 to 6 hours
Distance: 8.4 miles out-and-back
Elevation trailhead to lakes: 9,405 to 11,310 feet at Peacock Pool; 11,803 feet at Chasm Lake (+2,398 feet)
Restrictions: Parking lot fills early; overflow parking on road; stay on trail; use caution on snowfields; watch for rockfall; do not hike to Peacock Pool

Amenities: Toilets at trailhead; toilet at junction above timberline; Longs Peak Campground first-come in summer; ranger station at trailhead; services in Estes Park
Maps: *DeLorme*: Page 29, C6; Trails Illustrated 200: Rocky Mountain National Park; USGS Longs Peak
County: Larimer, Boulder
Land status: Rocky Mountain National Park, (970) 586-1206

Finding the trailhead: From the junction of US 36 and CO 7 in Estes Park, drive south for 9.2 miles on CO 7 to a right (west) turn past mile marker 9. Drive a mile to the Longs Peak Ranger Station, campground, and Longs Peak Trailhead (GPS: 40 16.2852, -105 33.3901) at the west end of the parking. From the south, drive 10.5 miles north on CO 7 from its junction with CO 72 and make a left turn to the trailhead. The lot fills early on summer weekends. Use overflow parking along the road below the parking lot.

The Hike

Chasm Lake, tucked into a glaciated cirque below the magnificent east face of 14,259-foot Longs Peak, is one of Colorado's most beautiful alpine lakes. Towering granite cliffs and talus fields surround the rocky shoreline of the 11,803-foot lake, giving a glimpse of raw, untamed nature. Chasm Lake sits amid toothed mountains including Longs' upper east face and the Diamond, a 900-foot vertical cliff which offers some of America's best high-altitude rock climbs, and Mount Meeker with its sweeping north wall enclosing the cirque's south side. The lake, fed by Mills Glacier, is a place encircled with views that you won't forget. Find a flat boulder on the lake's east shore to enjoy the scenery and a sandwich. The best time for photographs is in the early morning when the serene lake reflects Longs Peak.

Peacock Pool, a smaller lake in the valley below Chasm Lake, is best seen from the trail. The multihued pool is in a sensitive ecological area, so a trail doesn't descend to the 11,310-foot lake and visitation is discouraged to protect fragile alpine plants and avoid erosion. Admire it from a distance on your hike to Chasm Lake.

The soaring east face of Longs Peak towers above Chasm Lake, one of Rocky Mountain National Park's iconic alpine lakes.

Peacock Pool and Chasm Lake

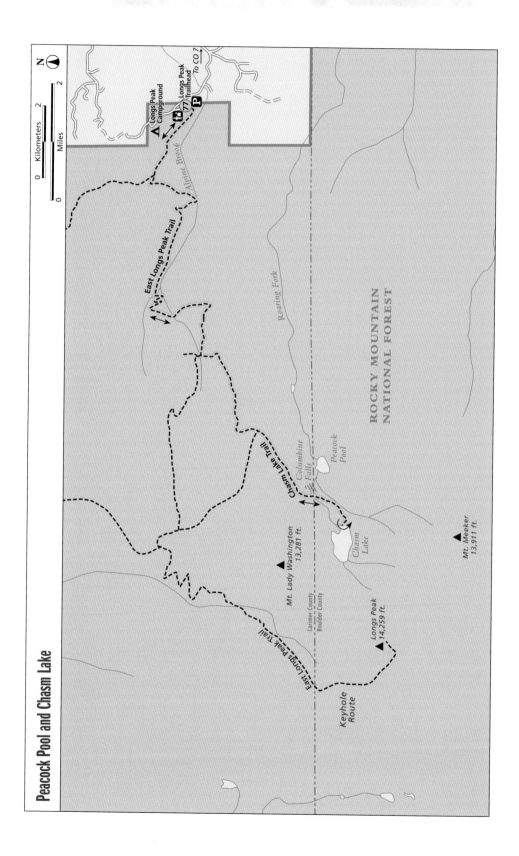

N

0 Kilometers 2

0 Miles 2

Longs Peak Campground

Longs Peak Trailhead

77

P

To CO 7

Alpine Brook

East Longs Peak Trail

Roaring Fork

Chasm Lake Trail

Columbine Falls

Peacock Pool

ROCKY MOUNTAIN NATIONAL FOREST

Chasm Lake

Mt. Lady Washington 13,281 ft.

Mt. Meeker 13,911 ft.

Larimer County
Boulder County

Longs Peak 14,259 ft.

East Longs Peak Trail

Keyhole Route

The Chasm Lake Trail traverses the lower slopes of Mount Lady Washington to Columbine Falls and Chasm Lake below Longs Peak.

The lake hike, starting at Longs Peak Trailhead, follows the East Longs Peak Trail alongside sparkling Alpine Brook, passing twisted limber pines in Goblins Forest and Jims Grove to timberline and a major trail junction and toilet at 11,540 feet. Go left on Chasm Lake Trail for the hike's second leg. A right turn continues to the Keyhole Route up the northwest face of Longs Peak. Chasm Lake Trail contours west across the southeastern flank of Mount Lady Washington, edging above 100-foot-high Columbine Falls below the trail and giving views of Peacock Pool. Finish with a scramble up a rock slab to the lake's eastern shore. Snowdrifts sometimes cover the trail in June; cross them with extreme caution. Bring poles and MICROspikes for traction.

Miles and Directions

0.0 Start at the Longs Peak Trailhead at the south end of the parking lot and hike west on the East Longs Peak Trail.

0.5 Reach junction with Eugenia Mine Trail on the right (GPS: 40 16.5006, -105 33.856). Keep left toward Chasm Lake and hike uphill to a bridge over Larkspur Creek. Continue to a bridge over Alpine Brook.

1.1 Junction with a spur trail to Goblins Forest Backcountry Campsite.

2.4 Junction with a spur trail to Battle Mountain Backcountry Campsite.

3.3 Arrive at a major junction with the Chasm Lake Trail and a toilet with a view at 11,550 feet (GPS: 40 15.9394, -105 35.5529). Go left on the signed Chasm Lake Trail and cross rocky slopes on the southeast flank of Mount Lady Washington.

4.0 Hike over the top of Columbine Falls (GPS: 40 15.652, -105 35.9760) and continue past "Chasm Lake Falls" above the trail (GPS: 40 15.552, -105 36.03). Continue to the base of a granite slab. Scramble northwest up it to the lake.

4.2 Arrive at Chasm Lake's rocky east shoreline below the east face of Longs Peak (GPS: 40 15.512, -105 36.1768). After enjoy the view, hike east down the trail past the waterfalls.

5.1 Return to the junction with East Longs Peak Trail. Go east on it and hike downhill.

8.4 Arrive back at the trailhead (GPS: 40 16.2852, -105 33.3901).

78 Sandbeach Lake

Enjoy spectacular mountain scenery and Colorado's highest sandy beach at Sandbeach Lake, a lofty lake on the northern edge of Wild Basin at Rocky Mountain National Park.

Start: Sandbeach Trailhead
Difficulty: Moderate
Trail: Sandbeach Trail
Hiking time: About 5 hours
Distance: 8.6 miles out-and-back
Elevation trailhead to lake: 8,315 to 10,283 feet at lake (+1,968 feet)
Restrictions: Fee area; no dogs; wilderness rules apply

Amenities: Vault toilets at trailhead; services in Estes Park
Maps: *DeLorme*: Page 29, D6; Trails Illustrated 200: Rocky Mountain National Park; USGS Allens Park
County: Boulder
Land status: Rocky Mountain National Park, (970) 586-1206

Finding the trailhead: From the junction of US 36 and CO 7 in Estes Park, turn south on CO 7 and drive 12.5 miles to Wild Basin Road/Boulder County Road 84W. Turn right or west on Wild Basin Road and drive 0.3 mile to a marked right turn to Rocky Mountain National Park's Wild Basin Trailhead and the park entrance station. The parking lot and Sandbeach Trailhead is opposite the entrance station (GPS: 40 13.1879, -105 32.0624).

The Hike

Sandbeach Lake, lying on a wide bench below 11,724-foot Mount Orton, is exactly that—a glacial lake bordered by a soft, sandy beach on its north and east shorelines. Visit the unique, 16.5-acre lake on a summer weekend and the scene isn't much different than the swim beach at Lake Pueblo or Chatfield Reservoir with hikers tanning on beach towels and kids frolicking in the frigid water. The 50-foot-deep lake, one of the deepest in the national park, was expanded by an earthen dam before the area became a national park in 1915, with the water stored for farmland irrigation. After the Lawn Lake Dam failed in 1982, the park removed the dam, leaving little trace of its existence. The sandy beach was deposited during its dammed years.

The hike to Sandbeach Lake follows a well-marked trail with mostly easy grades. The lake area usually isn't snow-free until mid-June. With eight wilderness campsites and a group site, the trail and lake are also popular with backpackers. Besides the alpine beach, the lake offers astounding views of the surrounding mountains, including 14,259-foot Longs Peak and neighboring 13,911-foot Mount Meeker to the north.

The south face of Mount Meeker looms above Sandbeach Lake in Wild Basin.

Sandbeach Lake

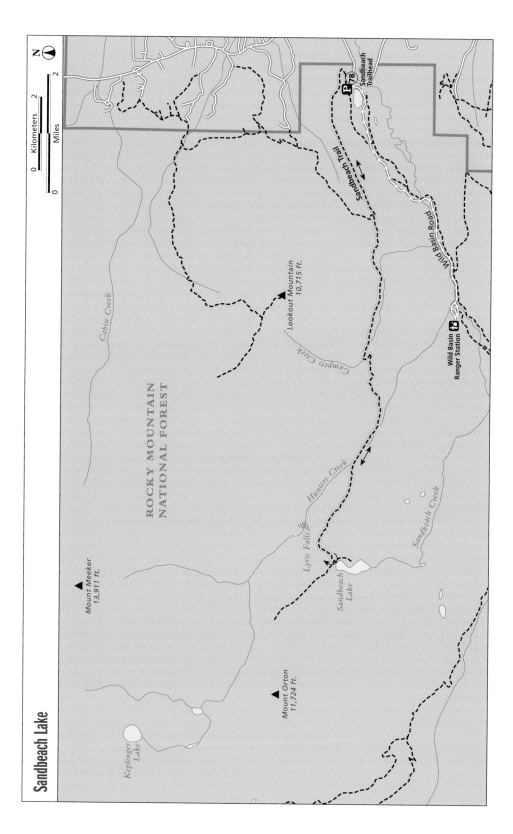

N

0   Kilometers   2

0   Miles   2

Mount Meeker
13,911 ft.

Keplinger
Lake

Mount Orton
11,724 ft.

Cabin Creek

ROCKY MOUNTAIN
NATIONAL FOREST

Lookout Mountain
10,715 ft.

Campers Creek

Hunters Creek

Lyric Falls

Sandbeach Lake

Sandbeach Creek

Sandbeach Trail

Wild Basin Road

Wild Basin
Ranger Station

P 78

Sandbeach
Trailhead

Set amid scenic splendor, Sandbeach Lake reflects peaks and sky on a summer morning.

Miles and Directions

0.0   Start at the Sandbeach Trailhead on the north side of the parking lot opposite the Wild Basin entrance station. Hike north on Sandbeach Trail and after 150 feet, keep right at a trail junction and hike up the steep trail to the top of the Copeland Moraine, a rocky moraine left by a large glacier that filled Wild Basin. Continue west atop the moraine through a pine and aspen forest.

1.3   Reach a junction with a trail on the right that leads northeast to Meeker Park (GPS: 40 13.0297, -105 33.201). Continue straight, passing two backcountry campsites—Hole-in-the-Wall and Campers Creek.

2.4   Cross Campers Creek, jog left, and continue west on the trail past two more backcountry campsites—Beaver Mill and Hunters Creek.

3.4   Reach a crossing over Hunters Creek, which begins at Keplinger Lake below the south slope of Longs Peak. Continue northwest on the trail.

4.3   Reach the north shore of Sandbeach Lake (GPS: 40 13.2374, -105 36.0722), passing four sites at Sandbeach Lake Wilderness Campsite and a hitching rack. After working on your alpine tan, follow the trail back east.

8.6   Arrive back at the trailhead (GPS: 40 13.1879, -105 32.0624).

79 Bluebird Lake

The Bluebird Lake Trail passes Calypso Cascades, Ouzel Falls, and Ouzel Lake before climbing to a sparkling alpine lake in a cirque below the Continental Divide.

Start: Wild Basin Trailhead
Difficulty: Strenuous
Trails: Thunder Lake Trail, Bluebird Lake Trail
Hiking time: 7 to 10 hours
Distance: 12.6 miles out-and-back
Elevation trailhead to lake: 8,566 to 10,978 feet at Bluebird Lake (+2,412 feet)
Restrictions: Entrance fee; parking lot fills in summer; obey wilderness regulations; dogs not allowed

Amenities: Toilets at trailhead; ranger station; services in Estes Park
Maps: *DeLorme*: Page 29, D5 and D6; Trails Illustrated 200: Rocky Mountain National Park; USGS Allens Park, Isolation Peak
County: Boulder
Land status: Rocky Mountain National Park, (970) 586-1206

Finding the trailhead: From the junction of US 36 and CO 7 in Estes Park, drive south on CO 7 for 12.5 miles to Wild Basin Road/Boulder County Road 84W. Turn right or west on Wild Basin Road and drive 0.3 mile to a marked right turn to Rocky Mountain National Park's Wild Basin Trailhead. Pass through the entrance station and drive 2.1 miles to a parking lot for Wild Basin Trailhead and a ranger station at road's end. Trailhead is at south end of lower parking lot (GPS: 40 12.4667, -105 33.99).

The Hike

The Bluebird Lake Trail climbs to shimmering Bluebird Lake nestled in a glacier-carved cirque on the southern end of Rocky Mountain National Park's Wild Basin. The hike, gaining 2,412 feet of elevation, follows rushing creeks, passes three waterfalls and Ouzel Lake, and crosses high meadows. The hike, best done from mid-June through September, also offers mountain views, wildlife, and solitude. Despite the park's popularity, the trail is never crowded, with most hikers only trekking to the waterfalls. Arrive early at the trailhead to grab a parking spot since the lot fills fast on weekends.

The first hike section starts at Wild Basin Trailhead. Head west on Thunder Lake Trail past Lower and Upper Copeland Falls, two small waterfalls on North St. Vrain Creek, to a footbridge over the creek. Climb south alongside Cony Creek, passing a horsetail cascade called "Lover's Leaps," to a junction with the Allenspark–Wild Basin Trail and the base of 200-foot-high Calypso Cascades. This waterfall, named for pink

Hikers relax on Bluebird Lake's rocky shoreline below Ouzel Peak and the Continental Divide.

fairy slipper orchids, tumbles over boulders and fallen tree trunks. Continue another mile to roaring Ouzel Falls, one of Rocky Mountain's most beautiful waterfalls. The 50-foot falls, a popular hiking destination, is named for the water ouzel or American dipper, a small bird that lives along frigid mountain streams.

From the falls, follow Thunder Lake Trail another half-mile to the Bluebird Lake Trail, which climbs through the burn scar of a 1978 wildfire. Higher is a side trail that visits shallow Chickadee Pond and Ouzel Lake, a lovely pond below the north face of 13,176-foot Mount Copeland. The last hike section climbs 1,000 feet from Ouzel Lake to Bluebird Lake, crossing open slopes sprinkled with wildflowers, traversing through moist evergreen forests, and scrambling up polished slabs to an overlook above Bluebird Lake. The gorgeous lake reflects rugged peaks including 12,632-foot Mahana Peak and 12,716-foot Ouzel Peak on the Continental Divide. The now-pristine lake was enlarged by a dam for Longmont drinking water in the early 1920s. In 1974 it was ruled unsafe, and the National Park Service removed five million pounds of concrete by helicopter and restored the lake. If you're energetic, hike to three more alpine lakes—Pipit, Junco, and Lark Pond—hidden in the cirques above Bluebird Lake.

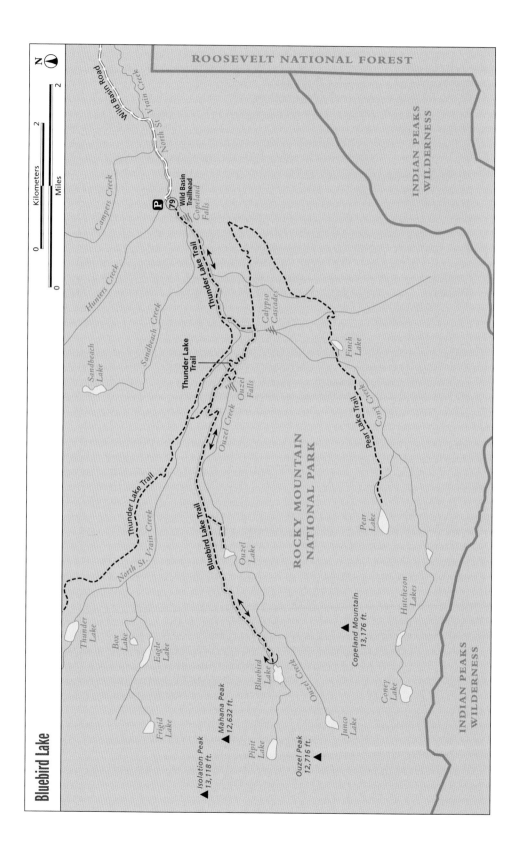

Bluebird Lake

N

Kilometers
0   2

Miles
0   2

ROOSEVELT NATIONAL FOREST

Wild Basin Road

North St. Vrain Creek

Campers Creek

Hunters Creek

Sandbeach Creek

Sandbeach Lake

P
79
Wild Basin Trailhead
Copeland Falls

Thunder Lake Trail

Thunder Lake Trail

Calypso Cascades

Ouzel Falls

Ouzel Creek

Finch Lake

Pear Lake Trail

Cony Creek

ROCKY MOUNTAIN NATIONAL PARK

Bluebird Lake Trail

Ouzel Lake

Pear Lake

▲ Copeland Mountain 13,176 ft.

Hutcheson Lakes

North St. Vrain Creek

Thunder Lake Trail

Thunder Lake

Box Lake

Eagle Lake

Frigid Lake

▲ Isolation Peak 13,118 ft.

Mahana Peak ▲ 12,632 ft.

Bluebird Lake

Pipit Lake

Ouzel Creek

Ouzel Peak ▲ 12,716 ft.

Junco Lake

Coney Lake

INDIAN PEAKS WILDERNESS

INDIAN PEAKS WILDERNESS

Cony Creek tumbles over worn cobbles on Calypso Cascades, a 200-foot-long waterfall.

Miles and Directions

0.0 Start at the Wild Basin Trailhead. Follow Thunder Lake Trail west alongside the north bank of North St. Vrain Creek.

0.3 Reach Copeland Falls on the right. A short side path leads to the falls (GPS: 40 12.2989, –105 34.2548).

1.2 Reach a junction with a trail on the right. Go left, cross a bridge over the creek, and hike uphill alongside Cony Creek.

1.8 Arrive at a junction with the Allenspark–Wild Basin Trail (GPS: 20 11.7338, –105 35.4235). Go right to Calypso Cascades, a long, tumbling waterfall, on a boardwalk.

2.7 Continue west on Thunder Lake Trail for 0.9 mile to Ouzel Falls, one of the park's prettiest waterfalls, on the left (GPS: 40 11.9257, –105 35.9752). A rough trail heads left from a footbridge to a viewpoint below the falls. Continue west on the trail, contouring across the mountainside.

3.1 Reach the junction with Bluebird Lake Trail on the left (GPS: 40 12.0954, –105 36.2057). Go left on Bluebird Lake Trail and climb south up slopes to a rounded ridge. Continue southwest along the ridgetop.

4.5 Reach a trail junction on the left. The path heads 0.4 mile into the broad valley to tree-lined Ouzel Lake (GPS: 40 12.1409, –105 37.5167). Return to the junction and go left on Bluebird Lake Trail across a slope above Ouzel Lake and Chickadee Pond. The trail ascends through old forest below cliffs, then climbs up glacier-scraped rock ribs and gullies.

6.3 Reach a granite bench above the northeast side of Bluebird Lake (GPS: 40 11.5509, –105 39.1495). Revel in views west of mountains lining the rim of the cirque, including Mount Copeland, Ouzel Peak, and Mahana Peak. After lunch, return back down the trails.

12.6 Arrive back at the trailhead (GPS: 40 12.4667, –105 33.99).

80 Lone Pine Lake and Lake Verna

Two of Rocky Mountain National Park's most remote and lonesome lakes—Lone Pine Lake and Lake Verna—nestle in the narrow floor of a dramatic, glaciated valley on the rugged western slope of the Continental Divide.

Start: East Inlet Trailhead
Difficulty: Strenuous
Trails: East Inlet Trail
Hiking time: 7.5 to 9 hours
Distance: 13.4 miles out-and-back
Elevation trailhead to lakes: 8,391 to 9,860 feet at Lone Pine Lake (+1,469 feet); 10,180 feet at Lake Verna (+1,789 feet)
Restrictions: Follow wilderness regulations; permit required for backcountry camping; no dogs, bicycles, or motorized vehicles or equipment
Amenities: Trailhead toilets; services in Grand Lake
Maps: *DeLorme*: Page 28, C4 and page 29, C5; Trails Illustrated 200: Rocky Mountain National Park; USGS Shadow Mountain, Isolation Peak
County: Grand
Land status: Rocky Mountain National Park, (970) 586-1206

Finding the trailhead: From US 34 in Grand Lake, drive to a Y-junction at the Grand Lake Visitor Center. Bear right on CO 278/West Portal Road and drive northeast for 0.3 mile to an intersection with Grand Avenue. Bear left and continue straight on West Portal Road. Drive 2 miles on the paved and then unpaved road to a parking lot and the East Inlet Trailhead on the road's left side (GPS: 40 14.3658, –105 47.9935).

The Hike

A ladder of five lakes hides in a high, glacier-carved valley on the west side of Rocky Mountain National Park. The lowest lakes—Lone Pine Lake and Lake Verna—are reached by a long hike up the East Inlet Trail from Grand Lake. The higher lakes lie in the upper valley below the Continental Divide in one of the park's wildest and least visited places. East Inlet, originating on the rugged north slope of 13,118-foot Isolation Peak, dashes northwest down the deep valley, filling the lakes and splashing over waterfalls, before emptying into Grand Lake, Colorado's largest and deepest natural lake.

Visiting the two lower lakes is a major hike with plenty of miles and elevation gain. Plan on a long day, so bring food, water, a headlamp, extra clothes, and rain gear. Trekking poles and MICROspikes are essential if there is any chance that snow and ice cover the trail. Use caution on the narrow and exposed trail section above the rocky gorge and East Inlet Falls, especially in wet or snowy conditions. To see the three highest lakes, book a wilderness campsite at Solitaire, Slickrock, Upper East Inlet, or Lake Verna to spend a starry night and explore them the next day. A faint path continues past Lake Verna to Spirit Lake.

Reached by the East Inlet Trail, Lone Pine Lake offers still waters for meditation.

Isolation Peak and the Continental Divide loom over Lake Verna in Rocky Mountain National Park.

Lone Pine Lake and Lake Verna

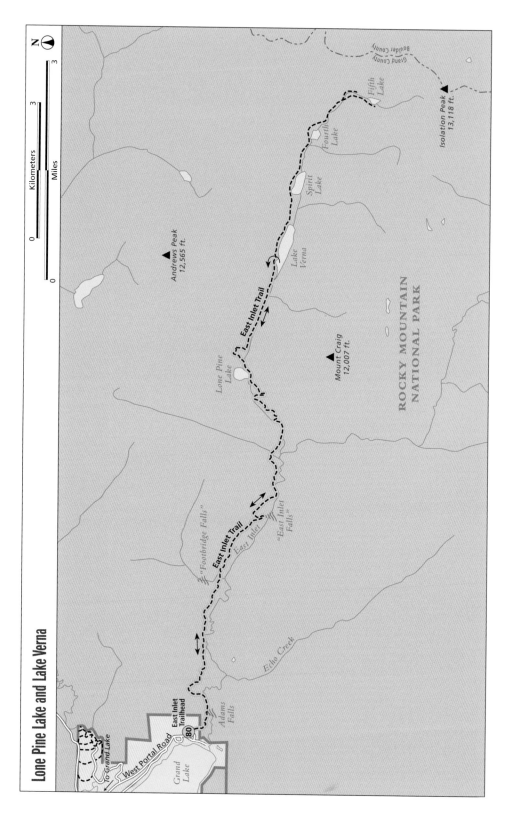

N

Kilometers
0   3

Miles
0   3

"Footbridge Falls"

East Inlet Trail

East Inlet

"East Inlet Falls"

Echo Creek

East Inlet Trailhead

80

West Portal Road

To Grand Lake

Adams Falls

Grand Lake

Lone Pine Lake

Mount Craig
12,007 ft.

East Inlet Trail

Andrews Peak
12,565 ft.

Lake Verna

Spirit Lake

Fourth Lake

Fifth Lake

Isolation Peak
13,118 ft.

ROCKY MOUNTAIN
NATIONAL PARK

Grand County
Boulder County

Miles and Directions

0.0 Begin at the East Inlet Trailhead and hike southeast on the trail.

0.3 Reach a junction with a short trail that goes right down steps to a viewpoint of Adams Falls (GPS: 40 14.197, –105 47.886). Return to East Inlet Trail and go right, passing an alternative side trail that goes right to Adams Falls. Continue east, skirting along the northern edge of a wide meadow. Look for moose. Cross low hills and continue east, following the northern fringe of more meadows and wetlands along meandering East Inlet creek.

2.2 At the trail's second footbridge, step left to see "Footbridge Falls" (GPS: 40 14.146, –105 46.311), then continue east into wooded hills studded with cliffs.

3.0 The trail twists along a bench between cliffs before traversing an exposed, narrow section above a high cliff (GPS: 40 13.754, –105 45.5565). Use extreme care and avoid loose, wet, or icy rock here. Exposure is extreme and a fall would be fatal. The creek dashes through a rock-walled gorge below the trail.

3.1 Reach a viewpoint of "East Inlet Falls" in the deep canyon below (GPS: 40 13.737, –105 45.5431). Past here, make a switchback left and climb over a rounded granite dome, then head east on rocky benches and hills in a wide, glaciated valley.

4.2 The trail crosses East Inlet (GPS: 40 13.5667, –105 44.5631) and switchbacks northeast up a long rocky hill and then levels off, passing a small pond, and then climbing again.

5.3 Reach the southeast side of Lone Pine Lake (GPS: 40 13.9059, –105 43.8421) below a high, slabby cliff covered with trees. After enjoying the pretty lake, head east of the lake through slickrock hills and then follow the creek's left side east up a narrow, rocky valley, passing the turn to East Inlet Backcountry Campsite just past a small lake formed by a landslide. Continue climbing to the narrow outlet bay of Lake Verna and hike along its north side.

6.7 Reach an open viewpoint on the north edge of Lake Verna (GPS: 40 13.6606, –105 42.6415). Look up the valley for dramatic views of the glaciated gorge to 13,118-foot Isolation Peak. More lakes hide in the upper valley—Spirit Lake, Fourth Lake, and Fifth Lake, tucked in the high cirque below Isolation Peak. After admiring the view, head back down the trail for the long hike out.

13.4 Arrive back at the trailhead (GPS: 40 14.3658, –105 47.9935).

Appendix: Land Status Contact Information

Bureau of Land Management Field Offices

Gunnison Field Office
210 W. Spencer Ave.
Gunnison, CO 81230
(970) 642-4940
blm.gov/office/gunnison-field-office

Campgrounds

Recreation.gov
(877) 444-6777 (Reservations)
www.recreation.gov

City, County, State, and National Monuments, Open Spaces, Parks, and Recreation Areas

Barr Lake State Park
13401 Picadilly Rd.
Brighton, CO 80603
(303) 659-6005
cpw.state.co.us/placestogo/parks/barrlake

Chatfield State Park
11500 N. Roxborough Park Rd.
Littleton, CO 80125
(303) 791-7275
cpw.state.co.us/placestogo/parks/Chatfield

**Colorado Springs Department of Parks,
Recreation and Cultural Services**
1401 Recreation Way
Colorado Springs, CO 80905
(719) 385-5940
springsgov.com

Curecanti National Recreation Area
102 Elk Creek
Gunnison, CO 81230
(970) 641-2337 x205
nps.gov/cure/index.htm

Denver Audubon Nature Center
11280 Waterton Rd.
Littleton, CO 80125
(303) 973-9530
denveraudubon.org/nature-center/

Denver Mountain Parks
(720) 865-0900
Park Rangers: (720) 913-1311
denvergov.org/Government/Agencies-Departments
-Offices/Parks-Recreation/Parks/Mountain-Parks

Eleven Mile State Park
4229 CR 92
Lake George, CO 80827
(719) 748-3401
cpw.state.co.us/placestogo/parks/ElevenMile

Fort Collins Natural Areas Program
1745 Hoffman Mill Rd.
Fort Collins, CO 80524
(970) 416-2815
fcgov.com/naturalareas/

Lake Pueblo State Park
640 Pueblo Reservoir Rd.
Pueblo, CO 81005
(719) 561-9320
cpw.state.co.us/placestogo/parks/LakePueblo

Lathrop State Park
70 CR 502
Walsenburg, CO 81089
(719) 738-2376
cpw.state.co.us/placestogo/parks/Lathrop

Mancos State Park
42545 Road N
Mancos, CO 81328
(970) 533-7065
cpw.state.co.us/placestogo/parks/Mancos

Rocky Mountain National Park
1000 US 36
Estes Park, CO 80517-8397
(970) 586-1206
nps.gov/romo

State Forest State Park
56750 CO 14
Walden, CO 80480
(970) 723-8366
cpw.state.co.us/placestogo/parks/StateForest

Steamboat Lake State Park
61105 CR 129
Clark, CO 80428
(970) 879-3922
cpw.state.co.us/placestogo/parks/SteamboatLake

Trinidad Lake State Park
32610 CO 12
Trinidad, CO 81082
(719) 846-6951
cpw.state.co.us/placestogo/parks/TrinidadLake

National Forests

Arapaho and Roosevelt National Forests
2150 Centre Ave., Bldg. E
Fort Collins, CO 80526
(970) 295-6600
fs.usda.gov/arp

Grand Mesa, Uncompahgre, and Gunnison National Forests
2250 S. Main St.
Delta, CO 81416
(970) 874-6600
fs.usda.gov/gmug

Pike and San Isabel National Forests
2840 Kachina Dr.
Pueblo, CO 81008
(719) 553-1400
fs.usda.gov/psicc

Rio Grande National Forest
1803 W. US 160
Monte Vista, CO 81144
(719) 852-5941
fs.usda.gov/riogrande

Roosevelt National Forest
2150 Centre Ave., Bldg. E
Fort Collins, CO 80526
(970) 295-6600
fs.usda.gov/arp

Routt National Forest
2468 Jackson St.
Laramie, WY 82070
(307) 745-2300
fs.usda.gov/mbr

San Isabel National Forest
2840 Kachina Dr.
Pueblo, CO 81008
(719) 553-1400
fs.usda.gov/psicc

San Juan National Forest
15 Burnett Ct.
Durango, CO 81301
(970) 247-4874
fs.usda.gov/sanjuan

Uncompahgre National Forest
2250 US 50
Delta, CO 81416
(970) 874-6600
fs.usda.gov/gmug

White River National Forest
900 Grand Ave.
Glenwood Springs, CO 81601
(970) 945-2521
fs.usda.gov/whiteriver

Passes

CORSAR Card

dola.colorado.gov/sar/cardPurchase.jsf

National Parks Pass

nps.gov/planyourvisit/passes.htm

shop.usparkpass.com/

State Parks and Wildlife Areas Pass

cpw.state.co.us/buyapply/Pages/ParksPassInfo.aspx

Ranger Districts

Aspen–Sopris Ranger District

620 Main St.

Carbondale, CO 81623

(970) 963-2266

Blanco Ranger District

220 E. Market St.

Meeker, CO 81641

(970) 878-4039

Boulder Ranger District

2140 Yarmouth Ave.

Boulder, CO 80301

(303) 541-2500

Canyon Lakes Ranger District

2150 Centre Ave., Bldg. E

Fort Collins, CO 80526

(970) 295-6700

Clear Creek Ranger District

2060 Miner St.

Idaho Springs, CO 80452

(303) 567-3000

Columbine Ranger District

367 Pearl St.

Bayfield, CO 81122

(970) 884-2512

Conejos Peak Ranger District
15571 CR T.5
La Jara, CO 81140
(719) 274-8971

Dillon Ranger District
680 Blue River Pkwy.
Silverthorne, CO 80498
(970) 468-5400

Divide Ranger District
13308 US 160
Del Norte, CO 81132
(719) 657-3321

Dolores Ranger District
29211 CO 184
Dolores, CO 81323
(970) 882-7296

Eagle–Holy Cross Ranger District
24747 US 24
Minturn, CO 81645
(970) 827-5715

Grand Valley District Office
1010 Kimball Ave.
Grand Junction, CO 81501
(970) 242-8211

Gunnison Ranger District
216 N. Colorado
Gunnison, CO 81230
(970) 641-0471

Hahns Peak / Bears Ears Ranger District
925 Weiss Dr.
Steamboat Springs, CO 80487-9315
(970) 870-2299

Leadville Ranger District
810 Front St.
Leadville, CO 80461
(719) 486-0749

Ouray Ranger District
2505 S. Townsend
Montrose, CO 81401
(970) 240-5300

Pagosa Ranger District
180 Pagosa St.
Pagosa Springs, CO 81147
(970) 264-2268

Paonia Ranger District
403 N. Rio Grande Ave.
Paonia, CO 81428
(970) 527-4131

Parks Ranger District
100 Main St.
Walden, CO 80480
(970) 723-2700

Pikes Peak Ranger District
601 S. Weber St.
Colorado Springs, CO 80903
(719) 636-1602

Saguache Ranger District
46525 CO 114
Saguache, CO 81149
(719) 655-2547

Salida Ranger District
5575 Cleora Rd.
Salida, CO 81201
(719) 539-3591

San Carlos Ranger District
3028 E. Main St.
Cañon City, CO 81212
(719) 269-8500

Silverton Public Lands Center
1246 Blair St.
Silverton, CO 81433
(970) 387-5530

South Park Ranger District
320 US 285
Fairplay, CO 80440
(719) 836-2031

Colorado Parks and Wildlife

Colorado Parks and Wildlife Headquarters
6060 Broadway
Denver, CO 80216
(303) 291-7227
cpw.state.co.us/

Hikers enjoy a quiet view across Bear Lake to square-topped Hallett Peak.

About the Authors

Susan Joy Paul has traveled around the United States and beyond to forty-seven hot springs, more than one hundred lakes and 150 waterfalls, and to the summits of more than 700 peaks. Her memorable adventures include hikes and climbs on the *Keyhole Route* on Longs Peak, the *Knife-edge* on Capitol Peak, the *Mountaineer's Route* on Mount Whitney, the *East Arête* on Mount Russell, *Otto's Route* on Independence Monument, the *Emmons Glacier* on Mount Rainier, the *Gooseneck Glacier* on Gannett Peak, the *Jamapa Glacier* on Pico de Orizaba, the *Ayoloco Glacier* on Iztaccihuatl, and the *Whymper Route* on Chimborazo. Her other books include *Touring Colorado Hot Springs* (second and third editions), *Hiking Waterfalls Colorado* (first and second editions), *Climbing Colorado's Mountains*, and *Woman in the Wild: The Everywoman's Guide to Hiking, Camping, and Backcountry Travel*. Susan lives independently in Colorado Springs, Colorado.

Stewart M. Green has hiked, climbed, photographed, and traveled across the American West as well as the world in search of memorable images and experiences to document. Based in Colorado Springs, Stewart, a freelance writer and photographer for Globe Pequot and FalconGuides, has written and photographed over fifty travel and outdoor adventure books, including *Best Easy Day Hikes Colorado Springs*, *Scenic Driving Colorado*, *Best Hikes Colorado Springs*, *Best Climbs Moab*, *Best Hikes Albuquerque*, *Rock Climbing Colorado*, *Scenic Driving New England*, and *Rock Art: The Meanings and Myths Behind Ancient Ruins in the Southwest and Beyond*. His photographs and writing are also published in many magazines, books, catalogs, and ads. Visit green1109.wix .com/stewartmgreenphoto for images and information.

THE TEN ESSENTIALS OF HIKING

American Hiking Society

American Hiking Society recommends you pack the "Ten Essentials" every time you head out for a hike. Whether you plan to be gone for a couple of hours or several months, make sure to pack these items. Become familiar with these items and know how to use them. Learn more at **AmericanHiking.org/hiking-resources**

 1. Appropriate Footwear

 6. Safety Items (light, fire, and a whistle)

 2. Navigation

 7. First Aid Kit

 3. Water (and a way to purify it)

 8. Knife or Multi-Tool

 4. Food

 9. Sun Protection

 5. Rain Gear & Dry-Fast Layers

 10. Shelter

PROTECT THE PLACES YOU LOVE TO HIKE

Become a member today and take $5 off an annual membership using the code **Falcon5**.

AmericanHiking.org/join

American Hiking Society is the only national nonprofit organization dedicated to empowering all to enjoy, share, and preserve the hiking experience.